MYSTERIOUS HORSES

OF

WESTERN

NORTH AMERICA

To the Memory of
CHIEF JOSEPH
The Great Nez Percé Warrior
Who Was Very Kind to a Very Small Boy

MYSTERIOUS HORSES

OF

WESTERN
NORTH AMERICA

William A. Berg

COACHWHIP PUBLICATIONS

Landisville, Pennsylvania

Mysterious Horses of Western North America, by William A. Berg
Originally published 1960.
Copyright © 2010 Coachwhip Publications
No claims made on public domain material.

ISBN 1-61646-027-X
ISBN-13 978-1-61646-027-3

Front Cover: Pinto © AncientImages
Back Cover: Appaloosa © Lorraine Swanson

CoachwhipBooks.com

CONTENTS

Students of the life that existed when the earth was young find among the earliest creatures the ancestors of the horse. That ancestry extends back farther into time than that of any important animal extant today.

Strange though it may seem, the mystery surrounding those earliest ancestors of the horse is not much greater than that attending some of the horses of western North America today. For instance, there is the spotted horse, now known as the Appaloosa. How did it happen that the Nez Percé Indians of the northwestern United States had these Appaloosas by the thousands at a time when the breed was virtually extinct elsewhere, although they were among the earliest of horses—the very first, as I indicate in the pages that follow.

Then, too, there is the Pinto horse. There have been pinto-colored horses far back in time, but only as occasional specimens. Then, as white men began crossing the upper Mississippi River into the western plains country, they found great numbers of Pintos being ridden by Indians. Doubts about the origin of these Pintos is common. These, as well as some other mysteries, are cleared up in this book. Still other mysteries, such as the origin of the Nez Percé Indians and the propriety of their name, must enter the story as part of my claim concerning both the Appaloosa and the Pinto.

My parents did medical and missionary work among an independent band of Nez Percé when I was a very small child. My earliest memories have to do with life in a Nez Percé Indian camp.

My father's oldest brother had trapped in Nez Percé lands as a youth, beginning in the early 1840s. Fortunate circumstances brought him to the Nez Percé Salmon River villages. There he saw things that were the starting point to a solution of the Nez Percé mystery. He had some unique Indian relics that had been given him there, and both he and my parents used to wonder and puzzle about them. Their discussions fascinated me, and my interest in Nez Percé Indians has never slackened.

My first horse was a spotted animal, not then known as the Appaloosa. A boy never forgets his first horse, and memories of him have kept me wondering about the Appaloosa throughout these many years.

I explain the mystery of the Appaloosa, the Pinto, and some other mysteries connected with western horses in my own way. To substantiate my position I introduce much relevant history and, I believe, present sufficient collateral facts to prove my claims.

W. A. Berg

1

THE PRE-HORSE AGE

Modern horses are the result of millions of years of evolution. Their early ancestors did not step upon the world scene in the regal form or the prancing step the horse displays today as it is being ridden by some member of a proud sheriff's posse in parades throughout America. On January first of each year these posses lead the advance echelon of the Parade of Roses at Pasadena, and, at closely spaced intervals in that longest of processions, they add a splendor to the occasion that is unexcelled by any other feature.

A friend of mine did not believe in evolution. She claimed that one cannot change a nasturtium into a rose, or a dog into a horse, by evolution or any other method. And she is so right. Evolution does not imply the transformation of one life form into another, different, life form without some previous hereditary relationship between them. Evolution connotes the transformation of forms and characteristics that enable life forms to meet the changing conditions that occur in this world. Nature does not permit the changing of one genus of life into another genus. But my friend was not convinced.

She has a library whose walls are lined with books. The subjects vary from the most elementary to some that are beyond my understanding. In times past, I have browsed among those books. Now I have found one that tells of the whale and something of its evolution. At one time the whale had been a land animal that later took to life in the water. It no longer needed legs, so nature tucked away the legs under thick layers of blubber, but atrophied leg bones have remained to give certain evidence of earlier body formation. That picture of an evolved whale succeeded where all my oratory had failed. Evolution won another convert.

Some forms of life have been reluctant to accept changes of form, but the equine species accept such changes quite readily. However, they seem to have clung tightly to various habits of their earliest existence. Had they not possessed a ready ability to change, they would most likely have died out together with certain contemporaries of theirs, the Dinosaurs.

Millions of years ago, during an early period in the formation of the earth, after rock began to solidify out of the matrix that was then the earth, land formations began to appear above the water. Mountain ranges were thrust up high into the air. Mostly they tumbled down again because of stresses and strains upon their bases, brought about by the cooling of the earth mass. Ofttimes the waters again engulfed them. Long before the present continents of the earth were formed, solids of the earth, both above and below the water, tumbled about breaking much rock into various sizes, from giant boulders down to sand in size.

We know these things to be true because the first important land animals had no teeth and used gravel to pulverize their food after it was swallowed; much as fowls do in the present era. Those first important land animals, known now as the Dinosaurs, lived so long ago that a guess of a few million years either way as to time is of no great matter.

Probably before the first great mountains were forming, obscure forces were forcing wide areas above sea level; some, though, had been formed previously. Be that as it may, for ages, large expanses of land were only slightly above the usual level of the seas and existed as great morasses or swamps, resembling somewhat the lowest elevations of the Everglades of Florida.

During those formation times the world climate was warm and conducive to vegetation, and in time vegetation grew there abundantly. Much plant life grew before the coming of land animals.

Such areas of land existed in various places about the world. One of those districts of great importance to the earliest ancestors of the horse, and in recent times, too, of great importance to American horses, is the great plains district of central North America. In recent times, the greater part of that plains area has attained higher elevation than that achieved in the early periods of land formations, and now much of the area is semi-arid. Today, beginning at the Gulf of Mexico, the plains that were mostly marsh lands then extend as far north as Northern Upper Canada, and originally extended to areas now covered by ice and Arctic seas.

In the warmer regions of that marshy country, at a time not precisely known, strange creatures of flesh and blood made their appearance. The relative time of their appearance may be estimated by the fact that nature had by then established sex in life as its best assurance of an increase in, and expansion about the earth of, its more recent innovations of life forms. The time may also be more closely determined by the fact that creatures that lived as land animals had not been completely separated in form and living requirements from those creatures that lived in water, nor had a separation been completed between the types of creatures that laid eggs in the production of their young and those that gave birth to fully formed progeny.

The first creatures of consequence that occupied those marshy lands are now known as Dinosaurs. After a time there was a great variety of shapes and sizes among those creatures, varying, in the smaller species, from a size as small as that of a turkey to creatures as large as warehouses in the larger species. They were egg-laying creatures and must have had the promiscuous proclivities of our barnyard fowls, with a corresponding production of eggs, for they spread over the marshy areas at a great rate.

Nature is averse to any one form of life becoming so numerous, so dominant, as to lead to the extinction of other forms. Should one form of life threaten to become dominant, nature sets up limiting circumstances to prevent such a situation from maturing. In the Dinosauria Age, the deterrent took the form of giant predatory species that used other Dinosaurs for food. Those predator forms of Dinosaurs were terrible creatures, huge in size, almost beyond belief, their large jaws filled with tearing teeth strong enough to crush any bone. The lesser species were gregarious creatures. What a racket there must have been in the areas where they congregated; the great bulls bellowing, the females twittering, and large fleeing creatures wailing to high heaven for a succor that seldom came!

Sometime in the days of those giant Dinosaurs, there appeared among them groups of a certain small animal. Those little animals dared to run around among the greatest of the Dinosaurs, apparently without fear and certainly with great impudence. That small animal is now known as the Eohippus, and is thought to have evolved from an earlier animal type that has such descendants as the donkey, the zebra, and other equine forms. The Eohippus, though, is the first animal form that gives satisfactory indications of lineage leading directly to the horse.

Fossils indicate that the Eohippus ran about in small bands. It was about the size of a common fox, and from a distance they would have looked something like bands of dogs scampering about, but these small animals were equine, not canine. The Eohippus was strictly an eater of vegetation and did not eat meat. There was no grass in those times, so it subsisted by browsing upon brush, eating the leaves and tender twigs. Horses also relish brush and even at times have been known to eat their wooden mangers in an atavic urge, because of needs inherited from primitive ancestry.

The Eohippus was an unusual animal in several different ways. Some of its peculiarities have enabled scientists to trace its descendants down through the ages to the horse. Before me is a treatise on the conformation and habits of the little ancient animals, and it makes quite a volume in itself, but it is too scientifically complicated to make comfortable fireside reading. I shall condense that book into a few salient items, sufficient to assure any reader that scientists have found plenty of evidence to make certain that their conclusions are based upon sound and convincing data.

Teeth found in Eohippus fossils are unique. Scientists are able to trace later equine teeth into undoubtable connection with the teeth of the Eohippus. Later that same form of tooth, with some modifications, is found in the modern horse.

Then there were the unusual and queer feet of the Eohippus. No other animal has ever had that same foot construction, except its descendants, including the horse. Its front feet included four toes, but its hind feet had only three. That unusual number of digits in four-legged animals has enabled investigators to trace Eohippus descendants through all the eons of time and through all changes of form. Again, down to and including the horse.

There is one other Eohippus characteristic that has come down through the ages. That was its custom of roaming the country in small bands. The horse, in its free state, is the only animal of consequence that indulges in that habit, and has persisted in it regardless of efforts on the part of masters to change that habit. Ruminants, such as the buffalo and other wild cattle move mostly in great herds, with the male taking a chance on getting his share, or more, of mates from the common herd. Other important forms of life live either in pairs or insist upon a solitary existence, except at mating time. But the horse, against all opposition, will persist in forming small bands.

The Dinosaur neighbors of the Eohippus were unable to achieve the changes necessary to maintain a future existence and disappeared from the earth, leaving little to show that they had ever lived: some petrified eggs and some fossil bones. What a tragedy! Oh well! Easy come, easy go. The world wouldn't miss them for some millions of years.

The Eohippus, though, made some relatively quick changes, finally becoming the creature we know now as the Mesohippus. The Mesohippus was most certainly a different animal than the older in time Eohippus, but the scientists weren't fooled. Not hardly more than some minutes. To them it was certain beyond equivocation that the Mesohippus had followed the Eohippus in direct lineal descent. Again there are tomes assuring in detail that such statements are correct, but again we will limit ourselves to a very few lines. Pre-eminent in the evidence are the items of the teeth and the feet.

The teeth of the Mesohippus were so similar to those of the Eohippus and in both were so unlike that of any other contemporary animal that there could be no question as to the relationship. Then, too, there were the feet and the peculiar number of toe bones. Now there were only three digits for each foot, with the fourth toe bone having almost entirely disappeared from the front feet. The fourth bone was there all right, but it had become very small and was not used as a toe any more. Too, now each of the three toes had individual hoofs. A queer circumstance indeed, and probably the first instance of the hoof in animal existence.

By that time, too, the animal had become a grass eater, and some distance away would have looked to us like a miniature horse. It was about three and one-half feet in height and well proportioned. There were other changes, too. Some puzzling for a time. One puzzle was the change in some of the creatures' faces. By this time some of the heads showed an elongated face, the face below the eye sockets being long and narrow, then spreading wide at the nostrils. The investigators were puzzled, until they found a fossilized unborn colt in such a position that there could be no doubt or uncertainty. The fossils of the long narrow face with the wide-spreading nostril structure were the females of the species. The position of the teeth was slightly changed, and, of course, the teeth as a whole were slightly modified. The creature by that time had been a grass eater for some ages now and a transformation in the tooth structure was the result of that change from brush-eating habits. Other changes were minor. We now know that the changes made were merely steps on the stairway leading to the horse.

Most Mesohippus fossils are found in South Dakota. No one knows how long they lived there. Maybe it was such a long time that wise men are even afraid to guess. Anyway, it was a long, long time, for their fossils are found in several layers of the earth's formation that occurred while they lived there; and then, quite suddenly, they didn't live there any more. They didn't die off as had the Dinosaurs millions of years before. The Mesohippus simply disappeared from America, but reappeared shortly afterwards far away, in remote areas of Asia.

Some sixty, and a few more, years ago I first read of the Eohippus and later ancestors of the horse. At that time it was believed that all equine forms of life had left North America and that actually no true horses had ever existed here in pre-Columbian times; now there are dissenters from those ideas. Only recently another step in the evolution of the horse has been discovered. That creature is known as the Pliohippus. The Pliohippus actually was a horse, though it did not of course contain all the exact features of the modern horse. It had a single hoof for each foot, with the multiple toe bones still there, inside the single hoofs; the teeth were much the same as in the present horse, but the creature was an animal inferior, apparently, both in size and conformation, to present equine types.

Throughout succeeding ages some horse form must have actually developed in North America, for some fossils—a very few—have been found that suggest an actual horse type. A very few fossils have been found, and in widely separated areas, attesting to such a fact, and, too, a complete skeleton of such a creature has been recovered from the tar pits of La Brea (now in the Los Angeles city area). The conditions of that recovery were such as to suggest the horse-type creature lived in the time of the Saber-toothed Tiger and some other creatures that are now extinct. There are several puzzling circumstances to consider and these may have led to less than a general acceptance of a prehistoric horse in America.

One set of such circumstances that still is puzzling is the fact that fossils of the Mesohippus and preceding equine forms are so very plentiful in the fossil lands of the Midwest, while fossils of the Pliohippus and succeeding equine forms are almost non-existent throughout all of central North America. That situation may well cast some doubts as to the actual existence of the horse in North America prior to the time of the coming of the white man to this continent.

Could it be that changing conditions of climate or other necessary living circumstances forced the Mesohippus to leave the North American continent with a vigor and speed denied to some animals not in their prime, and that some of those remaining, those perhaps too weak to undertake such an arduous journey, or some few Pliohippus in a preferred and suitable, though restricted, area stayed on in America, and that further restricting circumstances reduced the remaining numbers as time went on, and to such an extent as to limit the numbers of the Pliohippus to some very few, with a similar scarcity of numbers among later American equine forms? Some such circumstances, or other combinations of circumstances, may account for the numerical scarcity, and it need not necessarily mean that horse forms in America did not develop following the Pliohippus. At any rate:

It is now an accepted fact that sometime in the distant past, animals such as the giant Mammoth, the huge Mastodon, the Saber-toothed Tiger, and other creatures long extinct before the coming of the white man to America roamed over much of this northern continent.

In the Yakima Valley of the state of Washington, in the approximate center of a high moraine ridge left by some dissolving glacier, a complete skeleton of camel bones was found. Such a circumstance is so unusual; so unexpected by common folk that who knows? It may be that some day remains will be found of prehistoric American horses that will settle the matter for posterity.

Another mystery of those early pre-horse times is: Why did the pre-horse Mesohippus leave North America and Migrate to Asia, and apparently in a comparatively very short time and almost, if not entirely, completely? Could it be that a long-continued, and severe drought completely denuded its pastures of grass? The Mesohippus was, as is the horse, very loath to leave its home grounds. Once a band was established in a pleasing location, not winter storms or scorching sun, neither Dinosaurs nor Saber-toothed Tigers could permanently drive them from an established range. Complete and prolonged frigid times could have driven them out, but their habitat was in the northern hemisphere. A cold spell there would have also affected the areas into which they moved in Asia. The movement of those pre-horse creatures may always remain a mystery, but that need not seem at all strange.

Climatic changes that severely transform large areas of the earth's surface are occurring all the time. The Sahara Desert of northern Africa, now a classic example of a growing desert area, was not so long ago a paradise of palm trees and pleasing verdure. Areas of the frigid north, not too long ago a pleasant land, have, for some thousands of years, been the frozen Arctic. One can scarcely imagine what changes occurred in the millions of years during which the pre-horse animals lived.

We may never know what caused the migration, but we are certain that the ancestors of the horse migrated from North America to Asia, and that the great continent has been the area of many final evolutionary changes in both plant and animal life. Among those forms has been the evolution of the horse.

The continent we class as Asia is the world's largest land division and, in addition, extends to include the land masses now classed as Europe. The size of Asia is almost beyond comprehension. It contains 17,255,890 square miles of land area, almost exactly one-third of the earth's land surface. That great expanse, in times past, was conducive to certain great specialized areas. There are, and were, in early geologic times, great areas of tropical lands, also great areas of frozen, frigid lands. In between those two areas lay great expanses of swamp lands. During an early period much of the area that is now and land, even desert areas, then were great morasses. That fact is proven by the numerous Dinosaur fossils that may be found over great areas. Much of China, Mongolia, and Turkestan, along with the great steppe lands of central Asia, were at some time a part of that great swamp area.

Forces beyond our knowledge gradually changed that enormous area. The fringes of the morasses receded northward. As land emerged from the water it was fertile with ages of plant nutrition. Vegetation grew in that new land in great abundance. Fossils indicate that the Mesohippus lived there for ages. How long, is an indefinite period. After a very long time conditions changed and their fossils are lacking in some strata of earth formation, but then are found, in a closely succeeding geologic time, one probably interspersed with a former period—the fossil remains of another creature, the horse.

The proof of a very early existence of the horse in Asia is the finding of its fossilized remains in certain geologic formations. The sun has come up and then gone down again so many times that an estimate of the actual time is not worth making. Be assured that it has been a long, long time. If we should be so fortunate as to find some earliest horse bones that have not been turned into stone, we may achieve some day a closely approximate time by use of the carbon method, and that would certainly be a step toward further knowledge. Our claim, that the horse form still extant today originated in the hinterlands of Asia in far past ages, will be proved beyond questioning when such a time arrives. In the meantime we have certain clues that are adequate to assure us of our conclusions, and which we believe are worthy of general consideration.

One interesting feature leading to our deduction as to the time of arrival of the horse in Asia is that in the geologic strata of Asia, unlike in those of North America, the pre-horse forms, or rather relics of those forms, are not found mingled with the fossils of the Dinosaurs—convincing evidence that pre-horse forms came into Asia at a later time. Where such pre-horse fossils are found in Asia, the fossils are of Mesohippus or later forms of equine animals. None of the earlier Eohippus forms has been, as yet, discovered there. A convincing fact that the pre-horse forms of animal life came to Asia from America.

Next, there have been found in Asia the fossilized remains of ancient horses that coincide exactly with the fossil remains of horses that lived at a time so recent that the fossils are intermingled with the artifacts of ancient man of a very remote era. Too far in the past for any reasonably accurate estimate as to time of existence.

Fossils of the horse have been found in situations that indicate the existence of horses among human beings at a time before the horse was domesticated. One such discovery was made in the remains of an ancient garbage dump just outside the entrance to a cave. An indication that the horse at that time probably was used by human beings exclusively as food.

Among the several known facts tending to substantiate the theory that the horse originated in the interior of ancient Asia is the great expanse of grazing lands that extended for countless miles along three sides of the receding morasses of that period. Those areas were, in that ancient period, blessed with an equable climate and the lands must have been the greatest grazing lands that ever existed. Perfect horse country, you may be sure.

Nature has a system of developing new forms of life that fit right into new natural situations. An illustration of such a situation has been so recent and so prominent as to be well known. It is the situation of the American plains buffalo and the great plains country of central North America. That western plains country was certainly an area that had been seemingly designed expressly for the plains buffalo. No other creature, not even the long-horned cow, was fitted so completely for that plains country as was the plains buffalo. The buffalo could move into the northern reaches of that country, acquiring on the way the finest, most perfect coat of hair as protection against cold ever granted to any land creature. At the other extreme, it might find itself, in the hot season, in a torrid expanse of and land far in the southland. There it would shed its heavy, shaggy covering. The first new hair growing out would be actually silky. The animal could wrinkle its hide and the fine silky hair would wipe away the spring insects that were so annoying to other creatures. By early autumn the winter hair would be growing. That hair would be quite stiff until cold weather actually came along. So stiff and so long by mosquito time that only a really super mosquito with a very long feed tube could reach through the hair. Even when such a well-equipped pest did happen along, all the buffalo needed to do was to wiggle its hide and the coarse new hair wiped it right off.

The camel is justly famed for its ability to drink sufficient water at one time to carry it over and lands for several days. The buffalo was not far behind the camel in ability to travel over large expanses of waterless country without suffering. The camel has a hump, or humps, expressly for storage of water. The buffalo had its hump too, but the buffalo hump had a more utilitarian use than the mere carrying of an extra water supply. The buffalo hump did double duty, being both a food and a water storage supply. Should a great prairie fire destroy all feed in areas of several days' travel, or should snow become so deep that even a buffalo could not get through to feed, the fat of the buffalo's hump would nourish it for some days with almost no loss of energy to the animal. In time of water shortage, in the hot season of the year, before the hump had become refilled with fat that had been used up in the previous winter, the hump would contain mostly water. In case of need the hump would release its water supply to the needful parts of the body. Too, the plains buffalo had paunch arrangements as a part of its innards that could carry an enormous supply of water. Water enough to take care of any but the most severe water shortages. It was not uncommon for buffalo to be found grazing on the plains four or five days away from a water supply.

The sagas of the plainsmen tell of their preference for the hump of the buffalo above that of any other meat, but that preference was greatest in the autumns or early winters. At that time of the year the humps would be heavy with new fat and have a low water content. The feed in early spring would be scant. The cows would be nursing their calves and the bulls would be doing their seasonal fighting. By autumn, the most pressing interference with feeding would have been taken care of; the buffalo grass would have stood thick and rich. By the time snow began to fall the humps would again be full of hump fat; a delectable kind of fat that cooked up into a tasty dish for famished plainsmen. Of course, many Indians preferred it raw and ate it quickly, before it lost its animal heat. At any rate, the buffalo was in prime shape for another winter.

All in all, the American Bison (the plains buffalo) was perfectly suited for its life on the great North American plains. Such, too, must have been the situation for the Mesohippus at the time its numbers arrived in the lush lands adjacent to the jungles that rimmed the great morasses that then existed in central and northern Asia.

The lifting of land areas above the water that covered the earth in primordial times happened in Asia at approximately the same time that the uplift occurred in the great central plains area of the North American continent. Both areas originally were great expanses of marsh and swamp lands. Both swamp areas began to shrink as world climate conditions changed. The morass areas of Asia were so very much larger than the swamp areas of North America that the Asian swamp lands receded more slowly. It could well have been that the lush lands bordering the Asian swamp lands were still in condition to be a preferred habitat of the Mesohippus at a time when the North American area had become much like an and desert, and for that reason was disliked by the Mesohippus of that time. That would have accounted for the movement, en masse, of the Eohippus from America into Asia. Beyond a doubt, the land masses of Asia and North America were joined at that time, so that situation could well have developed. After some thought about the situation, it may not seem as impossible as it does at first thought. At any rate, the Mesohippus did go from North America into Asia at some very ancient time.

At the time the pre-horse forms came to Asia and for many, many years thereafter few, if any, of the great predator forms that came into being later had appeared. For thousands of years—the span of time would perhaps be beyond either our comprehension or belief—the Mesohippus, and little-changed succeeding pre-horse forms of pre-horse equine existence, grew and multiplied. With little to disturb them, their numbers must have reached staggering figures. And then nature again took a hand.

Nature will not allow any single type of creature or any other form of life to become all predominant. For whatever reason, or whatever cause, the pre-horse equines disappeared in a relatively short time and horses appeared in their stead.

Now, by the time horses appeared in those wonderful grazing lands bordering the jungle, great jungle predators had developed. With ideal conditions during those times, their numbers grew until food became a pressing problem and of course food means meat to a predator, and, further, it means meat on the hoof.

2

HERE COMES THE HORSE

Fossils indicate that a short period of time elapsed between the time of the Mesohippus and the coming of the true horse, but actually, the disappearance of the one must coincide very closely with the appearance of the other, for the relationship of the Mesohippus to the horse is definite and cannot be mistaken. As proof thereof we have a like formation of the teeth, the bones of the feet, and the hoof formation, although the shape of the foot achieved its final perfection, in the single hoof for each foot, in the horse. That, and the wide spread of the nostrils at the bottom of a long narrow face, are the chief points of similarly unusual conformation that give us assurance of direct succession between the two. In addition, there is another feature of the first horses that they could have inherited only from their immediate ancestor, their predecessor, the Mesohippus. That is the camouflage of spots of diverse or opposing color, worn by both the pre-horse animal and the first Asian horse. Allow us to consider the situation, please.

Nature always seems to establish new forms of animal life in situations most favorable to their existence, but at the same time arranges deterrents to prevent such an increase in numbers as to allow one species to completely eliminate another.

The jungles of Asia, during the time the first horse appeared, contained the greatest variety and heaviest accumulation of great predators of any area of this earth. That situation, due to proximity of the best grazing lands, could easily have gotten out of balance because of the great hunting skill and prowess of those predators. But nature supplied both the Mesohippus and the first horses with a perfect camouflage as an aid to survival. The natural camouflage given to the earliest horses has never been surpassed under any circumstances.

Kindly pardon now a digression from the subject of horses while we consider the matter of natural animal camouflage. Here will be an appropriate place to display some of the reasoning on the spotted horse—the Appaloosa—that gives it a preferred position as the first horse.

Nature is insistent that no area of the earth shall be without some form of life. Some forms of animal life have ample weapons with which to defend themselves. Some with no weapons of defense have the speed necessary to escape the killers in their environs. Some, without the weapons for defense or the speed needed for safety in emergencies, have been given a camouflage as a means for survival. Instances of such protection are numerous in insect forms of life and also, of course, in animal life. One most prominent example of such a characteristic, one that is known to nearly everyone, is the camouflage given to baby deer before their birth. The deer is the favorite meat of predators of many lands. The baby deer—the fawn—is the greatest treat of all. The most favored meal of any normal predator.

What complicates the situation for any baby deer is the fact that the fawn is the most helpless of any important meat animal for several hours following its birth. In that situation it would seem that coyotes or wolves, cougars, wild cats, or bears would enjoy many a toothsome meal of young deer meat, but such is not the case. Nature has arranged means to prevent that.

The fawn in a comparatively short time will grow into a mature deer. To kill a fawn would be a waste and nature detests waste, and then, of course, there is the survival of the deer species that must be considered. Nature has taken protective steps even before the fawn is born. First, nature has halted the operation of the mother deer's scent glands some hours before the time of the fawn's

birth; then, as the mother's time nears, she makes a circular back-
track to smell or see if she is being followed. When satisfied, she
selects a site for the birth, then, as quickly as the fawn is born, she
nudges her baby with her nose in a warning to lie *perfectly* still
until her return; a warning that the fawn obeys to perfection. The
deer mother slips away some distance to where she can watch the
place where her baby is hidden. Should a killer come near, the
mother will do her best to lure the killer away, behaving, if necessary, as though she is badly crippled, and if that fails, employing
sundry other lures; enough to either draw the killer away or at least
to ruin its concentration on its hunt for the fawn.

Coyotes, though, are clever too. They have been known to disregard the tempting on the mother's part and to persist in a search
for the fawn. At least one has been seen within feet of a hidden
fawn without being able to find it, finally giving up in discouragement and attempting to capture the mother. Now, when a coyote
cannot find a baby deer, the baby is well hidden indeed, for the
coyote is probably the cleverest of all predators. The camouflage
that prevented the discovery was a series of large white spots
mingled in its basic tawny coloring. Apparently those round white
spots, about the size of a tennis ball, in the baby deer's coloring, are
nature's most perfect camouflage in animals of any appreciable size.

Nature equipped both the Mesohippus and the first horses with
an identical camouflage of large round spots of diverse coloring as
a protection against the many and great predators of those early
times. There were some special differences in the nature of those
white spots in the cases of the deer and the equine animals. The
fawn's white spots were usually in rows along its back and sides,
and as there very seldom was any difference in a fawn's body color,
the spots always are white. Too, in a few weeks, the fawn would
grow sufficiently to be able to travel with the mother regardless of
the mother's speed, and then the baby's camouflage would no
longer be needed. For that reason, the second growth of hair on
the fawn, when a few months old, would not have the camouflag-
ing white spots, for the fawn would then have no need for that
extra protection.

There were differences between the situations of the deer and the horses. The deer animal matured much faster than did the horse. Too, it preferred brush as a diet, so it frequented timber lands and brushy areas and brush was a most perfect protection for it. The horse creature was much slower maturing than was the deer species. It would be some months before baby colts could keep up with the horse band in flight from danger. While the earliest ancestors of the horse were brush eaters, that diet had changed in past ages and now horses ate grass exclusively, except at such times as dietary requirements needed some additions. The horse, then, lived entirely in the best open grass lands, and as the best grass lands lay close to the moist jungle areas, the horse lived most of its life in close proximity to the great jungle predators.

The horse is fast; maybe was even faster then, but it was unable to generate the speed needed to avoid the rush of great predators who attained phenomenal speed before they were detected by the horses. Nature took care of much of that difficulty by giving those early horses a body coloring of very diverse colors, no two animals being colored exactly alike, and then added perfection to that diverse coloring by adding a plentiful supply of round spots of a color the opposite of that of the general surrounding color. Unlike the baby deer, the horse always needed its camouflage, so it carried its diverse coloring all through life.

Just in case some may feel that this camouflage matter has been unduly stressed, let us consider the conditions and dangers that must have been a menace every day to those earliest of horses.

The earliest ancestors of the horse spent much of their time in close proximity to huge and dangerous Dinosaurs. There must have been other areas that would have met their living requirements. It seems as though those early little creatures found pleasure in an impudent invasion of Dinosaur territory. The horse too has much of its earliest ancestors' impudence in dealing with situations that might be inimical to its well-being, or at least its fundamental desires.

As illustrations we will offer samples of common recent occurrences. It has often happened that some rider will become unseated in a situation far from home. A situation requiring many miles of trudging a dusty and hot road. In such a situation, the horse most often will not disappear over a far horizon into safety and a chance at its natural circumstances of living, but will most often stop to graze at a distance that is encouraging to the now walking person. The horse will continue to nibble and graze, apparently paying no attention whatever to the person approaching closely now in an attempt at recapture, and success will seem assured, giving all the thrill accompanying an event of importance, and then, when success is at hand (darn it), the horse will move away just beyond capture, repeating this until pressed too closely, when it will canter away, carelessly and disdainfully stopping again at a distance that extends an invitation for another try. The impudence of the horse, the intentional impudence of that horse in such a situation, is so plainly evident that a rider has been known to become so exasperated as to shoot the horse at the very next try.

Too, in the wild horse country of America, horses in recent times have been known to stay in a favored location despite of danger from wild predators or human horse hunters. Sometimes perversity, or impudence, is revealed in the every move. Something like that must have prevailed in the early horse bands that lived near the ancient jungles in Asia.

What kind of predators menaced those horses? We do not know them all, but we do know of some, and those are plenty. Probably the worst predator of that time and area was the Saber-toothed Tiger. That creature was really a predator supreme. Added to that was the fact that the rim of the jungle lands was not a straight line, but deeply indented in many places, and commonly such indented areas were the most luxuriant of the horse feeding places. The horses therefore would persist in feeding in them even though danger was near.

The Saber Tooth was, when mature, often as heavy as many a horse. The shape and form of its body gave it the ability to creep along with fair speed close to the ground, so close that detection most often could be avoided. It too had a very fine camouflage of coloring. Its conformation enabled it to spring clear off the ground and through the air for a remarkable distance, and in addition, should it be detected before it reached a springing position, it could generate, for a short space, enough speed to bring down a surprised horse. The Saber Tooth did not like to feed out in the open. It was a jungle creature, but that was no real inconvenience. It had the strength to carry or drag a full-grown horse into some area of trees almost regardless of the distance. Yes, that Saber-toothed Tiger was a terrible predator.

Of course, the Saber Tooth's relative, the Asiatic Tiger, was almost as bad a predator. It was inferior to the Saber Tooth in size and strength, but most likely made up for those deficiencies by being more clever. It would use more time, more strategy, in its approach, but its rush too was very speedy. It certainly did its full share in keeping horses from becoming too numerous in a hurry.

A predator almost as destructive to horses as the two mentioned was the Jungle Bear. The few fossils that have been found of that creature display an unusual conformation. Its proportions were very long as to body and very short in the legs. When it traveled in a hurry, its back must have humped up and down like a boat on very choppy water. It was able though to travel underneath much of the jungle growth, so it had ready access almost anywhere in the jungle and was not confined to game trails. Legend has attributed to the Jungle Bear much of the cunning found in the American Wolverine, and that would have made it one of the greatest predators of the jungle.

Another bad feature of the Jungle Bear was its continuous hunger. It was the worst glutton of the jungles. Its appetite was almost never completely satisfied. It would eat anything; alive and kicking or dead and putrid. An example of its power and eating ability could be of interest.

The humid Asian jungle was a perfect home for snakes, and snakes grew to great size there. One form was a giant constrictor that crushed its victims to death, broke the bones by its constrictions, and then swallowed them. The size of the creatures it could swallow is almost beyond belief. After feasting on a kill, it would retire to some favorite spot until that meal had been digested, then would come out along some game trail and await the coming of another victim. Sometimes a meal would be a long time in coming and the snake would become ravenous. At such times it would attack anything that moved along the ground beneath its waiting place on the lower limbs of a tree.

For a time meat had become extremely short in the jungle. A great Jungle Bear, ravenous, was slipping along on trail in the hope of capturing a meal. Looking down, the giant snake saw its movements and dropped down upon it. That snake got the surprise of its life. The bear went into full action before the snake could realize it. He did not try to get away. He welcomed the attack. The snake did manage to get a coil around the bear's body, and was hammering it with blows from its great head, but the bear turned over almost completely within its skin, began to rake the snake with its inches-long claws, and quickly clawed its way into the snake's vitals. Now, even a snake would feel all cut up in such a situation and would like to disengage itself and get away, but the bear was enjoying himself no end and would have none of that. Finally he began to eat that great snake, and for once that bear had more than he could eat at one sitting.

Sometimes the bear would be unlucky in the jungles and would then be forced to go outside in search of meat. Its best chance there would be a horse. It might take some time to locate a band of horses in a desirable situation, but the bear would be patient and along towards evening would take a chance. If the situation was not too favorable, the bear would use strategy. It would find a mud hole and roll itself thoroughly in that mud. That would mask its feral scent. Then it would trail back on the horse movements, find some quite fresh manure, and roll itself well in that, providing itself with a horsey smell. As dark came on it would creep ever so cunningly toward the band of resting horses. The horses would be enjoying a well-fed evening's snooze. The bear would charge them. Often it would miss, but woe unto some feeble one among them. The bear could feast then, and how it did enjoy a feed of horse meat!

In addition to the jungle animals already mentioned there were others. Leopards were forever on the prowl and they too loved horse meat. There were a few Asiatic lions, who lived outside the main jungle, but they preferred a different environment from the jungle lands, so they were no serious menace to the horses. They were not nearly so dangerous as the great wolves of Asia that existed at that time. That early Asian wolf was so terrible that its name has come down in history as the Dire Wolf. The Dire Wolf posed a different type of threat to the early horse than did the jungle predators. Whereas the horse could not achieve a sudden burst of speed that would surely carry it off safely before the onrush of some jungle beasts, it did have the speed to outrun the great wolves. To compensate for this the wolves had the staying power to remain for long hours at top speed, and, in addition, devised methods of group strategy that secured them meat on many occasions.

The Dire Wolves, capable of long-sustained speed, had the persistence that enabled them to maintain a chase for hours, and woe to any creature that was unable to outlast them. The wolves were hungry almost all the time but preferred to hunt by night. When extremely hungry they would sometimes attack by day. On a fresh trail their sense of smell was satisfactory, but they could not follow an old trail well. Their eyesight was keen at close range but inadequate at a long distance. They made up for their deficiencies of sight and smell by traveling in small packs, widely scattered, and when game was sighted in quantities, they could call in other packs from miles way. Thus they could range over wide areas quite thoroughly. They would take any meat that they could kill but preferred horse to any other.

After horse bands had multiplied and some had spread to northern latitudes and snow became deep, the bands usually moved about closely bunched and when attacked by a wolf pack would form a tight ring, heels to the outside and with the colts and infirm horses in the middle. The wolves would first try to break up the ring, in the hope of getting at a colt or securing some weakling being sheltered in the middle. If that failed, they would circle the band, keeping close, maybe hour after hour. Some tumbled around, close, in the snow, hoping to distract the attention of some unwary horse sufficiently for some confederate to get a nip at a hock or pastern joint. If some tendons could be severed, the damaged horse would be a victim sooner or later. The circle might be broken and then the colts or the old horses would be easy victims. The persistence of the wolves was phenomenal and discouraging. Occasionally, but not often, some nervous horse would charge out at some pestering wolf in the hope of doing damage. That would be against the precepts of long standing on the part of that horse and sometimes led to disaster, for the attackers would notice the nervous condition of that particular horse before the action and would be ready, surging in behind the charging horse and cutting it off from the circle. Then, all too often, that horse would be doomed. Such a horse, invariably, would have been a young stallion not yet of the maturity that would have caused its exile from the band at the will of the senior stallion. Sometimes the band stallion would charge out, kill or maim a wolf, and then quickly return to its place in the protective circle. That happened but seldom, for the senior stallion was smart, from much experience, and would not break the circle even for a moment, except under the most favorable conditions.

If nothing of advantage for the wolves materialized, they would keep up the pressure for hours, until finally some colt or other weakling in the ring center would weaken and go down. The wolves would then stop their circling maneuvering and bunching together against the weakest side would combine into an attack that would soon force the circle away from the fallen animal. Then, soon, all that would be left of that doomed creature would be some white bones. The wolves seldom left even one spot of bright red blood to show where their kill had occurred.

If a pack of wolves slipped up on a scattered band of horses, spread out grazing on growth that they could reach through the snow, these wolves, keeping out of sight while deciding on some strategy conveyed to each other by some means as yet not certain, would then, at an opportune time, rush in and endeavor to separate one or more horses, crowding them away from the band, and when successful, consumed the separated animals, sometimes tearing an unfortunate horse to pieces while it was still struggling to

escape. Should the situation be such that the snow crust would bear
the weight of the wolves, but break under the weight of the horses,
there would be a massacre, unless the horses had been close enough
together to form a protective circle before the wolves could complete their havoc. Those that failed to achieve the circle were sometimes actually eaten alive, the wolves beginning at the soft parts of
the belly or flank or at the soft parts beneath the tails. Horses were
more protective-minded than were some other animals, so that
such incidents did not occur too often to a horse band. But even
so, it did occur occasionally. Deer and some other ruminants
suffer great losses in that way in times of deep snow.

Having survived the winter, horses usually outfoxed the wolves
for another year. In the spring wolves occupied a different terrain
because of their cubs. In their spring locations there would be much
feathered and other small game, and that was important, for the
cubs needed a lot of meat, and small game could be carried easily
to the dens. Later, when the cubs had grown sufficiently to be able
to join in the hunt, larger game was preferable. Then a few families would form a pack and go on the prowl for larger game. If a
horse could be taken, that would surely be a prize. Horse was preferred meat for wolves at any season of the year.

With no snow on the ground, and the cubs lacking experience,
the pack leader would keep the pack out of sight while he recon-
noitered the horse band, hoping to discover a cripple or an old
horse separated from the rest. After he had engineered a plan he
would order up his pack, which converged upon some lone animal, cutting it off from the band and forcing it into flight.

The Dire Wolves possessed a lot of speed, but experience had
taught them that a horse could outrun them and they could not
figure on a quick kill. Oh, well! The cubs needed experience
anyway. So the pack settled down to a long chase, with the leader
hoping for a chance to work out a relay for his young hunters. First
the lone horse would try to gain the protection of the band, but,
failing in that, would take off for the far horizon. In affairs of this
kind the running horse invariably was a mare, for there would be
only one stallion to a band of horses. The rest would be mares or

colts; the colts would be mostly near their dams, and the older mares with colts would, because of their long experience, be clustered somewhere near the band stallion. That clustering would partly be based on family experiences with the band stallion and partly on the fact that mares in a band commonly form a strong attachment to some other mare of that band, and that leads to a clustered core in any normal band of wild horses. The lone animal might be either a young mare who was inquisitive about something close that was unusual, or, of course, it could, occasionally, be some immature stallion who might be working off excess energy chasing a tumbleweed or just naturally cavorting around. In most cases it would have been a barren mare.

Now, with their prey running ahead of them, the stronger wolves would press the chase, but after some time and miles of running some of the pack would peel off, some to the right, some to the left, scattering out so that if their quarry should circle and head back for the horse band they would be in a position to head it off, or at least be fresh to take up the chase from there. That kind of plan often worked with deer and antelope.

If the quarry was old or in poor condition for any reason, the chase would not last over an hour or so, but if the fleeing horse was in good condition, it would hold a satisfactory lead by evening, and when it became quite dark, would make a wide circle so as to evade its pursuers and in many cases make its way finally back to the band. That would be a most likely occurrence if the running horse had come to a considerable stream. The stream would be waded and followed long enough to wash off all sweat scents, whereupon the wolves would then be badly handicapped in their efforts.

Some people may question the ability of a horse to run at high speed for the better part of a full day without becoming completely exhausted, but remember, please, that we are discussing a spotted mare of the earliest breed of horses known. The reason why the Spotted Horse (hereinafter called the Appaloosa) mare could make such a wonderful run before the questing wolves was due to the fact that she had been specially adapted for it by nature under nature's most perfect process: survival of the fittest.

What sort of horses were those earliest Appaloosas? Let's try to describe them.

3

EARLY-TIME APPALOOSAS AND SOME OTHER OBSERVATIONS

When we of the present time first begin to think of horses, we should remember that the present-day animal is mostly the result of many years of human selective breeding. Generally speaking, each of the modern breeds was achieved under human-controlled breeding. The first horses, though, were established by nature, and because of its equine heritage the horse was able to adapt itself quite readily to any reasonable desire of its breeders. Many creatures, some of immense size and great strength, but without the ability to adapt to changes, no matter how vital for their continued existence, have disappeared from this earth.

After man took charge of the breeding and production of horses, he developed many breeds, each for its special purpose, and I believe that every breed developed has been a credit to the men who developed them. Man first made notable progress in the breeding of horses in the age of chivalry. After that stage in man's advance in civilization, his greatest need in horses was for large and strong work horses. It was during that period that many great strains of work horses were developed in Europe. Under man's selective breeding program, the stallion was the key to progress and the success of his program. So, in the course of a few hundred years, man, by selective breeding, developed lines of descent in which the stallions were great and impressive animals far overshadowing the mares in every respect except endurance. The stallion was the lord of the horse creation. The mare, more in the nature of a chambermaid. Regardless of how we admire the stallions, it was a well-known fact in the early days on the farm that the mares were the chief producers of the labor. In the early days of wheat farming on a large scale in the Pacific northwest, it was general knowledge that the mares could outwork any stallion, irrespective of size and whether or not the stallion had ever been used for breeding purposes. Someone may offer his views as to the reasons for that situation, someone else can think of some other reason. As far as I can remember, no one ever offered a satisfactory reason. But as a matter of fact it was nature's most important way of insuring the reproduction of the equine species and their spread over the earth. That is a certainty, for it is proved by the situation that existed among the earliest true Appaloosa horses.

The Power that planned the world and its future may have had in mind the horse as merely a servant of man to slave life away in front of a plow or a combine. As to that I cannot say, but one thing is certain: nature's purpose in establishing life in this world was to have some form of life growing in every possible place on earth— on and in the land and on and in the water. To accomplish that purpose she started different forms of life, both plant and animal. One of the important and interesting forms of life thus developed and established was the equine species. Nature meant for that species to reproduce and to spread over the earth, and, in order that they might accomplish that purpose, endowed them with special and unusual forms and characteristics. The males of that species, the equines, were given certain attributes not common among the males of some other important known animals. The females acquired some characteristics not generally enjoyed by the females of other important well-known animals.

The unusual attributes of the males were to insure that there would be no deterioration in the species. Those of the female, to insure the continued existence of the species. The females of the early horses, those that lived exclusively according to nature's plans, had need of a larger body than did the males because of the foals that the females would be carrying for much of their productive lives. The larger body demanded more lung capacity; larger lung capacity required exceptional nostrils to assure the needed oxygen for those larger lungs, and because of the mare's need for these things, nature supplied her with them.

The Appaloosa horse, when its blood lines are not too greatly diluted by other strains, exhibits these features most surely, as well as one or two others not yet mentioned. These will be brought in later as substantiating evidence is introduced.

The Appaloosa mare that was making the long run in escaping the wolves, as described a page or two prior to this, had all of these extra elements needed for her long run and final escape.

Without making a critical study of that mare, one might have passed over her size, which was greater than that of the stallion in a band of comparable age, but not even a casual observer would have missed noticing her large ears, suggesting those of a mule, nor also her special, enormous nostrils. Those nostrils were set wide of the face and were very long in their horizontal line as well. Then, too, the nostril itself had a spongy, expansive formation that could be expanded into an air scoop during a hard or long run, thus assuring great amounts of oxygen for the lungs of the mare during a time of need. This feature of the extraordinary nostrils was so prominent that early plains Indians noticed it and it brought about a custom among some of these Indians of slitting the nostrils on their best hunting and war horses. That fact is part of well-known history.

(Additional confirmation of this unusual difference between the bodies of the male and female Appaloosa will be given at an opportune time when I write of Appaloosas under observation by early explorers of the American Far West.)

A question that a reader may have in mind at this time is: What did the early-time Appaloosa horse look like? I had better describe them from what I remember as a child. Some present-day Appaloosas contain so much foreign blood that there is great variation in their appearance and conformation. When I first wrote on the subject I went into considerable detail, using so much technical nomenclature that I actually lost my mental picture of the Appaloosa horse when the description was complete. I have before me now an issue of the *Appaloosa News*, George B. Atley, editor—the official Appaloosa Horse Association publication. In that issue, a man knowing the correct technical names for the various physical features of the horse gives us a rather professional description of the Appaloosa. It is to be doubted that the average reader will acquire a good mental picture from that description. Such words as pastern, coffin bone, or fetlock may mean little to anyone not actively engaged in the horse business. Perhaps a description can be given in words not at all technical but that will supply a mental picture of the Appaloosas to anyone only slightly familiar with horses. As a basis for this description I will call upon my memories of the Appaloosas I knew as a very small boy.

The Appaloosas, as I knew them, stood from 14 to 15 hands high; that is, they were about 5 feet tall. The stallions and the mares were about alike in this aspect and that was the only feature that I recall in which both the stallions and the mares were equal. The stallion's head was rather small, comparatively, the ears also small and carried upright and tight. The eyes were set wider than is common in other horses and were friendly and intelligent, with none of the wild look common in other range stallions. The face was pleasing in length but pinched in considerably at the nostrils. When the least displeased or uncomfortable, the muzzle would have a wrinkled appearance, just as though the animal had eaten, or just tasted, a bitter, green, wild plum. At least one of the stallions I knew had quite a Roman nose, that is, the lower face and muzzle curved down sharply to the lower chin in a sort of hook. Body length was normal, the withers high, and the chest wide, with the front legs wide. The neck was normal, but contained a very sparse and short mane. So nearly not a mane at all as to be forcefully noticeable. The hips were pleasingly round both towards the tail and to the sides. The tail emerged rather high and was so sparse, so little like a horse's tail, as to be laughable. Some of the parts, usually concealed under the tail and elsewhere, were of a mottled pink and other body colors. I recall that there were some white feet and that one animal had, what I now call, laminated hoofs; that is, the hoof shell looked as though it had been put together in strips and by some unskilled workman who had not been at all expert. (Today I

believe that this feature was a throwback to some very early ancestor who lived at some ancient time when the horse genus was
very young. That it was a specimen of the original, evolved, first
horse hoof.) The movements of both the stallions and the mares
were very smooth and made for easy riding. The two cowboys I
knew who had Appaloosa mounts really loved them and claimed
them to be the best cow horses that they had ever seen.

The only similar physical conformation in the Appaloosa stallion and mare that I can now remember was to be found in their
approximately equal height. In every other conformation the mares
were larger than the stallions. They were longer than the stallions,
especially in the barrel. Their hip structure jutted back almost level,
then dropped down directly to the tail, which emerged rather low.
Toward the sides the hips were almost flat, then dropped away
practically vertically at the sides. The barrel was deep, especially
just in back of the front legs. That feature may have been empha-
sized because of the unusually high withers. At any rate the impression is still with me after a good many years. That combination made the most pleasant bareback seat I have ever straddled,
and I was practically raised on horseback.

The chest was very deep and broad. That wide spread caused
the front legs to be set wide apart and those legs were extra sturdy
and strong above the knees. The neck began tapering about half-
way to the top and ended sporting a mane that was so sparse and
insignificant as to be scarcely worthy of the name, but the lower
throat was so wide as to be almost a deformity. The airduct and
the throat vein were so large and prominent, with the heartbeats
registering so strongly, that they both are features that are as plain
in my mind as though I had just noticed them yesterday.

The ears of the Appaloosa mare were a very distinctive feature,
exclusive with her out of all the clans of the horse. Facing a person, in a group, those ears resembled the ears of a group of mules,
or of a small band of cow elk as they first glimpse a hunter as they
come up a game trail. The position in which the mare carries those
ears or handles them is a true indication of what is on her mind.
When she is at rest, content and secure, her ears are carried loosely,

each one inclined to loll in an independent direction, and will change direction independently of each other to catch sounds from different directions. At a word of command or of something of definite interest, either of sight or sound, the ears will act in unison to concentrate upon a specific circumstance. If something of interest moves or comes into sight, the ears immediately point directly toward that object, acting as a perfect pointer toward the object under scrutiny.

The eyes, too, were set very wide-apart—unusually wide—so wide that a mare could see to the rear without having to move her head from side to side. A feature that could have been of great importance in the early times of the great predators. Those eyes were large, limpid, and bright, and usually gave the impression of complete serenity and indicated an intelligence not found in many other animals.

The face was long, exceptionally long, and narrow below the eyes until coming to the nostrils; there the muzzle spread so wide as to appear to be the next thing to a deformity. When a mare ran— and I have seen them immediately following a race—the nostrils expanded into air scoops that extended to each side of the muzzle. That feature must have supplied unusual amounts of air in case of emergency. It was, by the way, so perfect a feature that Indians became aware of it at some early time, for it is a matter of record that some tribes of Indians slit the nostrils of their war and buffalo hunting mounts in the hope that the surgery would give added ability to their most important mounts to secure air.

The hoofs of the mares were spread wider than those of the stallions; they were not nearly so dainty, it seems to me now, and did not display as much white. That completes my description of the Appaloosa as I knew them and we will now proceed with the progress of the earliest horses.

4

THE APPALOOSA SPREADS AND A NEW NATION IS BORN

Once the Appaloosa was established it spread quickly and widely across Asia. That is certain, because of its predilection for traveling in small bands that were widely scattered owing the stallion's innate opposition to competition for his mares. That characteristic of the stallion induced a faster and wider spread than that usually attained by other animals. A stallion good enough to collect and hold a harem of mares must have been a superior horse, for heaven knows he must have had plenty of competition, since the incidence of male and female births was fairly equal among horses.

When a male colt reached sufficient maturity to get that male twinkle in his eyes, the band's leader stallion was mighty quick to take note of the circumstance. He was forever on the watch for such a situation, while the female members of the band were interested only seasonally, at mating time. As soon as the band leader detected the new situation, dissension arose, and furor and much clamor and bickering were heard as the master endeavored to run the youngster out of the band. The young fellow hung around, making a nuisance of himself, but soon the lord of the band would become so irked that he would run the young one pretty well out of the immediate vicinity. That was quite a job, too, for the youngster, now that need required it, quickly began to exhibit traits of deception and persistence, inherited from, but nonetheless annoying to, his sire. If by chance, or fortunate circumstance, the youngster did manage to cut out a mare or two, he would hurry with his prize to some distant place, where he hoped there would be no competition and where he might hope to add to his harem from time to time.

If unsuccessful in his endeavors to secure mares and forced to flee and stay away because of the fury of his elder, the colt would wander about alone until joined by others in a similar situation, after which his time would be occupied by the usual requirements of daily existence, and by a daily simulation of battle with his fellows in preparation for successful action at some later time.

When instinct, and the urges within him, dictated, the young stallion would disappear by stealth from the band of his peers and search for a harem of mares in charge of a stallion he hoped he could vanquish. He would be by that time a wonderful young animal, really attractive enough to catch and hold the attention of flirtatious mares, and what is more, he knew it. When he had located such a band—with enough mares to suit his fancy—he approached them, shrilling and snorting his challenge to the band's master. Very seldom did the young stallion charge right in and start hostilities immediately. By inherited custom, certain amenities had first to be performed. It was in a way a matter of chivalry, and of course, he had to display his perfections to the harem.

As soon as the interloper was seen by the band's master, that oldster would take umbrage at once, and hurl himself some steps towards his adversary, also displaying for the harem his own splendid form, with his head up high and his tail twitching in a warning for his mares to mind their behavior. When the young challenger did not retreat or turn away but answered with another challenge of his own, the master would return quickly, collect his mares into a compact group, and hurry them away some distance, preferably out of sight behind some brush or a nearby knoll, giving many a painful nip to rumps as a warning to the mares to behave while the nearby conflict was in progress.

Then satisfied, if not content, with that particular situation, the monarch turned about and hurried to come to blows with his adversary. If ever stallions could look imperial, it was at such a time as that—heads held high, their eyes actually flashing fire, their tails whipping from side to side as fury mounted, their superb bodies displayed to each other by their sidling, prancing approach, their hair shining as though freshly groomed by some solicitous groom. A final challenge was blared, snorted, and answered. Both shrilled in a battle shriek loud enough to have startled angels in high heaven; then amenities were over and the battle was on.

All chivalry was forgotten once the battle was joined. Every trick either animal knew, every stratagem ever acquired, was used in an effort to gain victory. The glorious horses of but moments before were gone. In their stead were two beasts of different mien and character. Ears laid back tight against their necks, eyes partly closed but shooting sparks of greatest hate and fury, lips drawn back and large teeth bared in a hate that thirsted for the feel of a jugular vein and for a hold that could not be shaken, front hoofs flashing with a speed faster than sight, they struggled for supremacy, and woe to the horse that went down. Once the battle was on, no mercy would be shown by either.

True, a badly hurt or discouraged challenger might disengage himself and find safety in flight, but that was a rare conclusion. For the defending stallion, the battle was to the death, although it has happened that a badly stomped-on and much disfigured older stallion has later revived sufficiently to totter away after the younger victor had left hurriedly to lord it over his new-found harem and then hurried them away to greener pastures. Most commonly, it was a fight to the death. It was nature's way of insuring that the best males would keep high the quality of future generations.

In the course of time, some horses went to a far country, and at some time some band became isolated and found itself in conditions completely at variance with conditions general to the earliest spotted horses. Then, with the passing of centuries and partly because of much inbreeding, these horses were bound to change. With few predators about, possibly none, camouflage would be unnecessary. Generations of hoofs in sand would cause hoofs to spread, or conversely, continued use of severely rocky terrain would change hoof shape and structure; a potent sport form might develop, many circumstances could change the conformation of the isolated horses—they are very adaptable—and lo and behold, a new breed of horses had materialized!

At least one situation is definitely known where steady high temperature, with a daily sun beating down on desert sand, bleached out color patterns, leaving a light-colored breed of horses whose conformation of body had changed in the course of a few generations because most of their food was browse.

A change of coloration in animal life in order to conform with the predominant colors of a location in closely associated areas is very common in nature. For instance: In the upper Cowiche Canyon of the Yakima Valley in Washington State, in an area of black rock cliffs, black rock talus, and black scattered rocks, the rattlesnakes are as black as the rocks all about them. They show no light color whatever in their markings. One mile and a half to the east of the black cliffs, in a gray sagebrush area, with the intervals between the sage a light, straw-colored cheat grass, the rattlesnakes are a sagebrush-gray color, with markings the color of the straw-colored cheat. The horse, being among the most adaptable of creatures, would, in the course of a few generations, assume color patterns under the influence of the natural surroundings. Therefore, a change in the color of horse groups, even a change in conformation, to meet the requirements of changed conditions as these groups spread into distant lands should not be surprising.

Their color patterns would most certainly change to the requirements imposed by great areas of desert sand, the extremes of a searing desert sun, and continual high temperatures, and in but a few generations there would be but slight resemblance between them and those recently from a foreign locale into areas of desert sun. So much for color changes. But we also find changes in body conformation, for horses, being very adaptable by nature, achieved transformations to better meet changed living conditions. For instance, the original horses had very scant tails and manes and a very inferior forelock. In desert Arabia we find the Arabian horse with a large, thick, and long forelock, so immense that it can protect both eyes during the worst of sand storms, and with tails ankle-long and even longer, the better to keep pestering insects away from its body. And in early times, when many Arabian horses still ran wild, manes were seen that were so profuse that they covered both sides of the neck, thus protecting jugular veins from damage or rupture in times of battle.

(Experiments in breeding in recent years have indicated a close relationship between the Appaloosa and the Arabian horse.)

Leaving a proposition that may still seem somewhat speculative to some, and returning to known facts about the early horse, we find that the spotted horse was known to early man in very early times, for they roamed throughout Europe at the time of the prehistoric cave men. On a wall of a deep cave in southern France, a cave man, thousands of years ago, painted in lasting colors a spotted horse. That picture delights the eyes of every horseman who has ever seen it. The colored spots are painted in color, and the size and position are such as to convince anyone familiar with good Appaloosas that the painter of that horse knew his subject thoroughly.

Had other horses of distinction, or even of mediocre appearance, been at all common, one or more of the other types would have been portrayed in some painting in those age-old caves by some prehistoric painter. Actually, those cave men painted their pictures so long ago, few really modern animals are pictured. Most of the paintings are of animals so ancient that they have been long extinct, which proves that the spotted horse was indeed a very early visitor there.

It could be, in fact it is quite probable, that the earlier attempts at civilization in eastern Asia were already in progress at the time the picture of the Appaloosa horse was being painted in the cave of southern France. No one yet knows how long ago the earliest efforts towards civilization began in eastern Asia. No one yet knows how long ago the earliest attempts at civilization began anywhere. Even the better-known attempts in the well-known lands bordering on, or adjacent to, the Mediterranean Sea have been set further in the past several times in the last hundred years. Encyclopedic information more than thirty years old is out of date. Seventy years ago it was commonly thought that the world had been created less than 5,000 years earlier. Today it is known that creatures existed on the earth, or in its water, millions upon millions of years ago, and I am suspicious. I believe that science will continue for some time to place those years farther and farther into the past.

When we consider affairs of the past, it is astonishing how circumstances of benefit to each other mature at opportune times. For instance: The peak in buffalo population in the great plains country of central North America occurred at about the time that the American Indians of that plains country achieved the horse, and it so happened that white men were just arriving along the Mississippi River at that time, looking across into that Indian country—a combination of circumstances that eliminates coincidence as a factor. Actually, it is amazing how often a combination of circumstances of great aid to human progress does happen at most fortunate times.

It could well be that horses arrived in great numbers in eastern Asia at a time when their coming was of great help to Chinese progress. No one can know for certain how long ago the Chinese had forms of organized human societies. Authentic Chinese history dates back more than 4,300 years. Emperor Fo Hi founded the Chinese silk industry at that time. By that time, too, Chinese astronomers were making correct records of astronomic phenomena.

The Emperor Yu began one of the world's greatest reclamation projects approximately 2000 B.C. It could be that China was an organized society 6,000 years ago, and that is a very long time.

The Chinese Emperor Shi Hoang-Ti built the Great Wall of China and expelled the Mongols from China around 200 B.C. Presumably, the Great Wall kept out re-enforcements of Mongol horsemen, which circumstance enabled the Chinese to get the upper hand of those aliens within the Great Wall, and thus the emperor got rid of those pesky Mongols who had been raiding throughout eastern Asia since before the records, or memory, of man. The Great Wall of China was built to stop horsemen. The foot soldier has always had more tenacity of purpose than the horse soldier.

The soldier on foot makes his progress slowly and painfully, usually marching for days and days of seemingly endless hours. His
feet are sore; most likely blistered. He has won his way thus far by
toil and sweat and will not fritter away the gain his personal
energy has achieved. He will go into camp when faced with a great
obstruction, and figure and plan, trying to overcome the bar that
his enemy set up to thwart him. He will build towers or ramps to
surmount it, or burrow underneath it like a badger. It's a long,
long way back home. He has just walked over it. And grub will be
very, very scarce (commanders do not usually take too good care
of a defeated army). No. Foot soldiers would have breached that
wall, but not so the cavalry. Upon coming to a barrier that impeded
their onward march, the mounted men would not halt for long,
staring at a wall that barred their way. In honest rage, by the very
nature of men raised upon horseback, they would ride in a great
rush with ever-mounting fury, maybe to the right, maybe to the
left, rushing to find a place where they could ride over or around
the obstruction in their way. Then finally, in disgust, they would
turn away in the hope of finding some other objective to raid. It
was 1279 A.D. before the Mongols conquered any large part of
China the second time. The Chinese claimed then that it was the
superior Mongol horses that did it and went to work acquiring more
horses of their own.

For far too many years the Mongols had been making life miserable for the people of Turkestan. Only the Himalaya Mountains
had saved them. Now free China got together with Turkestan, swapping rice and other commodities for horses. Spotted horses. China
had the goods and insisted on the best. It was in those days that
the Chinese became lyrical about horses, calling the spotted ones,
"The Heavenly Horse"; "The Kingly Horse"; "The Dawn Horse";
"The Beautiful Horse"; and similar names. The Mongols got wise
to what was going on but they could not stop the traffic; greedy for
wealth, they had cut their own herds down too low, and then there
were those Himalayas. The Turkomen delivered their horses by way
of the Takla Makar, Yarkand and the Valley of Kashmir. It was a
long drag, but they had the time and did the job, and by 1368 A.D.,

the Mongols were driven out of China and never again became a menace. They in turn complained about the shortage of good horses, but it had been their own fault. Greedy for wealth, they had sold so many of their spotted horses that their numbers had disappeared, and too, the climate of inner Asia had been changing steadily for hundreds of years. The great jungle areas had disappeared, and what once had been lush pasture land was now desert. The spotted horses had not been thriving in that environment. The Mongolian horses now were desert stock, hardy enough but becoming ever more inferior to their neighbors. The Turkomen still raised them in large numbers, but Mongolia, as an independent country, was soon to disappear from history. The days of Genghis Khan and his hordes of warriors mounted on spotted steeds were past. *Sic Transit Gloria Mundi.*

The greatest commander of the China-Turkestan coalition was one Timur (Tamerlane), the Tartar, known to history as Tamerlane the Great. He became thereafter the greatest conqueror ever to come out of Asia, and used all the spotted horses he could find for his cavalry. By 1370 A.D., he had swept Mongolia bare of her best horses and had all of Turkestan with him; his warriors were mounted on the best horses in all of Asia. He extended his power to include all of Persia, all of central Asia to the Great Wall of China, and from there to Moscow. When he died in 1405, the spotted horses, the Appaloosa, were practically all dead with him. Kings offered great rewards for the delivery of a good sire. They could not find one. They should have disappeared completely from history, and probably would have, except for the fact that Queen Isabella of Castile and Aragon needed horses desperately in her final surge to drive the Moors out of Spain.

A plentiful supply of fine Arabian horses had enabled the Moors to force the Spanish armies away from the Mediterranean shore. For almost 700 years they had crowded the Spaniards ever northward until they had come to the land of Castile. There at long last King John had withstood them. But King John had died and then his daughter Isabella had become queen and had sworn at her

father's deathbed to drive the infidels across the sea. The task had
seemed hopeless at first, but then she engaged Manuel Cortés, a
childhood friend, to supply her with horses for her armies. Cortés
did so well that the queen prevailed over the Moors and now one
more strong campaign should prove their end, but more horses
would be needed. Horses would decide the issue. She appealed to
Cortés and he, staunch friend, promised her the horses. He was
confident, for he already had made contacts that would produce
them.

There were almost no suitable horses left in all Spain. For the
long struggle against the Moors had been draining the horses, not
only out of Spain, but out of all Austria and France too. Christen-
dom was doing what it could to back up the Christians of Spain; a
Cortés agent in Vienna had made a contact in Genoa (ancient
Genua) with agents from the Christian settlements in and about
Aleppo in Syria who also were fighting the infidels. They needed
weapons, almost anything in Spanish steel would be acceptable.
They had horses by the thousands to exchange. A deal was made.
The exchange was to take place in Beirut, a seaport of Syria. Ships
were assembled from Valencia to Barcelona, with steel and many
drovers aboard. The exchange was consummated in Beirut, the
horses loaded, and Cortés was about to sail, When a band of
Turkomen swept into the city from out of the mountains beyond
Tashkent, followed by a great herd of horses. The Turkomen were
primitive people. Their wants were few. Their price was very low.
Financial arrangements were completed with Jewish moneylend-
ers and Cortés purchased the Turkomen horses.

Among those horses were a dozen of a queer, spotted breed.
The Turks claimed that they were the last in existence. Cortés
bought them for his farms.

The great flotilla of ships unloaded its horses at Valencia. They
were driven across country into Cordova and Badajos army areas,
where they were allotted to various army elements. The spotted
horses were taken to the Cortés farms up in Estramadura, with the
exception of one fine mare, which Cortés presented to Queen
Isabella with his compliments. The queen is pictured on that mare

as she accepts the sword of Boabdil, chief of the Moors, in surrender. The horses furnished by Cortés had given her the power to vanquish the Moors and remove the menace of Mohammedanism from Europe, and now the queen was ready for further brilliant enterprise.

A certain impecunious sailor man from Genoa, Christopher Columbus by name, had believed that the world was round and that by sailing west a short way the fabulous land of India would be found. He had tried nearly every court in Europe during some years without securing backing for the making of such a voyage and as a last resort had petitioned Queen Isabella. The queen believed in him and his ideas, but was unable to be of assistance until after the Moors were expelled. Immediately after Boabdil's surrender she sent for Columbus and sent him on his way across the wide water from the Old World to where he found a New.

In the course of time, Don Diego Columbus, son of the great admiral, began to colonize the New World discovered by his father. Among the early colonists was Hernando Cortés, nephew of the Manuel Cortés who had procured horses for Queen Isabella.

The nephew had been a favorite of his childless Uncle Manuel, and the uncle, after a few years, presented Hernando with some of the Appaloosa horses. The colonial situation proved to be ideal for young Cortés. He soon developed into the most influential and moneyed man in the early colonies. So when the governor of Cuba decided to try the establishment of a colony on the newly discovered mainland in what is now the land of Mexico, Hernando Cortés was given command of the first serious attempt to form a colony there.

Through unusual circumstances (see *The White God of the Aztecs*), Cortés took Appaloosas from his Cuban farms on that enterprise, and later received more from re-enforcements from his Uncle Manuel of Spain.

Cortés (who was believed by Montezuma, ruler of the Aztecs, to be Quetzalcoatl, the returned White God of ancient Aztec legend) came into serious trouble with these Aztecs in Mexico City, their capital. During some severe fighting there, his party was in serious difficulty. Montezuma, ruler of the Aztecs, had been kidnapped by Cortés and held as hostage for the Spaniard's safety in the Spanish quarters. He became ill as the fighting between the Spaniards and the Aztecs was building up to a climax. His wife thought that she could save her husband's life if she could get him home where the Aztec medicine men could use their cures, so she sent Iztcuitl, favorite daughter of Montezuma, and a charmer, as hostage for the release of Montezuma, together with a retinue of Aztec royalty and a group of Montezuma's personal sacrificial victims, as assurance to Cortés that Montezuma would never again sacrifice humans upon Aztec religious altars.

As the Aztec hostage party was gaining entrance to the Spanish palace grounds, the Spaniards were in extremities, temporary, but nevertheless very disturbing and unnerving to some of them. When they were threatened with the loss of Cortés' favorite Appaloosas, they, with some of the Spanish horses and some wounded Spaniards, were placed in the care of the hostage party and rushed through the Tacuba Gateway, out onto the causeway leading from the city. As Iztcuitl and her party passed through the gates, a great Aztec wail could be heard. "Montezuma is dead; Montezuma is dead."

The sacrificial-victim part of the hostage party wanted nothing more to do with any Aztec, and of course they feared the white man. They took charge and proceeded to leave Mexico City with the horses and the wounded Spaniards, meeting with no objections from Montezuma's daughter, for she now believed her father dead and was actually in horror of Cortés, since he had frightened her no end at an entertainment extended him at an earlier date. By good fortune, and also by the use of some ingenuity, the hostage party escaped the Aztecs, but was forced by circumstances to go toward the north, which direction led away from the homelands of the sacrificial members of the hostage party. They continued making their way toward the north, happy to have avoided Aztec war parties. And now we had better give some attention to the personnel.

Juan Alvarado, one of the five Alvarado brothers with the Cortés force, had been its veterinarian and had done double duty as its doctor and with great success. He was a quiet individual, not given to great flights of fancy, but a staunch friend in time of need, and he truly loved animals and more especially horses. He had been struck alongside the head with a heavy Aztec boulder. It had struck with such force that Juan had not even seen stars. He had simply gone down as though he had been struck with a sledge. Fortunately though, the blow had been glancing rather than direct and although the concussion had been severe the skull had not been fractured. After regaining consciousness he had a bad headache for some time but was fully recovered in about ten days.

The three armored wounded Spanish were swordsmen. They were not so fortunate as Juan. They died, one by one, along the way and left nothing with the party who attended them in their last hours except three suits of chain-mail armor, and later Juan never was sure who the three had been.

The Indians of the party included Iztcuitl, royal Aztec princess, favorite daughter of Montezuma, descendant of a long line of Aztec rulers. A beautiful young woman, a wonderful dancer, in the Aztec style, who had, as well, been thoroughly schooled in the Aztec customs, her duties, and her perquisites as an important member of the royal family. As yet she was not imperious in thought, but she was not at all well acquainted with common people or the characters and ambitions of those of lower standing in Aztec society. Her maids, two royal cousins, were maidens of about the same general circumstances as the princess.

Cuitlolo, Iztcuitl's royal cousin, chief of Montezuma's royal pages, was a man of an equable nature who had looked forward to no more exciting an existence than service as an important member of a royal household. Had he mingled with the lower classes on the city streets, he most likely would have been considerable of a snob, for his royal mother had taught him to have a very high opinion of his place in Aztec society. The two page boys were of noble families, whose fathers' great deeds in battle had established the youngsters in the service of the royal household.

Chanco, most forceful of the sacrificial prisoners, had quickly assumed command of the hostage party as it paused on the docks of the Tacuba causeway outside the gates of the great city. He was not a Tenocha Aztec but a member of the Oaxaca people in the far south. Young Chanco had volunteered to assume his mother's place as captive, she having been taken prisoner, along with others, while most of the Oaxaca male population were away on a religious pilgrimage to the island of Cozumel. The Tenochas were glad to make the exchange, for Chanco was a noted warrior of his people, whereas his mother had been merely a noblewoman of her tribe. Chanco himself had been a crafty warrior and not at all averse to delivering prisoners of war to the Oaxaca temple priests for immolation on the Oaxaca temple altars. Six other Oaxaca males were released with Chanco, as were six women and several children.

Among the horses were one Appaloosa stallion, possibly two, four Appaloosa mares, and six Spanish mares, two of which were severely wounded, the others only slightly. (The figures given are estimates by the author after long consideration of all available data and are believed to be reasonably accurate.)

Cuitlolo carried his personal obsidian dagger, the rest of the Indians were unarmed, but carried personal possessions of the princess Iztcuitl, who would have needed them as a hostage of Cortés. The Indian women had their cooking utensils, and a small amount of crockery and food, as Iztaccuitl, Iztcuitl's mother, had urged this upon them as an assurance that they were not being taken to the Aztec temple altars for sacrifice.

The Cortés people had been so badly beaten in the Mexico City affair that the party really had no conception as to just what had occurred.

The narrow Chapultepec causeway branches off Tacuba Way approximately one-third of the way across the lake to the western shore. Chanco chose the Chapultepec road because it led away from the populated areas of Tacuba and old Tenochtitlan, and too, it was shielded from view by the great Chapultepec aqueduct that carried the waters of Chapultepec creek into Mexico City. As soon as the causeway was spanned, he led the party to the right into the brush along the creek and as much as possible along the dry stream bed. Scouts hurried ahead to the front, and later, after they reported the roads to be almost choked with Aztec soldiery on the way to the city, Chanco chose a path to the right that led to the farther areas behind the rise of Tacuba Hill. Two days later they reached Montezuma's hunting lodges, and as the place was deserted, and gave evidence of long vacancy, they camped there for the night. The three wounded Spanish swordsmen had died before that. Juan, by then, was conscious, but was troubled so greatly by dizzying headaches that he was still carried in a litter as the party proceeded northward from the hunting camp.

Iztcuitl knew the lodges well and, knowing that her father was dead and believing that Mexico City was in the process of being ruined, saw nothing wrong in outfitting her companions as best as was possible from the weapons and household utensils available at the lodges. As they started out toward the north, Iztcuitl, now astride an Appaloosa mare, decided that this was goodbye to all she had known. From now on her future would be up to her, and could be based only on her past experiences and upbringing. As she rode away, she made up her mind that regardless of future circumstances she would live to be a credit to her mother's teaching and her father's wisdom and foresight.

They made their way slowly northward, with scouts out ahead to keep them away from any inhabited places, spent the winter among some lakes where there was much water fowl, and arrived at the banks of a large river during the summer. They had seen no inhabited areas for weeks and set up semi-permanent shelters in the heavy brush land along that stream. The hunting was good and they stayed there for some time while the party recuperated and plans could be made for the future.

They lived along the banks of that stream for twenty years, men and women getting married and children being born, each person found a personal niche in the community. Iztcuitl, the princess, married Chanco and established a school program that stressed retention of class distinction and the matriarch system of home society. Others among the women gave instruction in their special personal skills. Chanco, as the mate of Iztcuitl, the social leader, was acknowledged as ruler of the band, which after some years claimed the dignity of a tribe, and he allotted various duties to each adult according to ability.

Juan Alvarado, as he grew older, became somewhat more religious than he had previously been, after some years built up quite a following among both men and women, and held weekly meetings, although he had no idea what day might be the Sabbath. His chief contribution to the welfare of the group was in supervising the care of the horse bands, which grew with each year. He taught his men selective breeding and kept Appaloosa blood lines pure, hoping some benefit would derive from this for his people in the future. Two small vagabond groups of nearby Indians blundered into their area and were taken in with pleasure. The horse bands were becoming impressive, and then, in the twentieth year of their coming to that place, a great array of white men, mounted on a miscellany of horses and with a horde of strange animals with long ears (mules) and loaded with great weights on their backs, splashed across the river a few miles above the village on the river bank.

Juan was out on the river bank working on a heating process for worn-out horseshoes. He had carefully removed every horseshoe before it became completely worn out and was improving upon his forging apparatus. At a mud bank along the river edge, he had built a clay furnace, fashioned for sturdiness, and with baked clay rods for a grill. With the fire reaching high heat beneath, being fed with rich grease-wood brush, and given draft by means of a homemade bellows, the worn horseshoes to be used that day would be placed on the grill to heat and when they reached the malleable stage of bright red, Juan would hammer them into shape with a stone hammer, using a large stone for an anvil. He got along very well except for his tongs. He couldn't make them hold worth a darn. If he could have just made some tongs that would have worked well, he could have turned out some real fancy work. But even as it was, the women thought his knives were very good. By the time Chanco told him of the army of white men that had gone across the river, those men were long gone. It didn't bother Juan. Not a bit. In fact, it was he that suggested it was now time to move on. Juan scarcely thought of himself as a white man any more, or maybe he didn't think of the Indians as Indians, just as good friends. At any rate, he said it was a good time to move on. The neighborhood was likely to get all cluttered up with people.

A meeting was held and nearly everyone agreed that moving on would be the thing to do. While the camp was preparing, scouts were sent out, north and northeast, to get the lay of the land two weeks or more away. The way to the northeast was agreed upon, for the reports from that direction indicated more water and feed for the horses, and soon then they were under way.

Everything was better on this move. Everyone had a horse; even the children. The younger horses were ridden and the older horses were used as pack animals. After some weeks' travel they came to a great plains country. Sometimes game was scarce. Sometimes they went hungry. The first winter up toward the north it got so cold they almost wished that they could freeze to death and get it over with. The second winter they nearly did. They saw some buffalo and antelope. They saw wolves and they saw coyotes by the dozen. They saw ground squirrels by the acre and found them very tasty. At one time they ate nothing for a week except grasshoppers. That's all there was. The Indians liked them. They had eaten them back home in the old days. Some of the people were getting older. They talked some about the old days, as old folks will, but never fretted. There, up ahead, always lay something new. In the late spring of the third year they began to work up into high country. Mountains to the right and to the left had caps covered with snow. Game was scarce along there, but the streams were full of fish. These Aztecs weren't much as fishermen, but Juan taught them how to net fish, and fashioned hooks, while some of the women ravelled out line. They didn't grow hungry. In all their travel they saw only two family groups of Indians, but they kept away from them. The second summer, they found an old couple in a wickiup. They were old and helpless and had been left to die. What can one do with helpless people when there are no means of transport? The plains Indians had left them to die. The old couple were

so nearly dead that they had lost the will to resist death, which
they would have done had they been stronger; then, by the time
they had recovered sufficiently to understand what was happening, they were willing to go on living again. Juan fixed up two
travois for them, the same arrangement that Sandoval had used to
bring helpless men across the Xocotlo desert on the Cortés way to
Tenochtitlán. The old couple never did become very active, but the
old woman taught the traveling women many a trick with food
before the summer was over. And then at last they were atop a
high ridge; no snow covered mountains loomed before them. None
either to the right or left. Before them, far in the distance, the
mountains stood up high, a dark blue in the summer evening.
Below and to their left front, a canyon opened up, dropping down
steeply. It seemed endless. For two days, they had been working
their way across a high plateau. The air was light. It was hard to
breathe. The horses sweated endlessly and every spot of leather
that rubbed the hot hide galled badly so that open sores formed.
There was no game. Almost no water. It looked cooler in that canyon dipping deep below. As Chanco looked down that way, with
some yearning tugging at him, his horse took a few steps and
began sliding down hill. A long line of horses soon followed. The
next day they were following a rippling stream (the Salmon River).
The pools were full of fish. Wonderful fish. They ate their fill and
forgot the miseries of the long way there. The day after they came
to a large river (the Snake). Large fish were actually choking the
riffles over across the stream to the left, on a triangle of ground
next to the largest stream, stood a grove of stately trees. Iztcuitl
broke into a smile and a girlhood song. She had found her home at
last and knew it. Alter some days they dug pits in the bank alongside some trees. Smaller trees were felled and burned into sections
and the pits walled up high. Roofs were fashioned out of long
straight limbs, then covered with sod and after that with thatch.
Now everyone was happy once more. The hunters came in with elk
and with deer. Mountain goats were high up on the rocks. Soon
they would get them, too. Deer were plentiful. One need not ride
out for them. Merely stay hidden in some covert and an arrow

would bring one down. Up in the young timber blue grouse could be had for the taking and the streams still were full of fish. It was a paradise. But now, late in the autumn, so late that it was impractical to do anything about it, trouble began to materialize.

The tall thick pine grass, that actually covered the hillsides and looked so rich and nourishing, was no good whatever for horse feed, apparently, for the horses would not eat it. The sunflowers, though plentiful, did the horses no good either, for they were bone dry, harsh, and mostly tasteless husks, although when cleaned and ground the seeds, when mixed with Quamash root and baked before the fires, made a good and nourishing bread. The sparse-growing clusters of some fine bunch grass were all too scarce and in just a few weeks the horses had cleaned the area of feed for some miles around. Juan noticed that the horses were not doing well and discovered the trouble, but by then the highest of the hilltops were covered with snow, and frost glistened on the side hills, although down in the flatland where the camp was it was perfect Indian summer.

Some of the young men had ridden a long way down river over a large game trail. After more than ten days on the trail they had come out upon a high point, they said, from which they could see to the north farther than they could find the proper words to express. That land, from where they were, looked like a land of maize that stood ripening in the field. Below the country lay before them, straight ahead, and to the right and to the left, farther than the eyes could see (the Palouse country). The young men were all excited about it, and when they were told of the local grazing trouble, they suggested moving at once to that far country.

Older heads are slower at coming to decisions. Then too, Iztcuitl was again heavy with child, as were some of the other women. Some girls, who had grown up during the long trek to this place, needed schooling in the precepts due their royal blood. Chanco talked it over with Juan and Juan was sure that the horses could be wintered where they were. There was much willow and many cottonwoods and such fare, and such feed had brought the horses through the last two winters of the plains country in very fair shape. Game was plentiful here, and a good supply of roots and sunflowers was on hand. They would stay here for the winter, then, next year, they would see.

Up high in the mountains, even up high in the hills, the snow became deeper and deeper, but down in the Indian village the season stayed much like Indian summer until very late. Elk and deer came down into the lower lands and browsed on buck brush and other browse, even competing with the horses among the willows. Meat was hung up in the tepees about the village and hides were stacked high. There was much work to do, but life was pleasant.

Iztcuitl, now nursing another baby, taught the young women much as she had been taught during her own young years, and performed the ancient rites as the girls attained womanhood. She herself pierced the septums, taught how to heal the slits properly, and insisted upon the precise behavior of the maidens. She taught the maidens of the royal line the importance of careful selection of mates, as was their due because of royal blood.

With the coming of spring the streams filled and rushed by merrily, but the willows anywhere nearby had been used up during the winter and the horses began to look thin and ragged as they lost their winter coats of hair. That fretted Juan even more than it did the Indian youths and he began to speak of the fine lands the youths had seen to the north the past autumn. With Chanco's agreement, some of the young people packed up and went north with Juan and the youths, taking the horses to the better feed.

Those people that moved to the grazing land did not erect houses out of poles and sod. They set up tepees of hides and fur. That type of dwelling was portable and could be moved with the horse bands, and anyway they were most convenient as a dwelling place should they wish to move on following the horses.

Then Chanco, with his eldest children away to the grazing grounds, became dissatisfied with the confined areas along the Salmon River. He had become used to wide open spaces and now wanted more room. He wanted to explore farther to the west. After some persuasion Iztcuitl agreed. Then, within a short time, the homes on the little river were vacant and the wanderers were on the move again. Keeping to the right of Big River, they crossed some streams and finally came to the grazing grounds. The young folks there were agreeable, so travois were loaded and the trek into the west begun.

After some weeks the travelers came to a river that really was big (the Columbia). There was no fording that stream. They camped awhile. The women dug roots and the men hunted. Chanco and Juan rode up stream, less than a day's ride. At a slight curve in the river, a long island lay athwart the stream. The flow of the great river had been dropping in volume right along. It was now about mid-summer. The camp moved up opposite the island. Some of the young men made it across without trouble. Some rafts were fashioned out of driftwood and these were towed across. It really wasn't too much of a chore. Up stream a short way, a wide valley led into the west (the Yakima Valley). They followed that valley and its stream until the valley turned due north. Scouts found a nice small valley coming in from the west (the Satus), with timber at its head, and Chanco led off that way. After some weeks they came out upon a high plateau. An occasional small stream meandered on toward the west. The grazing was wonderful and the hunting perfect. Camp was set up along a stream (Spring Creek) that came out of a side hill in large supply. Camas roots were in great profusion nearby. To their right, nearby, a high, snow-covered mountain (Mt. Adams) reared up into the sky. Farther toward the sunset another snow-covered peak (Mt. St. Helen's) cast a shadow eastward in the early morning. Up higher on the ridges they had, as they came into this prairie, seen more snow-capped mountains toward the southwest. One so near (Mt. Hood) it seemed to be just next door, but it could not be seen from the new camp. Some young men, from the top of a high ridge, looked down once more upon the Great River. It was a wonderful sight. Across the river prairie lands stretched into far mountains. Other men rode west and came to a deep and rugged valley. There tumbled a rippling stream they called the Klickitat (Singing Waters). A fish run was on, so the entire party moved down to the Klickitat for the fishing. A day's easy ride below, the Klickitat flowed into the Great River. The land west of the Klickitat was rough country. Much rock and the poorest of grazing. The timber was scrubby and a chill wind blew. Farther to the east along the Great River, they discovered a paradise. The land sloped toward the south from a high ridge. Sunflowers bloomed on the higher elevations.

Areas that reminded Iztcuitl of the park between her childhood home and the great Tenochtitlán temple were scattered here and there; some high, some low, close to the Great River. They found, less than a day's ride up stream, a waterfall that tumbled between rock cliffs (Cellilo Falls). The great eddy below was teeming with fine fish. Flowers were growing in a protected park-like area an hour's ride below the falls. There were wild honeysuckles, roses, and other flowers. Iztcuitl had one good look and said this was to be home. So there they stayed. That turned out to be a happy thought. They lived there for some years. The horse bands increased in numbers, so that they fairly swarmed over the grazing lands. Fish ran up the river twice each year. Deer were plentiful along the nearby Klickitat, and in chokecherry time the Klickitat valley held a great number of bear, all feasting on chokecherries and ripening acorns. There were camas and other roots, sufficient to feed a nation. At first someone built a crude oven in which to bake camas bread, but that did not prove satisfactory, so he built another out of well-placed slabs of rock on a sand dune below the falls. Some of the older women baked camas bread, while others helped care for the fish. It was a happy land and a very happy time.

Juan never forgot the religion of his youth. With help from the young men he set up some walls of rock, and built an altar in that protection. A small fire was built on top of the altar and girls kept the fire burning in honor of the Virgin Mary. Everyone by then knew well the story of the Mother Mary and her Son Jesus.

It was probably religious fervor of some kind that brought about the piling of the many stone walls by those people during their stay in the area below Cellilo. These walls are a complete mystery at the present time. The reason for their having been built where they are is due to an unusual situation regarding the talus rock

near their location. Roughly, from the Klickitat River area eastward to the vicinity of the Mary Hill Museum, probably twenty
miles following the lines of the talus, the rocks have crumbled away
from high cliffs in convenient building-block sizes. The stone walls
were put up close to those rock areas; very close. They could have
served no utilitarian purpose. They were not fence lines nor did
they constitute corrals for the enclosure of horses. They were built
where they are simply because of the convenience of the building
material. Some sections of the walls have been buried under drifting sand during the last forty years. Off and on, during those years,
I have tried to ascertain a reason for the walls. No one can offer
any idea that makes good sense. Maybe good sense cannot be used
in arriving at a solution.

The talus rock found there, below the basalt cliffs, is very rare,
even in a country of large basalt-rock areas. In all my various
searching during some years, I have located only one other talus
area of building-block-size rocks. That area is below the cliffs along
the south rim of Moses Coulee below Jamison Lake, in Douglas
County, Washington. There must be other such situations, of
course, but they are rare.

The lower Columbia River area does not have the distinction
of an exclusive talus-stone-wall mystery. Such another situation,
almost entirely identical, with mysterious talus-stone walls along
the base of cliffs, exists in the province of Sinaloa, central Mexico,
near the populous city of Culiacán. (See Valliant's *Aztecs of Mexico*,
plate 18.) Investigators have been puzzling over that Culiacán
series of walls for some centuries, and the nearest they have come
to a solution of that mystery is to hazard a guess that some religious purpose had been involved.

After some years of pondering about these mysterious stone
walls, I decided that they were of Mexican origin. Then, after dis-
covering the stone bake oven in the nearby Cellilo area, I was
certain of my conclusions. The following winter I made an extensive tour of Mexico, and in particular its Aztec areas, looking for
confirmation of my conclusions. These talus-stone walls are typi-
cally Aztec; ancient Aztec. Only their location here below Cellilo is

mysterious. We found, too, in Mexico, in areas not at all remote, descendants of the ancient Aztecs still using bake ovens of comparable construction with the oven below Cellilo, and in widely scattered areas.

Those walls and that bake oven below Cellilo Falls were arranged and built by Aztec people not too long removed from their native environment. Of that I am certain.

In 1956 the Dalles dam was completed and the water of the resulting lake has covered the stone bake oven, but should the water be lowered some day soon, I hope to clean up that structure and take photographs of it.

No one can know now how long those wandering Aztecs lived in the area immediately below Cellilo. Judging from the stone walls and collateral situations, I estimate that period as approximately twenty years. And then, possibly while Chanco, Juan, and some others were engaged in some enterprise at the mouth of the Klickitat—the beginning of slack water below the turbulent rush of water in the Great River, below Cellilo—some canoe-loads of warriors from lower areas of the Great River, Willamettes perhaps (The Willamettes, in early trapper times, had a reputation for belligerency and sudden murder), came up to our party in an assumed friendly attitude, but for some reason Chanco was killed. At least, for some reason the wandering Mexican Indians left the area. What could have been more natural than for Iztcuitl, princess-wife of Chanco, to wish to leave an area where murder had come paddling up the wide Great River? More would surely come. She remembered the well-liked locale up along the Salmon River, so isolated one could not conceive of hostile bands ever coming into that country bringing murder or other calamities. Aztec women have ever been noted for their love and constancy of home life. She and Chanco had been in the prime of life for some time before and during their stay in the Salmon River country; children had been born to them there. It would be natural for her to yearn for the security of that isolated sanctuary. She had been partial to it; had not really wished to leave it. At any rate, the wandering Mexican Indians left the country below Cellilo Falls.

Not all of them, though. A family or two, or maybe three, had separated from the main camp, moving up some distance to the wonderful fishing area on the lower Klickitat. It could be that some little faction had not controlled some disruptive tendencies and been exiled from the main camp. (During some early pioneer days the Klickitats had a poor reputation. Seemed like they couldn't keep their hands off other people's possessions.) At any rate, Klickitat Indians were established in very early times on the Klickitat River. They were of the Nez Percé people, which later became the name of the descendants of our wandering Aztecs.

Iztcuitl, Juan, and the main party most probably left that locale, heading away from the Klickitat area where Chanco had been killed, working up to the high ridge toward where their earlier scouts had first looked down into the Cellilo country from south of present Goldendale, possibly using the great canyon that comes down to the Great River from the high country in the vicinity of the Mary Hill country. The early pioneers tell of great Indian trails down that canyon in pioneer times—the Mary Hill canyon, where once each year in present times hot-rod addicts achieve gripping thrills as they race along its looping curves.

Beyond a doubt they stopped at their former hunting camp up at the edge of the timber where Goldendale now stands. There was water there and luxuriant shade. There they could exchange dried salmon for jerked venison before they headed for the high pass leading down to Satus Creek and thus down to the Tapteal (Yakima) country. Coming down into the wide flats along the Tapteal they would rest and secure fresh meat before continuing on downstream, and there a few more families left them, moving up into the great areas of fine grazing lands just to the north.

Don't ask why they split off from the main camp and went northward. It was just a few miles out of the way, and the way to the grazing grounds up on the Big River was scarcely more than a week's travel. Anyway, human beings have been forever looking for new lands that they can claim as their own, and it was wonderful Indian country they were going to occupy.

Those few families developed into one of the great western Indian tribes, known to the first white men as the E-Yakimas (Full Bellies) and nowadays as the Yakimas, who are achieving an important position in the economy of the Yakima country.

Arriving at their former grazing grounds, many families set up their tepees along some pearly stream. Their horses had increased to great numbers and needed room and much grazing land, but Iztcuitl, her family, and the other still-living old-timers, Cuitlolo and the others of royal or noble Aztec blood, their children, grandchildren, and some great-grandchildren, moved on up to the Salmon River location, renovated the old buildings, and settled down permanently.

Iztcuitl, now a woman of mature years, was becoming more punctilious than ever in the teaching of the old ways of her royal-family past. She was strict in bringing up the maidens of important lineage. She saw to it that each maiden, so entitled, had her septum pierced, her septum pin fitted, and knew the niceties of its use and favor, and was careful that none except those of proper family connection were barred from its use.

Young people, being what they were and always have been since the time of Adam and Eve, were ofttimes inclined to disregard the niceties prescribed by the wisdom of their elders, who with the added years attained greater control over passion, and Iztcuitl, always with her great family connections in mind—and now, of course, others of the original noble women in the lodge rooms who, with increasing age, had come to much the same state of mind—found great merit in prescribing the most sedate of courting and marriage procedure.

Iztcuitl followed a procedure used heretofore exclusively by the Tenocha Aztecs following their having been endowed with a preferred position by their men folk in ancient times after the defeat of their enemies during the fighting in the marshes along the western shore of the great lakes in the high valley of Central Mexico. The battle had been hard-fought, the attackers determined to wipe out those feral Aztecs once and for all. The coalition attackers would have succeeded, too, had it not been for the Aztec women.

Side by side with their men, they had given blow for blow, and sometimes two and more. When an Aztec was disabled, a woman took his place and fought with the ferocity of a woman defending her loved ones. Should some warrior falter because of long, strenuous battle, a woman was always at hand to urge him on and give him added strength. When the enemy had retreated and disappeared for good, the surviving Aztecs settled in the grazing grounds north of the Big River, the Snake, in an area now known as the Palouse Country in southwest Washington state.

Juan was a good Catholic, unobtrusive but faithful to its precepts as he understood them. He taught his Indian friends so well that religious services were still being held in the villages along the Salmon River 250 years later, when Captain Bonneville spent some months with them. In addition, maybe of no greater importance but a task that had required dedication and untiring vigilance and purpose, it was his work and teaching that preserved the Appaloosa horses in a direct line of pure-blooded descent. He laid the foundation of that cause so well that some 250 years later, when the white men came, they found the Appaloosa pure in line of descent and with its unusual qualities of original conformation and character unchanged.

To those who do not have any knowledge of the problems involved therein, this may not seem a matter worthy of praise, hardly of discussion, but horsemen can understand Juan's problem—the eternal vigilance required for assured selective breeding; the task of teaching the technicalities involved and instilling them in his pupils; the consecration of purpose that lasted as long as did those Indian people. Only those who can comprehend his problems and the extremes of dedication that held him to such a task can have full appreciation of the services he rendered in his preservation of the Appaloosa breed of horses.

Those Indian people called themselves by an Aztec name, both unspellable and beyond my powers of pronunciation. Lewis and Clark called them the "Choppunish" Indians, but that name never became common. Among other people, even before Lewis and

Clark's time, they were known as the Nez Percé; French for "Pierced Noses."

The name Nez Percé has stuck. However, historians are united in claiming that there has been no justification for such an appellation, but I have never concurred in that view.

My parents did missionary and medical work in the early 1890s among a small band of independent Nez Percé Indians in the wilderness of what is still mostly undeveloped north-central Idaho. My earliest recollections are of that time. My father's oldest brother was a mountain man of the old type, having trapped for twelve years or so in Nez Percé lands, beginning in the early 1840s. Fortunate circumstances led to friendship with some Crow and Nez Percé Indian youths and his first visit to the Nez Percé lands was to the Salmon River band. I can remember him discussing the pierced-nose situation with my parents. He claimed to have seen pierced noses among the Salmon River women. Later, when I was grown up, I read through voluminous notes of my father's on the subject of Indians, and then read a memorandum about the Nez Percé custom of the pierced noses, but without learning of a solution to the mystery as stated by certain historians of more or less note. That called my attention to the fact that the name "Pierced Noses" had been given them, beyond a doubt, by some very early French voyager. Now, I had noticed many names of natural circumstance that had first been bestowed by such voyagers and every name told a correct story. That, combined with my uncle's claim to having seen women with pierced noses in the Salmon River villages, gave me the clue, and I developed my thoughts to the conclusion offered herein. I knew that the Shahaptian had been a matriarch people up until such time as they were badly decimated by small-pox and other diseases, and had come to use the white man's ways, and was surprised to learn that the Aztec, Tenocha Aztec, had also been a matriarch society. I then discovered that the Tenocha had at an early time endowed their most important goddess with septum ornaments. I have yet to find an instance where a Tenocha Aztec god has been graced with a septum ornament. It is a symbol that was reserved for the greatest goddesses and for the royal and noble women. I was sure then, but had no proof. I tried every important library between Mexico City and Vancouver, B.C. (I think), but couldn't find anything to back up my position. But then, in January, 1956, in the great Central Library of Los Angeles, I was feeling poorly and leaving, when I discovered a large volume, entitled simply *Aztecs*. Leafing through its pages, I found an illustration showing one woman and six men above a caption reading, "Nobility Calling on Montezuma." The woman's face was turned partially toward the front, facing the reader, and it displayed, as though to my personal order, the lady wearing a colored flower at the ends of her septum pin. None of the men had any nose embellishment. I was ill for some time, and when I again visited the library, I was unable to find that volume.

This January, 1959, in our local Yakima library, I picked up Valliant's book, *Aztecs of Mexico*, and there found plate 35, almost a duplicate of the illustration in the Aztec book of the Los Angeles library. I hope to find more proof, but in the meantime I feel certain that my reconstruction of the "pierced-nose" name as applied to the Nez Percé Indians is correct, and was proper at the time it was bestowed upon those people. I offer it here as the solution of the mystery of the Nez Percé name.

The Nez Percé Indians, differing in that respect from many western Indian tribes, but like the Aztecs in that particular too, were very careful of their women. They expected them to be chaste. When the pioneers began coming in among the Nez Percé, and didn't see any pierced noses, they naturally asked about it, and were shrugged away. The Nez Percé did not wish to call a lusting white man's attention to their most valued women. This contributed to the idea that the Nez Percé name was an error.

The Nez Percé Indians were a different type of Indian than the rest of the Indians of the American West. With one small exception, they lived within the Columbia River basin, which includes the Salmon River area. Etymologists have classed the Nez Percé as part of the Shahaptian people, but that is about all the information that may be found on the subject. When it comes to their origin and kindred subjects the silence is wonderful. Who were the Shahaptian? We will tell you now. The first Shahaptian were the Nez Percé, the Upper Nez Percé first, and then the Lower Nez Percé. Next were the Klickitats. They were the first splinter tribe. Then came the Yakimas, a great nation. Then the Palousas, a splinter group of the Lower Nez Percé; the Warm Springs band, in northeastern Oregon; and the Umatillas to the west of them, to the south of the Columbia River in Oregon along the small river of the same name that became so important a section of the old Oregon trails. To the north up the Columbia, a hard day's ride on a good horse, came the Moses Lake bands, then west, just across the Columbia at Priest Rapids, the Wanapums, a tribe that took its religion most seriously, and lived a life of great austerity, doing harm to no man, and receiving none. Then, among the most important Indians and considered an integral faction of both the Upper and Lower Nez Percé, came the Cayuses, who chose for their home grounds lands in the Grande Ronde country, high up in the Blue Mountain elk and deer country, where emigrant trains paused to rest and gather strength for the final stretch to the Dalles in the lower Cellilo country.

All of the Shahaptian peoples had many horses when the white men came into their country. The neighboring Indian tribes had almost none, unless they were friends of the Nez Percé, but with the coming of the pioneers the horse situation began to change. In one way or another, the other Indian tribes began to acquire horses too, either by theft or as gifts from the Nez Percé or their heirs and assigns. Gold was discovered up towards the Upper Nez Percé; also pretty much through all of central Idaho. The Upper Nez Percé had acquired little immunity against the white man's diseases. By 1870, they had almost vanished. Gone were those of direct descent from royal Aztec lines. Gone the noble caste. The old customs died away. The Nez Percé promised to be faithful and true to the white soldiers. They never fired the first shot in any battle, but war with the United States army came anyway. When the war was over there was little left of the Nez Percé nation. In 1895 the Nez Percé tribe was disbanded, a few Nez Percé were scattered among some other tribes, and the Nez Percé as a nation was no more. But 1895 was an interesting year for still another reason than the dispersion of the last of the Nez Percé. In 1895 a white man became interested in the Appaloosa horses of the Nez Percé, and took steps to preserve the breed. Here we again resume our story of the Appaloosa, and that leads us directly to another of our mysteries of western American horses.

Since 1895, it has become known that the Appaloosa is one of the oldest breeds of horses. My claim, as disclosed herein, is that the Appaloosa is the oldest breed of all the horses, having evolved directly from pre-horse forms of life. If my proposition has been properly presented, you may be convinced, along with me, as to that fact. Following my claim that the Appaloosa was the first horse, I have led step-by-step, I hope, to the bringing of the Appaloosa into the hands of the Indians that became the Nez Percé tribes. Those Indians, as I pictured the circumstances, received possession of one Appaloosa stallion, some Appaloosa mares, and four Spanish mares during the fighting between Cortés and the Tenocha Aztecs in Mexico City. I believe these are substantially the facts and expect to prove them true by introducing now the next mystery among western American horses, the Pinto.

5

ABOUT THE PINTOS

An occasional pinto coloration has existed in horses as far back as history goes and apparently they were favorites from the start, for it is recorded that the Hebrews, some thousands of years ago, used various stratagems and endeavors in attempts to induce their pregnant mares to produce the multi-colored animals.

Some breeds of horses are so negligible a number as to be insignificant. Among such pintoless breeds are the Mexican mustang.

As white men began crossing the upper Mississippi River into the northern central plains, they found a great number of Indians mounted on pintos. So many as to be astonishing. Anyone at all interested in horses will have noted that fact in the early paintings of western horses. George Catlin and Alfred Miller, two noted artists of the western scene in the early 1830s and later, show a great proportion of pintos in their paintings. Even painters of a later generation, Charles Russell and Frederick Remington, display an important number of pintos in their paintings, and these were produced after the western horse blood had been greatly diluted with blood lines from the eastern United States. The unusual and great incidence of pintos in the northern plains country was so prominent that it could not escape the attention of students of the native western-plains horses.

Notwithstanding that situation, ever since the days of some early white-men travelers into the areas of southern Texas, the idea has persisted that the predominant number of horses that put the northern plains Indians on horseback were brought from Mexico, through the Texas area, and continued on north to the northern Indians. It was told that these horses were brought to the northern Indians as the result of raids in Mexico by Comanche and Pawnee Indians. The first instance of that type of thinking that I have found was offered in the 1790s. Several such statements were made in the next forty years or so. After the first few mentions of such movements towards the north, it is stated specifically that the horses being brought north were Mexican mustangs. Unfortunately for that claim of horses being brought north from Mexico, the Mexican mustang—if noted for anything—is noted for its complete absence of pinto coloration.

As time progressed, the numbers of mustangs being taken toward the north increased with almost every new statement, these numbers finally being specified in nice round figures, as running into the thousands, and unless my memory fails me, the amount eventually attained the figure of hundreds of thousands annually. Some writers have questioned these nice, large, round figures, notably Mr. Roe.

The earlier proponents for great numbers of horses being taken to far northern Indians by the lower Comanche and Pawnees may be excused for making an error in their conclusions, for Texas land for some distance north of the Rio Grande River was in those times Spanish territory and by the late eighteenth century must have contained many wild mustangs. The Comanche and Pawnee tribes at that time were very active predatory Indians and they already had all the horses that they really needed, except for meat. Undoubtedly they were very active in raiding neighboring tribes and of course raided into Mexico at their pleasure. They both were such formidable and noted tribes that the earlier white travelers of Indian areas were inclined to be somewhat in awe of them, and too, because of the more or less continuous raiding back and forth, there would, on occasion, be many horses moving about—some of them, naturally, moving, for a time at least, to the north, the east, the west, and some no doubt towards some southern place.

What would be the incentive for Indians in southern Texas to take large bands of horses far into the Missouri watershed area in the seventeenth or very early eighteenth centuries?

My father, when little more than a lad, to secure funds to complete his education, taught school in Minnesota and North Dakota territories when Indians roamed those northern areas quite freely. The Fort Snelling massacres and disturbances were but a recent occurrence. He performed medical and missionary work among far-southern Mexican Indians while still a very young man, and later, during the first years of this century performed the same work among Indians in the northwest. He knew Indian nature. He said, more than once, that, with the exception of the most backward of those far-southern Mexican Indians (those were aboriginal Aztec), Indians were all pretty much the same as to desires. And he knew Indians.

The Comanche and Pawnee Indians of lower Texas of those days, far from civilization and scarcely, if ever, having seen a white man, would not in the least be inclined to run horses across hundreds of miles of arid country that lay between more northern Texas and the watershed of the Missouri, for with the exception of scalps, the northern Indians had nothing that the Comanches and Pawnees wanted, and scalps aplenty were much closer in several districts south of the Rio Grande. Those Indians had no medium of exchange—did not even know that such a thing as money existed, nor would have had need for it if they did. They had no reason to build up estates of Indian wealth, because at each brave's death, immediately following final burial customs, a feast was held and everything the decedent had owned was given away to Indians outside of his immediate family. Ofttimes the family wickiup would be completely destitute, even of food.

The Comanche and Pawnee Indians of Texas of those days would have neither inclination nor reason for running horses from Mexico north to within the Missouri watershed. An Indian brave, in the situations we have just been considering, would have felt that a long trip north across many miles of arid, game-empty country, to be a sheer waste of time. There were many interesting prospects that were so much closer southward in Mexico, and with greater possibilities too, for in addition to the Mexican Indians there were the Spanish haciendas, any one of which might be taken by surprise, and sometimes was.

The defenders of the hacienda not killed in the fighting, together with the family and whatever white friends, male or female, they had would then be available for torture, and torture of a white person was the zenith of desire for any Comanche or Pawnee. Torture of an Indian captive was a pleasure, but the torture of white people, young or old, brought assailants the very acme of delight. Then too, in such a situation resided the opportunity for permanent honor and glory in their tribes and among the neighboring villages. Each brave had the privilege of devising and inflicting upon his captives any new and terrible torture that he could think of. If a new, more cruel, longer-enduring torture could be inflicted, the result would be greater honor among his own people and friendly neighboring tribes. Songs in his honor would be sung for generations. Many maidens, on pleasant evenings, would be enticing him to the willows that shaded some nearby spring. No. The Comanche and Pawnee interest lay nearer to the south rather than to the far-distant areas of the north.

Should some think that the above presentation of Indian desires and behavior to be mere wishful thinking, let us consider some recorded history of the horse situation in the early nineteenth century regarding large numbers of horses, or lack of numbers, being moved north from Mexico into the Missouri River basin.

6

Where Are the Horses Supposedly Going North?

In assessing the numbers of horses going north to the Indians of the Missouri River area in the late years of the eighteenth and the early years of the nineteenth centuries we will offer examples of the numbers of horses seen moving toward the north by experienced plainsmen at intervals during those times. The smallest diameter of the plains country, the smallest transverse diameter, should be the best situation at which to discover any considerable movement of horses going north either under human duress, as escort, or out of their own desires or persuasion. That smallest diameter lies approximately between north parallels 37 and 38 at about the north border of Arkansas.

Formerly I, and I believe that today Americans generally still do so, considered the great western American plains country to be a land of limitless horizons, stretching on into space seemingly without end. That may have been true in the days of Indians on foot and of trappers still hoping to find horses that could take them across the plains into mountain country, but the western plains country in the latitudes of the upper Arkansas River and for some miles on into Missouri are really not that wide.

Sixty-five years ago, when I first read of Daniel Boone, he was the principal national hero to every boy in the neighborhood. We all hoped to grow up and enjoy such adventures as Daniel Boone had found.

It so happens that Daniel Boone was the first white man to have crossed the Mississippi River in the upper country and to have made a record of his adventures west of the great river.

He was born in Bucks County, Pa., February 11, 1735, of the German parentage that is commonly known as Pennsylvania Dutch, and grew to young manhood in his native county, but later led the first white migration into the then wild lands of Kentucky. There he proved himself to be a brilliant man, standing alone in dealing with Indians, and being the first typical western man generally known to Americans; but he was of a trusting nature, and therefore not as businesslike as he should have been in his land acquisitions and other dealings, and when past middle age he was penniless and decided to go west in an endeavor to recoup his lost fortunes. About 1808, maybe a year or two earlier, he crossed the Mississippi, going from Kentucky into Missouri lands.

When Daniel was but a lad and for some years later, he lived among Indians much of the time and the Indian way of life came natural to him. He became a better Indian than some of the more famous Indians on the western frontiers. He learned their best hunting and trailing methods and improved upon them. Indians were very careless of their meat and allowed much of it to spoil, but Boone had learned from his mother many of the old country ways of keeping meat sound for long periods while at the same time the curing meat took on added nourishing power. Then, after he had led the way into Kentucky and had settled down as a married man, he readily acquired the skill to handle tools and erect homes and to make special conveniences for his wife. Daniel Boone must have had a nimble mind and a very versatile pair of hands. He knew how to handle a crowd and how to address a public gathering, but unfortunately he was too liberal; everyone near was his friend, and so he found himself broke, and crossed the great river to make enough money trapping to pay up his debts and to put something by besides.

After trapping a couple of years Daniel came back home to dispose of his catch of furs and other gainings, and spent the summer there. During the time he was away from Kentucky he had picked

up some of the traits common to old-time western men. He liked to
talk when he had company and did so at every opportunity, telling
mostly of his experiences west of the great river. His experiences
had been uncommon to most of his listeners, so it may be presumed
that old Daniel sort of ran off at the mouth. However, everyone
seemed to like to hear him talk and that made the matter even.

He made several journeys into the far west, coming home off
and on to dispose of his possessions, then taking off again; but
before leaving he left his folks a record of what the west was like.

He told of the great, snow-covered mountain peaks that stood
up high into the sky far out in the west. How, in the mornings, the
sun made castles out of the highest peaks, with colors past describing, and how in the evenings of early autumn, as the sun dipped
down behind those peaks, the tops of high mountains seemed to
be crowned with such glories of color as must surely grace the
thrones of the Heavenly Kingdom. (Daniel became very religious
as he became older.) He told of crossing the plains to those mountains. He called those mountains the Rocky Mountains, a name they
will bear as long as the United States shall last, as nearly every
day, from some position or area, they will continue to display their
golden glories at sunrise and sunset.

He told of killing a great bear there. Its fur had been sort of
sprinkled with white hairs, so he called it a Grizzly Bear. He told
that the bear was larger and weighed more than any horse in Kentucky. It was ten feet tall, he claimed, wide as a barn door, and
weighed (he believed) near a ton. He told of great colonies of
ground squirrels (great cities he called them), spread over the prairies for miles without a break; he claimed, too, that the ground
squirrels were good to eat, with seasoning or without, and that they
were good at any time, but really delicious when a man was nearly
starving. That story shocked some of his listeners. They believed
that the ground squirrel was no better than a rat—so some
thought—and who ever had heard of men folks eating a rat? The
very idea!

He told of sage hens that at evening time were so dull-witted
that they stayed put, so that a man could knock them over with a

stick. A good thing, too, in some Indian country where a man had to be careful of his hair.

He told of ducking and dodging Indians, once for weeks on end, for they knew that he was somewhere about but could not get their hands on him. He told too, once, of a time when he did not fool them, had failed to escape, had lost everything right down to his hide, and had been mighty happy to be released without losing that too.

Stripped right down to the hide, in a country bare of game, he was left to starve. Then he told—and he couldn't help grinning as he told it—of how he had loped just out of sight and then kept after the Redskins until two nights later, when he made away with two of the Injun ponies, a smooth bore gun, a bag of Indian war medicine, and some powder and lead in a buffalo-horn powder flask.

He must have been rough and tough when occasion demanded it. Once he told how he had taken refuge in a rosebush thicket that was surrounded with chokecherry trees. How the Indians yammered for his blood the while they were eating chokecherries; of how, as he was hunkered down behind a big ant hill in the center of that rose bush patch, that was actually alive with big black ants that kept gnawing at him while the Indians kicked around in the edges of the rose bushes, he never dared make a move; and then how later he killed six of the Indians with his Kentucky rifle and his pistol, along with the help of Old Slicker, his favorite skinning knife.

He told of great herds of buffalo that stretched to the farthest horizon no matter which way one looked and of how he was trapped up a tree for two days before he was clear of the herd. He told of droves of antelope, how fast they could run, and how they would gang up on a lone prairie wolf and cut him to pieces with their hoofs before the wolf could even start to streak away from them. How curious these antelope were; so curious that all you needed to do to get meat was to stick a gun rod into the sod with your cap on top and they could come up to investigate that slightly swinging cap and then there would be meat for supper. He told of waking up one frosty morning and finding a big rattlesnake coiled up against his belly.

He could and did, sometimes, talk steadily for a week without repeating himself once. Most of his talking was written down at one time and another, but one thing he never mentioned in all his talking (and he was a Kentucky horseman); he never once told of seeing wild prairie horses. He had established the finest herd of blooded horses in early Kentucky history; he had been born in the far end of a horse barn and until his later crossing of the Mississippi had lived continuously all his life in the midst of horses. Had he seen any appreciable number of horses on the western plains either under Indian control or free as he moved about the western prairies for most of ten years, he would have told it to someone. He never did.

Some may feel that although Daniel Boone did not see an appreciable number of horses on the plains, it might be just as well to ignore that fact, but his experience is only one of many such. We expect to offer several more of similar character and some that are of a scope that should make the complete testimony convincing enough to convert an entire jury of readers.

We of course realize that Daniel Boone had plenty on his mind besides being on the lookout for wild horses. But the fact that he lost his own horse early in his second year in prairie country would just naturally have interested him in any horses, unattached or free. And of course there were bloodthirsty Indians to watch out for. Some Sioux, together with lodges of equally bloody-minded Sioux sub-tribes, commonly spent their winter seasons in or near the area Boone trapped in during the winters. From the Arkansas River along the south, up north to the Platte and the Missouri, was an area that contained a greater number of Indians than any other area east of the Rockies in those years.

At so early a period in western-plains experience, the plains Indians, that far north, had very few horses, but they were on the lookout for scalps, and it is certain that Boone's scalp would have been the preferred trophy for any Indian.

Looking at the situation from any angle, if Daniel Boone had seen any free horses he not only would have endeavored to catch at least one but would have told of the experience to someone. He never did.

7

We Are Still Looking

A friend, a law enforcement officer, now retired, but a man of much experience in a large city of the east, once told me that in any investigation of a crime one coincidence was not taken too seriously; but two coincidences in facts fastened serious suspicion against a suspect, and the suspect was detained for further investigation; and that if three coincidences in the investigation of a subject occurred, the subject never escaped conviction of the crime as charged. The captain was a man of long experience. He had several medals of commendation, and two for bravery. He was careful of his statements, as a man that has dealt with criminal offenders should well be, and I believe that his statement is well based in fact.

Accepting then his statement that three coincidences are positive proof of a fact under investigation, conversely then, three coincidences of opposite fact should prove the contrary to a proposition offered as a fact. Accordingly, should I be able to give three well-substantiated sets of circumstances to the contrary, that should invalidate the claims of those that assert that the predominant numbers of horses that came to the northern Indians came from Mexico following drives northward, mostly by the Pawnee and Comanche Indians.

It is fortunate that we have at least three more most impressive propositions against the claims stating that predominantly great numbers of horses came into the far northern plains out of Mexico. These last three circumstances are facts vouched for as

authentic by American history. I will present the earliest of the
case histories first, and the last set of circumstances last, as I
expect that last presentation to clinch my position as to the
movement of horses to the northern Indians. I offer next a chain
of circumstances that should go a long way toward convincing the
most skeptical as to the merits of our position.

Captain Bonneville, a name well-known throughout the American west, came of a line of distinguished forebears whose individual
names were part and parcel of the baptismals that lent distinction
to a name that now needs no such accessories, for Bonneville is a
name well-known now, in lands that he once explored for the
American government. His full name was long and, for an English-
man, almost impossible to spell, as well as to pronounce. It is for
that reason, I sincerely believe, that Washington Irving, the noted
author who edited the captain's exploration journals, failed to re-
veal the captain's full cognomen. He entitled the journals, *The
Adventures of Captain Bonneville, U.S.A.* Now, Washington Irving
is an author of great renown, and I have yet to earn my salt, but if
the great Irving can get away with that who am I not to follow his
example?

During the early months of 1832, young Bonneville was a captain in the U.S. regular army, a fact that speaks wonders for his
brilliance of mind and resoluteness of spirit. A young man who
could attain a captaincy in the regular army of Uncle Sam in the
dull army years between the War of 1812 and the war with Mexico
in 1846 is deserving of careful consideration. As Captain Bonneville
was growing up his greatest ambition, his fondest dreams, had been
that he might some day become a captain in the army and accomplish great deeds for his country. Now he was a captain, but he
was most dissatisfied, and one can scarcely blame him, for instead
of riding steeds into great battle and accomplishing deeds of daring
and great danger, his high talents were used by the army on plans
for the army's future. The captain was possessed by ideas of exploring the great unexplored areas of the west. He dreamed of lands
that no white man had ever seen, of waters that had never been

forded or bridged. He had been pestering the high command for a furlough, for the express purpose of doing such exploring, but so far had received nothing but refusals. The high command in the end became rather irked at his persistence, suggesting that he finish the work he was now occupied with, and in the bitterness of the moment Captain Bonneville received his commander's assurance that as soon as that job was completed he could have time off for all that exploring.

The general did not know that the captain virtually had the job already completed, and was surprised as all getout when the youngster presented himself a week or so later with everything complete and in apple-pie order. The general would not go back on his word. The captain got his furlough, but the terms were as strict as the general could make them. Captain Bonneville was to have a furlough of two years only, and the general made it quite clear that if he wanted to keep his place in rank and seniority in the army he had better be at hand when the two years expired. The general specified further that the captain make careful records of all areas traversed by him, that all such records and the values thereof should belong to the army, and still further, that all the expenses of the exploration must be borne by the captain himself, for, the general said, the army had no funds to waste upon explorations that could be better made by men used to such work: mountain men, French voyageurs, and such like. The captain was not in funds (what young army captain ever is?), but he was determined, so with the assistance of friends and other interested men he organized a trapping expedition that would go to new lands in a search for furs, it being hoped that the furs secured would pay for the venture and give a profit to the backers. So, on May 1, 1832, Captain Bonneville led out of Fort Osage on the Missouri in search of new lands and high adventure. He found plenty of both.

Captain Bonneville used an entirely new concept in American exploration. His intention was to secure enough furs while exploring to pay for the entire cost of the exploration. In accord with that plan he organized a self-sustaining unit, with a personnel so varied that it consisted of members as inexperienced as recruit camp tenders to some of the best trappers in the business. A new, and it seemed to many a foolish, innovation of Bonneville's was a wagon train for the use of his party. Captain Bonneville had studied the reports of Lewis and Clark; he had talked with everyone he could find that knew the western country; and, as much of the reporting on such an effort was that it was impractical, the captain was the more certain that such a venture was feasible and made his plans accordingly.

His course out of Osage lay along the pleasant slopes to the south of the Osage River in order to avoid the high and rugged bluff areas north of the river some hundred miles to the west. The region there would have involved a lot of winding travel and there would have been much rough going and the captain wanted his outfit more seasoned before attacking such rugged country. He knew the area well, so kept away.

On May 6, the caravan passed the last border habitation and thereafter, almost at once, began coming to affairs of considerable interest. The captain's records are replete with Indians, but contain not a word of horses, either wild or in droves under the persuasion of masters. It does contain detailed information of the means undertaken to avoid the loss of their own horses to thieving Indians. Apparently their knowledge, at the time, of western Indians consisted largely of the Indian proclivity and skill in the stealing of horses. The Indians were masters at that. It happened often among the Indians of that area and time that a band from one tribe would steal the horses of another tribe, only to lose them back to the original tribe, by theft, a short time later. The theft of horses, by one tribe from another, led to much of the fighting between different Indian bands and Indian tribes.

Tied to the rear unit of the wagon train was a cow accompanied by her small calf. That calf was the first such animal ever seen by the Indians of the area and caused more wonder than did even the wagons that rolled along on four wheels. Word spread and Indian parties came great distances to see and marvel at that calf. Some of the interested Indians wanted to trade for that calf. Furs

in considerable quantity were offered in exchange, but Bonneville
was just heading into the far west in a search for furs and did not
see the sense in beginning to load up on furs and hauling them
over mountains and plains at that stage of their venture, so such
offers were flatly rejected without any consideration. Some Indians offered to swap horses for the call, but nothing doing.
Bonneville simply was not interested. The captain had become very
fond of the creature and saw to it that it had whatever attention
was needed so that it would not be uncomfortable or fatigued as
travel proceeded. Some bright buck among the Indians noticed the
captain's fondness for the little thing and conceived what he
thought was a very bright idea. He rode away in great haste, rushing for his home tepee. There he had his beauteous young wife
bedeck herself in her finest costume and most resplendent jewelry,
which consisted principally of bear claws, elk teeth, and the nails
from the fingers and toes of foes that had been vanquished by her
mate. Some of these last were highly polished and gleamed bright
under a warm spring sun. Some were colored a bright red; some
were blue and some were green. The Indian buck could not understand the young captain's interest in the assorted finger and toe-
nails, and his total lack of interest in the young woman as a bride,
for the captain could scarcely have shown less interest had she been
a mummy. There was no trade, and it was impossible for the captain to determine which of the two Indians was the most disappointed—the disgruntled Indian buck, or the disappointed prospective June bride—for the buck had turned surly and apparently had
mislaid any desire to speak, and the disappointed prospective
bride-to-be (apparently she had not as yet received sufficient
schooling as an Indian wife) vented her spleen of disappointment
in a flow of Indian invective that caught the attention and raised
the admiration of the most experienced among the men of the
expedition, and withal contained some choice bits of frontier
vocabulary that were delivered so plainly and with such force that
it was easily heard at the far end of the wagon train, and was so
pointed in expression that even the greenest rookie of the train
understood every meaning and intended application.

The captain, himself quite speedy at repartee when among his social equals, for once in his life found himself at a loss. Words alone could not hide his discomfiture and no other course was open in his dealings with a woman. He did the best he could by disappearing quickly among the crowd of his men, now gathered about and greatly interested in the matter of the rejected bride. He managed to relieve his angry feeling by shouting loudly for the wagons to move on, and quickly.

It was the first time in his life that the captain had found himself unable to cope with a woman with full aplomb and expediency. Among the lessons he was learning early in his journey west was to avoid complications of any kind with Indian womanhood.

For some days out there was little or no game, and some of the experienced among the men taught the rest about prairie-grown roots as a source of food and the use of rabbits and prairie grouse and other birds, but of an evening the men were disgusted with such puny fare, so some steers attached to the outfit for that purpose were slaughtered, and the men feasted in frontier plenty and content.

No wild horses are noted, but on the 14th the men killed their first buffalo and they then perked up wonderfully. Buffalo was what they had been dreaming of, and now soon they were among plenty. In just a few days they came to a plain that seemed to be literally alive and swarming with the animals.

On May 24 they came upon their first mounted Indians, a band of sixty Crow warriors, their horses bright with decorative colors. Experienced men said that they were Crows and in battle array, so the captain ordered battle formation and everyone took prearranged battle stations. The captain, with a bodyguard, rode out to meet the Indians. The Crows, still some distance away, put on quite a show. They were the most superb of horsemen, their horses putting on a show with complicated maneuvers, the rest prancing along in fine style. It was noted that many of their horses were piebald (pinto). And now bells could be heard, and that was evidence that the party was not a war party, for war parties did not advertise their presence with the ringing of bells. And now the Indian party broke into a furious gallop straight for the captain and his bodyguard, sweeping on as though to engulf them, at full speed, and yipping their war cries in a perfect simulation of their battle charges. Captain Bonneville knew of that Indian custom of greeting, but had just time to wonder whether this was pretense or not when the leading Indian threw up his lance in an order to halt and the rush stopped in a few jolting bounces of the Indian horses. And now the decorations of the Crow war horses flickered and jingled with the movements of the horses that quivered and pranced in an eagerness to continue the run. They were well acquainted with charges in battle and loved it as much as did their masters. The records say that the Crow steeds were very fine horses. They most likely were Nez Percé horses, they being friends and neighbors, living but a short distance from Nez Percé lands, and firm friends for a time beyond remembering.

The Indians and whites came out about even on this first meeting. The Crows had never seen a cow calf before, nor had they ever seen a wagon train; while many of the whites had never before seen a scalp dance, such as was exhibited by the Indians during the festivities that followed the meeting.

From that meeting on, until July 1st, the party saw many interesting things, as the records show, but did not see either more Indians or more horses. On the 1st of July the same band of Crow Indians that had visited them previously were seen on their way back toward the north. They did not stop to visit, but flaunted fresh Blackfoot scalps. Apparently, as opportunity offered, they had become a war party after all. It was during that stop that Captain Bonneville first saw the Indian method of shoeing their horses when their feet became broken and sore after much traveling. They shod them with improvised boots of buffalo rawhide.

Weeks later, up in higher country now, the party again came up to great herds of buffalo. Once more they feasted on the choicest of buffalo meat, and again the men became more lively, even jovial. The captain decided that buffalo hump meat must have something special. The men relished it above all other and quickly perked up tremendously after partaking of it.

On the 20th they came in sight of the Rocky Mountains and the young men were all greatly thrilled. They had been hearing of those mountains and had been anxious for a look at them, and now were more anxious than ever to get among them. On July 21st they captured their first horse. The horse was as tame as any barnyard animal. All they needed to do was to put a rope on him and they had one more horse for their pack string, and by this time a pack string was being used, for the extreme dryness of the plains, and some rough and rocky terrain, had shrunk the wheels so badly that there was difficulty in keeping the iron tires on their rims, and an occasional wheel collapsed even though careful attention had been given them much of the time. They never did find anyone to claim that horse, the record says. They probably did not lose much time looking too hard for some former owner. He was a mighty fine pack horse, too.

On the 26th, a great cloud of dust was seen up ahead and the Indian alarm was sounded. Preparations were made for battle, but when the horsemen appeared up front they proved to be merely a mounted band of trappers (50 or 60) on their way to the annual rendezvous.

Shortly, from there on, it was tough going for some days, for both horses and men. The weather was hot and there was no water. Horses began to play out. On the second day of no water they came to the slopes leading down to the Seeds-ke-dee River. They all made it down to water, though some of the horses were in very bad shape. The Seeds-ke-dee is one of the well-known rivers of the west, for it was a common meeting ground for trappers in summertime. Temporary fortifications were thrown up as a protection against attacks by Blackfoot Indians, who were reported to be the most feral Indians of the Rocky Mountain regions, and rumors were that some were lurking not too far away. It was said that the Blackfoot went about on foot in the summertime in search of horses. The party had no intention of losing theirs, security protection was strengthened, and the men were coached in methods of fighting Indians. A party of trappers over the next range of hills lost their

horses a few nights later and thereafter night guards were stationed. Some small bands of trappers came in and those bands
consolidated as a security measure against the Indians.

The meeting place of the trappers was known as Pierre's Hole,
and in later years the place became the favorite rendezvous of most
of the trappers in Rocky Mountain territories.

The consolidated group of trappers, along with some friendly
Nez Percé and Flathead Indians, anxious to be along for various
reasons, started out toward the west. The next morning they met a
large band of Indians. They turned out to be Blackfoot. A few were
mounted, but most were on foot. The whites, suspicious of the
Blackfoot, started a fight, and that developed into quite a battle
before the affair was over. Many good men were wounded on both
sides and some were killed. The Blackfoot lost all of their horses
early in the battle. They hadn't expected the whites to start the
battle (they were usually the ones who started any battles). They
had been surrounded as the fighting started and some of the horses
were killed almost at once, with the unhorsed Indians taking to
the brush. They lost 32 horses, all of which had been stolen just
recently. Most of them from some of this party of white men, and
recognition of their horses was what had started the fighting.

The Blackfoot holed up in the brush, behind some large logs,
and the whites, even though aided by the Nez Percé and Flatheads,
could not clean them out. They all lost men, trying. The Blackfoot
sneaked away during the night; the trappers and their Indian allies
then went into camp for a few days to recuperate, nurse their
wounded, and bury their dead. The affair wasn't a total loss, for
they had taken all the Blackfoot horses, which pretty well made up
for what had been stolen from them just a short time before. They
were a sorry-looking outfit when Bonneville came along a day or
two later. The captain set up camp nearby and did what he could
to aid the wounded. His help was important too, for he was well
supplied with medicines and remedies.

One of the chief elements, in his youth, that had most interested Bonneville in the west was the first published reports of the
Lewis and Clark expedition. These told of great hordes of beautiful

horses that roamed the plains of the Columbia country, where the land lay like the waves of a wildly tumbling sea, and whose wave tips were gold with waving grass in a western sun; of Nez Percé braves, tall, virile, and kind. They included accounts of the Shoshoni Indians who told of the Spanish settlements far to the south, where they themselves got many of their horses. They told also of a great salt lake in a country far to the south, high up among the mountains. The Shoshoni faces grew wistful and their voices gurgled more than usual, suggesting a yearning for that great salt lake so far away. There was salt there, while in their homelands they were forced to do without salt. The salt lake was so far away, and nothing is so precious to a human mind as that which he desires but cannot have.

During his pause at the trapper camp, taking care of the wounded, Captain Bonneville became surprised at not finding any wounded Blackfoot around or nearby. Some old trapper had a proper answer, he thought. "A good Blackfoot is a dead one," said that trapper. An opinion apparently agreed with by the Nez Percé Indian who was assisting in the dressing of the old trapper's wounds.

Captain Bonneville had only two years' leave of absence from the army. He wanted his trappers to explore as much unknown territory as possible in that time, so he split his forces, sending a party to the southwest towards the great salt lake he had heard talked about, giving them orders to cover as much country as possible and to map it carefully as they moved about, and if possible to recruit enough horses to bring their furs back with them. They would find headquarters in the Judith Basin on their return, he said, and showed them where that place was on their maps. Then, with that outfit on its way, he started for the Columbia Basin in the company of some Nez Percé Indians who were proceeding on the way home via the Judith Basin, their ancient hunting grounds.

The name Nez Percé had a magic sound for the captain and he was determined to stay close to those Indians until they had guided him to their homeland. He was determined to see those "hordes of beautiful calico horses" that Captain Clark had spoken about in an inspired hour at West Point. So, with a long pack train strung out along the trail, he followed his Nez Percé friends on their way into the Judith Basin buffalo-hunting grounds.

Arriving in the basin, they found the country empty of buffalo. A large party of Nez Percé direct from home, together with a large party of their friends, the Crows, had been there, killed great numbers of buffalo, and the herds had become alarmed and taken off across the hills and away.

The Nez Percé party that the captain had followed into the basin decided to make a winter's visit to the Crow nation in their homelands east of the Rockies, but as that was not in the direction that he wanted to go, he added his force to a small band of Nez Percé that was starting for their own homelands along the Salmon River.

This band of Nez Percé was in no hurry to get home; they had their families with them, so they just loitered along. That bunch of Nez Percé was in no hurry. They weren't going any place—only home; and an Indian tepee in those days was not a home to rush back to but a place to avoid as long as it was convenient. That is easy to understand in the present circumstances, for an Indian tepee has no place in which to hang a hat, and as every Indian buck in this party had managed to swap Nez Percé horses for hats at the summer rendezvous, they really were in no sweat to get home to such inconvenient lodges.

Captain Bonneville had been born energetic. It was some basic urge within him. Even when he was little more than a tot and things were dragging around home because of the humidity or something, he would each year, at least once, wrap up some belongings into a bundle, including a comb of honey—usually one that was leaking plenty—some biscuits, and whatever else came handy, and start out for points unknown. After a couple of years of that, the town policeman kept watch for him on a hot day, and if nothing matured in the daytime, the cop would advise the night watchman to be on the lookout, and sure enough, sooner or later, mostly sooner, the youngster would show up heading out for some place that would hold more action.

In the years when the future captain had found local things of interest, the two city officials had worked out a system for containing the young fellow until his folks could be notified that he was in hand, so that they might come to collect him. That situation invariably led to some stormy scenes. That is, they were stormy on the part of the captain-to-be. But the young wanderer had a certain addiction that came in handy at such times. A new dessert had just lately come into vogue in his home town. Nowadays we know it as ice cream, but young Bonneville's name for it was "Goody Good" and he stuck with that until he managed to talk his mom into allowing him to wear long pants. After that, he forgot the name "Goody Good." Not only that, he forgot all about the dessert too, claiming along with his fellow-upstarts that eating ice cream was sissy.

Regardless of such former issues, the captain was extremely irked at the dilatory progress of those Nez Percé. His time was limited and he had places he wanted to go and more places he wanted to see. Coming one day to a valley that had a pleasing southern exposure with a pleasant location of many small streams all dammed by beaver before coming into the valley's main stream, with each area pleasantly timbered with sweet cottonwoods and willows that would be just perfect for horse feed during the coming winter, he decided to split his force again, leaving the main body here to trap beaver over the winter, while he, with a few companions, forged on ahead of the slowly moving Nez Percé, making his way into their home grounds before the coming of the severe winters that were bound to make a journey tedious and chill later on.

There were a lot of elk and deer in the valley, and after a day's hunting, following which elk and deer carcasses cluttered up the landscape, assuring the captain that his force there would have no shortage of meat, he loaded up most of the dried buffalo meat and hustled out for a rendezvous in the Salmon River lands of the Nez Percé Indians.

Hurrying past his friends, the lazy Nez Percé, he was told that he would find a few Indian families ahead, maybe a week or so of

travel along the trail. He couldn't miss them, it was said, for they
had many horses, and he was shown the hoof-prints left by those
up ahead.

Hurrying ahead then he did catch up with the advance Nez
Percé in a couple of days. He found that a small band of Flatheads
had joined the Nez Percé, for safety, he learned, for it had been
reported that a large band of Blackfoot were somewhere near. There
had been lots of Blackfoot signs reported by their scouts, they
claimed, although Bonneville had seen no such indications. They
claimed further that the Blackfoot were a thieving, rascally lot, and
professed to be pleased to have the addition of the white men to
their party.

As they traveled along slowly—this outfit of Nez Percé was
scarcely more rapid on their way home than had been the earlier
band of those Indians that the captain had just left behind—a few
more small bands of Indians joined their group, mostly Nez Percé,
but also a small band of Shoshoni. The Nez Percé were more than
haughty with the Shoshoni, and would have liked to have driven
them from this group that was traveling toward the Nez Percé
homelands, but the Shoshoni, appreciating the security of the
larger band—they too had seen lots of Blackfoot signs—put themselves out in being friendly to the very (just then) high-nosed Nez
Percé.

These Nez Percé had not been as fortunate in their hunting as
had been other bands of Nez Percé encountered by the captain.
Actually, they were rather destitute, but tried as best they could to
hide that situation from their neighbor travelers. The Shoshoni
were commonly a most destitute people themselves and it wasn't
even a full day after their coming before they understood the situation of many of these Nez Percé. They ingratiated themselves with
the destitute people by unobtrusively slipping into the Nez Percé
party certain of the best cuts of buffalo meat. Their first efforts at
being friendly were rejected by some haughty, but very hungry,
Nez Percé, but the Shoshoni were wily. They made presentations
of meat through the Nez Percé children and when once the way
was opened and the aroma of roasting buffalo hump was wafting

through that day's camp, the Nez Percé reserve melted away, much as snow melts away in the spring. One hour it is frosty with no signs of ever leaving, and by the next, the pleasant kindness of a warm Chinook wind is melting it and the snow is disappearing at a great rate. The Nez Percé had been morose at first when the Shoshoni had sought refuge in the larger combined force, but by the next morning one would have thought that they always had been the best of friends. Apparently the old horse-thieving days of the Shoshoni were to be forgotten—at least while the Shoshoni buffalo meat held out—and the party moved forward in great harmony.

This band of Nez Percé was virtually unarmed, being equipped so poorly that they even had a hard time securing game. That was a circumstance unusual to western Indians. Upon Bonneville's questioning them about that situation, they claimed that they never carried many weapons with them at any time, for their lands lay in sheltered seclusion. They had come into the buffalo lands in the early autumn with sufficient weapons to take care of the buffalo, but a Blackfoot raiding party had relieved them of their weapons on a dark and stormy night. It was that situation that had brought about their food shortage, for, they claimed, they were commonly the best-fed of any Indians. They claimed also that they never took the warpath except to help their friends, the Crows, in their wars against the Sioux, who in the past few years had been encroaching upon their friends more and more each year.

The Sioux were survivors of the Iroquois nation that in the period before their domination by white men had lived mostly along the coast of the Atlantic Ocean. They had been forced, more or less, steadily westward in avoiding too much Of white men's western surges, and now that white men were crossing the Mississippi in droves, they were in turn crowding the Indians that lived there further to the west again, although they were still endeavoring to hold onto their latest homelands in western Minnesota and in the northern Dakotas. With the exception of the thieving Shoshoni, the Nez Percé claimed, they furnished many horses in trade with neighboring tribes and had little use for weapons except for hunting.

Bonneville was surprised at the Nez Percé's lack of weapons, but was even more surprised at the religious meetings held by them and their generally devout behavior. These Nez Percé, who said that they were of the Upper Nez Percé people, held religious services regularly every Sunday. How they could have managed to keep that day regularly through many years is itself something of a mystery. Under questioning by the captain, they professed to have no remembrance or knowledge as to when their religious services and circumstances had come among them. They said it was a matter of old tradition that at one time a white god had lived among the people and had taught them, and that they had been worshipping a Great Spirit ever since those times and had found the custom good. Nothing could happen, apparently, that would change them from their custom of regular Sunday services; neither lack of food, nor threat of the Blackfoot, had any effect at all. On Sunday, travel stopped and most other affairs of labor or daily duties were voided. On a weekday, while on the trail, should some worthy get an inspiration, travel would halt, and the inspired one would hold a meeting, while the great truths of their beliefs were delivered and expounded in priestly tone and manner, the speaker urging that his neighbors follow the ancient Nez Percé teaching to always treat their fellow-man as they themselves would wish to be treated. Such episodes varied in length with the moods of the speaker. Some were short in speech, probably because of a lack of inspiration, but on occasion some worthy might allow his zeal to overcome his good judgment and he would sermonize on and on, with apparently no end in sight.

In such cases, the good Captain Bonneville might become so provoked at the long, exasperating delay as to forget or mislay temporarily his usually Christian impulses and wish that the worthy speaker could be stricken with a paralysis of the tongue, or something; to stop unending talking, he even did wish once that the speaker, by some Divine interference, might just drop dead. Later in the evening, following a fine supper of buffalo ribs and such, the captain in reviewing the day's events would recover his customary genial disposition and regret his heathen wishes of the day,

and to make amends would gather up a lot of food and present
that to the speaker who that day had been the subject of his most
horrid hopes.

These Nez Percé had many fine horses with them; mostly they
were piebald, or shall we say multi-colored. They compared favorably with the better horses back in the east. They had with them
really more horses than they needed, but since the young boys took
care of the work with the horses, the large number did not inconvenience the mature braves of the party. But the captain complained that the Nez Percé were most woefully careless of their
horses, turning them loose to graze unguarded through the night,
and such procedure was worse than gall and wormwood to the
captain's military training. He remonstrated with the Nez Percé
about such carelessness, but the Indians were not impressed. They
replied that they had many horses and should they become short,
there were plenty more where these came from. He more than
pecked at them on that subject but the Nez Percé weren't bothered. They said that with the exception of the Shoshoni and occasionally a Blackfoot raid, nothing much ever bothered their horses,
and after repeated preaching about it on the captain's part, they
remarked, rather pointedly, that they were also tired of listening
to warnings about lost horses.

The captain did, however, achieve a bit of surcease for his disturbed emotions, for after he gave the Flatheads and the Shoshoni
a lurid lecture on the dangers of leaving their horses unguarded,
they followed the white man's example of carefully guarding their
horses at night, bringing them right into camp. Some of them even
brought the tethers into bed with them and slept on them, so that
any great amount of movement on the part of the horse would be
quickly detected even though that fact would bring them out of a
deep sleep. The captain wouldn't, he simply couldn't, lay off of
those Nez Percé though. Every evening he had to give them a little
lecture, and of course, sooner or later, he was bound to be right.

One evening a small band of Flatheads rode into their camp in
a great hurry, claiming that they had seen evidences of a large band
of Blackfoot early in the day and were in a hurry to get out of the

neighborhood. As they noted the size of the captain's party as it was now constituted, they decided to hang around awhile. Now the Bonneville party had grown into respectable proportions indeed.

That evening the captain took his usual precautions for the safety of his horses, and again chided the Nez Percé for their carelessness. Those Indians did not mind at all that evening. Hunters had brought in some elk and several deer and everyone was well-fed, and a well-fed Indian is usually a happy one. There were many horses, they said, and they were quite right. They did have a large number of fine horses with them. The Flatheads were more careful. They had no surplus of horses with them and horses, for them, were sometimes hard to get. After their horses had grazed until nearly sundown, they were brought into the center of the camp and securely tied up. The Shoshoni brought their horses up so close that they practically slept with them. They themselves were experts at relieving other people of their horses and were taking no chances on those thieving Black-foot warriors should they actually be near.

That night those pesky Blackfoot stole about one-half of the Nez Percé horses. In the morning the captain wanted to leave a guard for the camp and lead the Nez Percé in a chase of those thieving Blackfoot, but the Nez Percé shrugged off the suggestion. Someone might get hurt, they said, and just shrugged the idea off.

The next night, the Nez Percé lost some more horses, and during the middle of the night there had been a lot of commotion in the Flathead camp for Blackfoot raiders had tried to make away with the Flathead horses as well as those of the Nez Percé. Neither the captain nor the Shoshoni had lost a one. The Nez Percé were now looking mighty glum. Their features weren't brightened up the least bit either by the yapping of their squaws. Some of them, it looked like, would be afoot. Now that most of their horses had been stolen they began to take the captain's advice and followed his methods of protecting his horses. Closing the barn door after the horses have been stolen is a step in the right direction, but it does not replace the stolen horses.

The Blackfoot trail led away as plainly as though an entire squadron of cavalry had passed by in the night. Captain Bonneville believed that the Blackfoot, in their turn, might become careless. The Blackfoot, he reasoned, would be tired with their several nights' efforts at collecting those horses. They had not been bothered in the least by the aggrieved camp and might well believe that no retaliatory action would erupt this day. Worn-out and hungry they might stop and cook up a meal of horse meat and then rest for the day. Determined to teach those thieves a lesson, the captain ordered his men to prepare for the chase, and enlisted the Flatheads, and furnished the plundered Nez Percé with mounts, replacing some they had lost. In spite of their pacifistic characters, somehow that morning, the Nez Percé were raring to go.

That was a most pleasing retaliatory action; pleasing to Bonneville, we mean, but certainly most displeasing to most of those Blackfoot warriors. Of course we have no way of knowing how those Blackfoot felt about the situation—the ones that went to the Happy Hunting Grounds, as most of them did—but one thing is certain: the Blackfoot who left that scene of carnage left in such a hurry that plainly they were most displeased with the entire situation.

When the rescue party got back to camp with the horses that had been recovered, they found a large party of Pend Oreille Indians visiting the Nez Percé camp. Those Indians were close relatives of the Nez Percé and were on their way home now, after a long visit in the Nez Percé villages. They had plenty of horses, having just come from Nez Percé lands, and were a happy lot. A sister-in-law and two brothers-in-law were here in this band of Nez Percé, and the whole gang threw quite a party, and before it was over, all the Shoshoni and Flathead Indians, and even the whites, somehow became included, if not involved. A great time was had by all. The Nez Percé party had enjoyed their in-laws so much that they had gladly accepted the Pend Oreille invitation to come and spend the winter.

Captain Bonneville was somewhat disturbed about that at first. He had expected these traveling Nez Percé to guide him directly to the Upper Nez Percé villages. However, he scarcely had time to become perturbed, for one of his friends among the Nez Percé brought forward a Flathead chief, who, he said, could guide him directly to the home trail leading down to the Salmon River villages.

8

Efforts to Find the Nez Percé Horses

It is not our purpose to give a complete account of Captain Bonneville's tour of the western countries. Such a story would take up quite a volume of its own. Our purpose in bringing him and his explorations into our story is to combat the erroneous idea that the predominant number of horses acquired by the northern Indians came from way down in Mexico, instead of, as we claim, from the far northwest.

It will have been noticed, surely, that on the way across the central great plains in 1832 Bonneville saw only one strange horse, and that was a tame one, until they came into the high eastern areas of the Rocky Mountains. Those first horses had been ridden by Crow warriors who had received their first horses from the Nez Percé. The second group of mounted Indians they came in contact with was a band of Blackfoot, who (I believe) had stolen their mounts from either the Nez Percé or from some Indians who had secured them from the Nez Percé, for the horses were all Nez Percé horses.

Horses did not become plentiful until the party arrived at the headwaters of the Seeds-ke-dee River. Those horses had originated on the western slopes of the Rockies, and had all been in the hands of Nez Percé owners or in the possession of neighbors and good friends of the said Nez Percé.

We found that only two tribes neighboring on Nez Percé lands, the Shoshoni and, a little farther removed, the Blackfoot, were not friends of the Nez Percé, because of their propensities for stealing

Nez Percé horses, and we found further that those two tribes, unfriendly to the Nez Percé, were the only two far-western tribes that were short of horses on their annual hunts in the plains buffalo country in 1832.

During the time of the opening of the west by white men, the Blackfoot Indians were the most notorious thieves among all the Indians of America. When not engaged in stealing from other tribes, the Blackfoot bands would keep in practice by stealing from each other. It could be possible that their thieving activities among themselves, added to their proclivities of thievery outside their homelands, tended to create such a shortage of food at unfortunate times that they were forced to use their horses as meat for home consumption, thus creating a common shortage of horses in their community lands. At any rate, in spite of all their thievery, the Blackfoot were usually short of horses and did much of their traveling, their horse stealing, and their wars on foot.

The Blackfoot had come out of the far north at some recent time, settling in the rugged Rocky Mountain areas just across the summits to the northeast of the Nez Percé, with small bands of Flatheads separating the two peoples. Their thieving quickly became universal and as the Nez Percé had hordes of horses, they were among the first victims of Blackfoot thievery. Whenever a new Nez Percé village chief was installed as the head of his band, his first act in such office would be a declaration of enmity against the Blackfoot, but the Nez Percé, too content at home to carry a war into obscure lands, never carried a war to the enemy, being content to do their fighting on the buffalo-hunting grounds.

One result of the Blackfoot arrival in these lands was a strengthening of the friendship between the Flatheads and the Nez Percé (it is believed by some students of the American Indians that the Flatheads and the Nez Percé were closely related at some ancient time). During the severe fighting between the Flatheads and the Blackfoot in 1807, the Flatheads appealed to their friends, the Nez Percé, for help. The Nez Percé sent over a great band of their best horsemen and gave the Blackfoot such a whipping that open warfare between those three tribes never flared up again. As a result

of their cooperation in that war, the Nez Percé furnished the somewhat impoverished Flatheads with numerous horses, and they had
been friends ever since.

Following the last incidents in the previous chapter, the Flathead chief did guide the captain's party close to the trail leading
into the Salmon River country, but while they were still some days
distant, a blizzard came up, piling snowdrifts as high as the scrub
trees that grew at that elevation. The Flatheads, now approaching
quite near to their home lodges, wished to take a shortcut that
would take them home by nightfall, so an old Nez Percé warrior,
who had not wished to go with the Pend Oreille for the winter and
stayed with Captain Bonneville, claimed that he could guide the
latter from where they were then situated, but suggested that there
should be a wait in the hope that the blizzard would abate, for the
swirling of the snow was often blinding and could confuse the direction. A camp was then made in a field of scrubby willows; the
willows were tied into cone shape, the snow was cleared away down
to the ground, the short section of framework willows above the
snow covered with hides, and within a short time everyone was
comfortable, except the horses. The packs were placed inside the
shelters that had been prepared for the men, but the cold was griev-
ous for the horses, for their back hair was short and gave almost
no protection. The horses could have died that night, but Captain
Bonneville, in addition to being clever, was also a kind-hearted
man. While some men tied hides over the horses' backs, others
were sent out into the storm to fashion windbreaks as shelters
against the wind, and the snow was banked up high to prevent drift
into the shelters. Other men were breaking frozen willow twigs for
horse feed, so that as the blizzard raged and the snow drifted, the
horses were snug in their shelters.

The light was then growing dim. It was not night nor even
evening, but the sun was long past the meridian. There was no wood
for fires nor, as far as anyone could see, the least chance for any.
The old Nez Percé was huddled up against a bale of hides inside a
shelter, trying to keep some warmth in his old body, but without

very much success. One of the trappers, sorry for the old Indian, and wishing to give him the pleasure of human companionship, grinned through his whiskers at the oldster, spread his hands out as though holding them over a camp fire, then rubbed them together in an age-old gesture that has been performed since the time men first battled cold, continuing to grin at the old man. The aged eyes of the Indian woke into life. He nodded his head, pointed a finger at his chest, stood up, and made a few prancing steps, with every step falling into its previous footplace. The old man was saying in sign talk that he could get some wood. His white friend shook his head no; but in response the old man nodded his head up and down in a vigorous yes. The trapper called for Captain Bonneville, who was opening a bale of dried meat in the protection of the shelter. More sign talk followed, and shortly the old Indian was leading a dozen men, trappers and camp tenders, each with a hand on a string that would guide them back to shelter through the swirling snow. The old man must still have had in full his age-old Indian instinct for direction, for he led them straight as could be through the brush tops and the swirling snow into the shelter of some rimrock. The high wind there had carried the snow some four to six feet past that rock, drifting it away from the rim and leaving a vacant place between the rimrock and the snow that left the ground as bare as it must have been before the storm, and there, just before them, lay the remains of what once had been a great gnarled old rock pine.

Parts of it were crumbling away in decay, but much of it broke up fairly well into firewood, and the great twisted limbs, upright and dry, full of pitch and firm as the day the tree had fallen, broke away at the tree heart and soon there was enough wood for every man to carry.

They followed the long string back. The old Indian had been the first one out, he was the last one in, and he was nigh frozen, but fires were soon going bright and warm. Soon the old man was all thawed out, and as the fires crackled beneath the cooking pots, that oldster, an admired man for once in his life, was hoisted up high upon a pile of bales, where the heat brought out a smile upon his old, seamed features, and there he was granted the honor of having the first puffs on Captain Bonneville's personal pipe.

Times of stress, times of heartbreak, of frigid cold or other tortures have their compensations if one has sufficient determination to overcome or withstand them. From that time on, the aging gent (he really was one, you know) was accepted as a full equal by every man in that camp.

It could be that the designers of the Declaration of Independence, drawn up by members of the Continental Congress in Philadelphia assembled, knew very well whereof they wrote when they said: "We hold these truths to be self-evident, that all men are created equal. . . ."

The blizzard raged for some days. The snow drifted for a time in drifts so high that most of the scrub willows were covered and the horses needed help to feed on them deep in the snow, and then, when the wind died away, the cold was all the more intense; the snow was as light as the finest down, with even less body to it than the finest ashes. There was meat in the packs, and the men were not too restless. There were chores to do. Horses to help and take care of; wood to bring in from the fallen tree; and, when that was gone, felling the two standing trees, first one, then later the other, when it was needed. Two old-timers among the trappers made up some webbed snowshoes, such as Captain Bonneville had once seen the Ojibway Indians wear in the north woods some years before. Enough were made for ten men and the captain. One terribly cold morning a force of that number led out from camp; most of the men, including the captain, were awkward in this new type of footwear. (Snowshoes are seldom worn by mountain men as long as they have horses.)

The second day out of camp the men stood high up on a snowy rimrock and looked down into a shallow valley where a herd of elk was trapped in deep snow. The elks were all slaughtered, dressed, etc., and then the men were faced with the problem of what to do with the meat. True, the meat was freezing fast, but it would do them little good here in this gully. How could the situation best be managed?

Toboggan-like sleds were fashioned out of hides by bringing up the leg hides and tying them together; then ropes of rawhide were used to pull the loaded sleds towards the top. That worked fine. Back-packing would have been impossible. All the meat that could be sledded at one time was taken to the main camp, with three men left at the meat site to guard the meat until the sled party could return.

The captain was determined to get to those Indian villages on the Salmon River. That had been his original idea when he had started planning for this trip. With the whole world, it seemed, buried deep in soft snow, the prospects looked glum for the immediate future, but as you may have noted, the captain was a lucky man. As he neared the home camp, Joe, the aged Nez Percé, hustled out to meet him. He had been practicing on snowshoes while hustling wood and was doing so well he just had to show off a little; and that gave the captain an idea—Joe could guide him. Joe would find his way home no matter how deep the snow. But there were all the men. What to do with them while he was away? This snow might melt any day, and he could not leave the men in idleness while he visited the Nez Percé village during the winter.

A solution was worked out by much sign talk and jabber with Joe. Joe could by now string a few simple words of English together and that helped to keep the situation clear, but it was mostly sign talk. "Yes," Joe knew where there was beaver. It was a wet and cold place. Nez Percé did not trap there. Nez Percé no like trap anyhow. Have plenty horses. Swap. No need beaver skins. Yes, maybe can do. Draw 'um map. So. Like this. Go maybe five days; maybe ten days. No can tell. Too damn much snow. Come to high mountain. Here. See? One more here. See? Big rimrock fall down here. To the right. To the west. Another big rimrock here. On left, east. Go around rimrock here. On right. Down bill. Maybe one day. Maybe two. Can't tell. Too much snow. Purty soon big flat. Much small water. Lots of brush for horses. Much beaver."

And so it was arranged. The men would go trapping. They were to blaze their trail well, so the captain would have no trouble finding them when he headed back. They knew well the Bonneville

markings. Don't be careless, the captain said, then started away
with three men for company and with Joe to guide them.

The going wasn't at all bad with the snowshoes. They didn't
hurry, but kept moving, except for part of two days when the wind
was drifting the snow so badly that they became uncertain about
their directions. The weather remained very cold, but they holed
up in deep snow and got along well by drying off before a fire before rolling into their blankets. The going was all downhill after
they headed due west. There was no brush, no rocks, no down
timber—nothing—to bother them as they mushed on downhill.
Snow covered everything. There were no mosquitoes, no gnats, no
pests at all to bother them. They eased down some on the grub the
last two days, then, all of a sudden, dogs were barking and yapping at them from up ahead, and they were right up to the villages.

Captain Bonneville had noticed sometime before, just after
coming down that last long, steep pitch into the lowlands, that they
had come into a different country. The brush stuck up through the
snow at the south exposure of the hillsides. The twigs making lines
against the snow background were as fine and clear as the lines of
a good etching. The willows along the low places had all been
browsed down to the heavy wood, the limbs of the cottonwood trees
had been torn off, and some of the smaller trunks had been chawed
on—a sure sign of horses. And then the men came to a trail of horse
tracks. The trail surface stood up inches above the other areas,
making the trail a slippery ridge instead of a sure pathway. Now,
too, the men were suddenly wearing too much clothing. Bodies were
steaming, for even though they were moving downhill there was
considerable exertion in moving their footgear.

What a terrific lot of excitement there was in this first village
as the barking Indian dogs announced their coming! The hair stood
up on the dogs' backs just as though they were charging mountain
lions. Encouraged by the barking of many dogs in their rear, some
of the leaders charged so close it seemed as though they might try
for a bite, but the stern command of old Joe's well-remembered
voice halted them into tail-wagging impotency, and then, quickly,

it seemed as though everyone in that village was out to greet them. Some of the men were armed, ready to give battle, but within moments they too were smiling and hilarious. It had been a long time since they had greeted a returning wanderer, and they all were hungry for gossip.

Captain Bonneville had never before seen Indian villages such as these of the Upper Nez Percé. Very few of the homes were tepees. Mostly they were substantial structures made out of logs. The larger buildings contained two floors. The lower floors were sunk into an excavation in the ground; the sides of the excavation were walled up with green logs that had been freed of bark, and then the excavation dirt had been banked up against the walls up to window height. The windows were not real windows, but approximately three feet above the dirt line to the roof had been left free of logs at space intervals so that the air could circulate throughout the house in times of high temperatures, or the free spaces could be closed with long mattings that would keep out the cold in freezing weather. It was really a good arrangement. Ramps led up through the banks to the doors, which also were covered with mattings, though these were doubled to give added weight so that normal winds would not move them around.

The upper floor rested on poles that were notched into the wall logs at the desired level, and consisted of poles split down the middle and notched for evenness in the floor; the piers that held up the cross members were of unpeeled lodge-pole pine; the upper lengths had strong limbs protruding as a place on which to hang clothing and weapons. The roofs sloped all one way, being fashioned out of long thin poles supported by the walls at the ends and resting o uprights at intervals. The high side of the upper rooms was 6½ feet in height while the lower was very little more than 5 feet. The roofing consisted of long, narrow, spliced poles fitting tightly together and covered with a layer of heavy matting that in turn was covered with sod, which held the matting in place. That style roof tended to coolness during the summer and warmth in the winter. The windows for the upper floor were merely openings that could be covered with tule matting. Open vents in the roof allowed the smoke out and they had a clever arrangement to assist in drawing the smoke upwards in days of high winds.

The captain found that the larger buildings were dormitories, some for the unmarried women, others for the unmarried men or youths not yet of marriageable age; still others, of course, for families. He found, too, that each sex held its dormitory inviolate and this was respected. Some married people and their children lived in small homes, set up in about the same fashion as the dormitories. The captain was almost surprised to notice some tepees set up on the outskirts. Those tepees were probably shelters for some folks that were not permanent residents.

The captain and his small escort moved into the center of one of the dormitories where it was warmest and found the place clean, comfortable, and pleasant. No vermin were about and that surprised the captain, for he had found many of his Red friends rather plagued by various and assorted little pests. He was considerably surprised when the next day he found few horses about the village. He was told the horses were below in the good prairie-grazing grounds with the Lower Nez Percé, for winter grazing was good there. He was greatly disappointed in not finding them here, for those beautiful horses were what he had been most anxious to see. He rested a couple of days, visiting mostly, but the captain could not be idle for long. Besides, there was a lot of work waiting for him.

Now, the good captain would not have thought of laying a claim at being a doctor. Actually he may have been a good veterinarian at that state of his experience, but while he had been a lad about home he had acquired much medical experience, all at the receiving end. Being a lively lad amid rough surroundings, he had been plagued with the usual contusions and abrasions, the cuts and punctures customary to a lively boyhood, and at one time had suffered from a multiplicity of large boils, some of them in the darnedest places. At school, too, he had picked up some experience in fixing up his buddies for one thing and another, so that after a time they began to brag about his doctoring, and during his tenure at West Point his dormitory room had someone in for medication nearly every day.

That year in the Nez Percé area the winter had been one of the hardest remembered by the local people. First, there had been weeks of rain and the darkest kind of weather, and then it had snowed, without end it seemed. Everybody had been kept inside for a long time now, a situation unusual with Indians. In consequence, many of the children had been breaking out with boils and carbuncles and one thing and another. Some had watery eyes, running noses; some had the sniffles; one young fellow had a broken arm. Even the grown folks had an unusual number of troubles. One of the men in his dormitory had a cough so bad that the captain was surprised that it did not shake the roof when the sick man turned loose in a spasm.

He set the young fellow's arm; first giving him a couple of slugs of spirits to sort of keep the lad's attention off the accompanying pain. He had a bottle of some sort of tar emulsion, and mixing that with honey he dosed the coughing man so liberally that the racking cough disappeared in self-defense, and believe me, he was in business right thereafter. Pretty soon he was doctoring nearly everyone, from the youngest baby up to the patriarch of those local villages. The dormitory where he was domiciled was inconvenient as a dispensary, because the women could not bring their sick children there. So the captain, following an agreement with the village chief and assisted by the two village police, moved his medical practice into a lean-to hut, open on the west side where the sun gave plenty of light, and with a warm spring that never froze over right alongside. That spring bubbled up so clear and sparkled so in the sunlight that it reminded the "doctor" of the carbonated water back home.

It was really surprising what a lot of sick babies and ill children there were in those three closely associated Indian villages. After a few days the three men who had come with the captain began to kid him, suggesting that his number of women patients would drop in a hurry if he would only shave off that beard—and there may have been something to that.

Captain Bonneville, though black of hair and beard, did not have the type of beard as was often sported, with pride, by mountain men. His beard did not envelop his entire features from the top tips of his ears to the tip of his nose and hang down into his jacket. It was not unknown for mountain men, after some months of wintry weather, to have so much beard on their faces as to completely hide their features, including most of their eyes. Really, it was not at all unusual, toward the end of a hard winter, to see a mountain man with hair growing out of his nostrils, out of the top of his nose, out of his ears, and out of the tops of his ears, a man actually more hairy of face than a hairy baboon from the Cameroons. The captain's beard was not like that at all.

His beard hair was fine, almost silky in texture, it did not extend upwards over his cheek bones, nor did it grow out of or over his nose, nor out of his ears or over them. It did not begin at the back of his neck and continue on past his chin, finally disappearing beneath his undergarments as an added covering for his chest. The captain's beard was only of medium length and was slightly and pleasingly curly, leaving the cheek-bone areas fully in view with all their fresh pinkness. His eyes were in no way hidden, but looked at his patients with such an expression of kindness and good will, exhibiting a look of pleased surprise at being of help, that babies and little children cuddled up to him in happy confidence after a first look, and, strange as this may seem to some, his glance had the same effect on the Nez Percé women. They all looked as though they, too, would like to cuddle up to him. Yes. As a doctor, the captain sure was on his way to becoming a great success. And why not? We know now that healing is not all a matter of pills and (may we say) Epsom salts. A kind, and more especially, a pleasing temperament often brings a cure when pills and nostrums have failed.

But life has its bad moments as well as its good ones. A chinook blew out of the west for the greater part of a day, melting the fluffy snow covering, and then it turned cold again immediately, freezing a heavy crust on top. It would be the best opportunity for the white men to leave. A few hours later the captain and his three companions were on their way, slogging it up toward the top of the Bitter Root Mountains and his trappers at work up that way.

The captain never did forget those Nez Percé. His notes are filled with memos that praise their kindness, the stature and noble forms of their warriors, their dwellings, and their religious worship. Nor did he forget the women. His notes tell of their beauty of form and feature. Of their kindness of heart and other virtues. Apparently it was not the Nez Percé women alone who were sad at his departure.

Some months later the captain was still waiting to hear from the men whom he had sent to explore the Country toward and beyond the great salt lake far to the south. He waited until his patience was spent, then, fearful lest they had found difficulty and trouble, he decided to take some of his best men, mounted on the best horses, on a speedy trip in that direction, hoping to locate the lost men and be of assistance should they need it.

A hurried start was made. The captain covered much country, riding toward the south for weeks, seeing neither his men nor Indians nor horses. Coming out at a high point one bright morning, he saw far below him, and to the west, a lake within a vast flatland that glistened in the morning sun as though the sands were composed of jewels or brilliants. He knew that this could not be the great salt lake. It wasn't large enough, being only 30 miles long, while the great salt lake was said to be 150. The men made their way down to have a look.

Arriving at the lake, they found it to be but a mere puddle—if a body of water that stretches out for 30 miles can be classed as a puddle. Regardless of that, puddle was the right name, for as near as the explorers could ascertain, the lake was but a thin sheet of water lying upon a shallow, flat, impervious base. Its sides encompassed it in all directions as flat as a board—it seemed—and the mineralized sparkling base, though but sand in appearance, was as solid as a (let us suggest) concrete floor. It was, and is today, a queer formation. The hoofs of the horses made nary a dent, leaving no footprints nor any trail after having passed. A strange odor, slight but persistent, permeated the air. The horses seemed to like it. They kept putting their heads down low and sniffing as though they were inhaling something pleasant. That area, that once was a lake, is now known as Bonneville Lake. There is little, if any, water there now at any time of year, and it is the site of many attempts to test the speeds of automotive equipment of numerous makes.

It was a hot day and as both men and horses were in need of water they did not tarry long, but turned away in the direction in which they hoped the great salt lake lay. After some miles a dry water course gave promise of water at higher elevation, and as the height above lay across the direction they wished to follow, they took their way upward and did, after about an hour, come to water holes containing good water. After all had drunk their fill, they headed over a divide that stood between them and a southerly direction. After passing over that ridge they came to a most rugged land. Boulders, rocks, and ridges of cliffs tumbled in every direction. High, and farther to the west, timbered heights were seen, and since they needed grass for the horses they made their way in that direction.

It had seemed but a short distance to that timber, but night came, and finding a swale that had good grass for the horses they made camp there for the night. The next morning, in a tangle of hills and a wallow of gullies, with all sorts of impediments to progress, the captain was limbering up his legs from saddle soreness. He was up ahead, picking out the most desirable route, and carrying his gun at ready for a shot at a deer (there were many deer signs), when he stepped around a clump of buck brush and was face to face with a scarecrow of a man.

Both men, in perfect unison of frontier thought and action, were automatically lining up the muzzles of their rifles for a quick shot should emergency require it, when, by golly, they both recognized each other simultaneously. To Bonneville, the scarecrow in front turned into Mr. Walker, the man in command of the party that had been sent the autumn before into the south in search of beaver and the great salt lake.

To Walker there, his opposite was the man he had least expected to see in this forlorn country. While on the watch for a deer or any other meat, he had also been keeping a sharp lookout for Digger Indians, varmints that had been making life miserable for his party for weeks. They had run off most of his horses, shooting them full of arrows and apparently eating them without either salt or cooking. They had pestered the white men past endurance, until the latter had become so fearful of them that they had, recently, at a time that had seemed most opportune, shot down several dozen of them, men, women, and children. Since then, those Diggers had recruited numbers from elsewhere and had been hanging around, just out of sight, ready at any moment. They became so pesky, so onerous, that the white men had nightmares about them and would wake from sleep because of bodily pains and inconveniences, sweating and springing up in terror, sometimes firing into the night and doing damage to some of their own horses and whatever.

The party just then found by Bonneville had been barely existing, being almost entirely out of food, using whatever roots and other plant growths they could stomach, with an occasional animal to add flavoring to their unsavory vittles. Walker had nothing but complete failure to report to his commander, but was so happy to see him that he gave so great a shout of delight that the noise racketed back and forth among the huge boulders and rimrocks with such a volume of cheer that the men of his force, working their way slowly and painfully in the rear, could not fail to know it as a paean of delight. And Bonneville, regardless of the circumstances of his subordinate and party, was so happy at coming upon Walker that he too was halloing with joy at the simultaneous meeting with Walker. For the captain, for some days now, had been debating the advisability of going on or turning back. Only his determination to keep on with a project until completed, regardless of the odds, had kept him going onwards, and now, with the parties united, bad luck seemed to turn into good. Four good deer were killed in a glade less than half a mile from the meeting place, and that evening all the men ate to their stomachs' content.

Mr. Walker told of the great salt lake and of his party's journeys in attempting to ascertain its dimensions; of the wastes that surrounded much of the salt water and the shortage of food of any sort near, a situation that had forced the men away from the salt water and into high hills in search of meat; and of the lack of game

and near starvation, and then of desert wastes lying ahead, westward, seemingly without end. No men had been lost, but at times
it had seemed as though no one of them could possibly survive. He
told of coming later to great and pleasant valleys occupied occasionally by pueblos or haciendas. Of how gracious and kind the
people were; of great missions, with their priests and Indian
peoples, and of how finally they came to the western sea, to a village named Monterey, whose people, though Spanish, were the salt
of the earth.

Between recounting his troubles, the wonders of the country,
and the great ocean, Walker was still talking as both men fell asleep
that night. It was a happy occasion.

The next morning some of the men were indisposed from over-
eating, a circumstance unusual with mountain men, but these had
gone far too long on scanty rations. Their systems could not handle
such an overload at the first feeding. The horses were grazing in
fine grass and in a few days would be ready for the long journey
north to headquarters up on Green River. In the course of more
talk it developed that Walker had lost all his furs and most of his
horses while crossing the deserts toward the west. Many of the
horses, the most decrepit first, had been used for food. They had
seen no horses since leaving headquarters until they came into the
great valleys of central California, and there horses roamed in
countless numbers, but mostly they were a different type horse and
originally came from Mexico. Walker grew wistful when talking
about those great valleys; its horses, and wonderful people; the
gardens that grew at the haciendas and occasional missions. During the winter they had trapped in the country inland from
Monterey and had traded the pelts for horses and whatever other
objects were available and suitable for their use, including some
dried beans and chili, a food that they had come to relish. Then,
after some fandangos and other celebrations, they, with the assistance of the kindly people, had started for the eastern mountains,
avoiding the deserts by keeping farther to the north, but later had
come into the lands inhabited by Digger Indians, who eventually
almost completely despoiled them.

MYSTERIOUS HORSES OF WESTERN NORTH AMERICA

It was a woeful tale. Bonneville could sympathize with Walker. He had been going through much of the same mountain country. Its sinks, its valleys, its hills and terrible mountains. He could visualize without the use of any imagination some of the troubles that Walker and his men had been through.

Two days later they started out for the northern country. The weakest of the men were on horseback, for Bonneville had brought extra mounts with him and added to that were his pack horses whose packs were unfilled. As they moved northward, Captain Bonneville could summarize that the trip had been a total failure. And he wondered where all the horses were that were supposed to be in the territory.

Captain Bonneville's usual urgency to get a matter completed urged him on, but speed was out of the question; he was limited to the slowest among his party, which now consisted of some men in precarious circumstances. This situation, combined with the fact that his salt-lake expedition, from which he had expected so much, was a complete failure made the captain's mood far from hilarious.

He was not alone in that situation. Walker, the leader of the salt-lake southern enterprise contingent, was a man of spirit and courageous endeavor, a man not accustomed to failure, and the very poor results of his journey were gnawing at his insides as well as keeping an unpleasant taste in his mouth.

Fortune may treat us illy, and the prospects ahead may seem to be of little value, but if we persist, the winds of fortune will turn into a direction that brings surcease to ills and Dame Fortune will smile on us again. And so it was with our friends, now struggling through a terrible area of loose rock and tearing chaparral, the horses sweating under the strain of poor footing and the men tense with the fear of possible mishap to the horses; and then, rounding the shoulder of the rocky ridge, they saw before them a paradise that stretched in front of them for many a mile.

The urgency within the captain's usual nature was driving him north at the best speed he was able to muster, but alas, he was limited to the speed of the slowest among the men, and that, for him, was slow indeed. This situation brought no hilarity to the captain's mood. Failure of his venture, total and complete, was the prospect before him. Loss of money for his associates in the business and disgrace with the general public. The situation ahead looked very gloomy indeed.

Mr. Walker was in no better circumstances. He was far from being a man familiar with failure. The captain and all his associates had known him as such, and his present situation galled his spirit worse than the rough saddle smarted the saddle sores on his bottom. The future looked as gloomy to him as did the prospect immediately before him, for the party had just then come to a side hill composed of loose and shaley rock that tumbled and slid beneath the tread of their horses' feet. The horses, in very poor condition anyhow, tender of foot and weak of knee, were likely to tumble at any step and that brought the spirits of their riders to another new low. The two leaders, keeping up a front as best they could, had just come to a mordancy of spirit that could in a few more hours of such rough going lead to a state of mind that would result in a burst of profanity at the continued perversity of fate; at the rolling of boulders under foot and the tearing grasp of chaparral from all sides; when, upon rounding a sharp point in the terrain, there loomed before their eyes a scene so pleasing that they could not, for some moments, believe their eyes. Up ahead, slightly to the west of north, sloping down to the east into a green and pleasant valley, lay a hillside of the greenest grasses, where purling waters flowed. Deer sprang from coverts at their approach and grouse took up into the trees as they came near and from their perches craned their necks as they watched the travelers proceed below them.

A pleasant pool with sylvan surroundings demanded that all should halt and dismount. Both men and horses slaked their thirst from the flowing stream the while trout slipped backward downstream, not the least alarmed at their presence. Horses were relieved of their loads, their sore backs doctored with the exudations from some balsam trees, and were soon feeding to their hearts' content and the satisfaction of their bellies which for too long had been growling at the emptiness of their situation.

Shortly thereafter, hunters were returning with fine deer, grouse, and diverse other fowl, and now a fisherman, long discontented with the lack of fishing waters, came up to the cooking fires with a string of trout that would have made Izaak Walton himself slightly acrid with envy.

This was paradise, enough for today at least, and tomorrow was another day, and almost a full day away at that. Let us eat, drink, and be merry, for no one can know what fortune tomorrow may bring.

As they were consuming their first good meal since a time beyond certain recalling, the two leaders were seated beneath the shading boughs of two tall conifers. The captain, a man of concentration upon the food in both hands, was immune to extraneous circumstances, but Walker was annoyed by a light but persistent buzzing above. As both his elbows brought hands full of food up to his mouth, he glanced upwards and was surprised to note that veritable swarms of bees, up high, were moving into the verdure up there and that many were also going away in, it seemed, almost equal numbers. Mr. Walker then, with the edge of his appetite dulled by reason of the fact that his capacity was limited to the confines of his body, watched the goings on up there for some time, finally deciding that bees were coming, feeding for a time, then departing for home with a load of material.

Now, Walker was no expert on bees, though I'll bet he had received the usual supply of bee stings common to a rural boyhood; but he knew that it was bee custom to feed upon the blooms of plants and that their food consisted of the nectar from such flowers. How they could secure nectar from the fronds of balsam trees, however, was completely beyond his comprehension. Then, in attempts to ease the pressures of his overloaded innards, he inhaled and exhaled some deep breaths, and he thought that he could smell honey, and lots of it. Once, when but a lad, he had opened a five-gallon crock of stored honey for his mother. The crock had been standing in the sun for approximately two hours and the honey was warm. As the lid came off that crock, that honey smelled sweeter, better, than anything he had ever smelled. His mouth had actually watered with the sweetness of it. He never had forgotten those pleasant moments, and now, although he was full as a tick, his lips grew moist with a longing for honey.

Assisted by two of his men, Walker now managed to raise his overloaded body erect and began an investigation.

He discovered that the leaves—the needles—of these two solitary balsam trees were covered with a thin coating of soft wax. He had never seen such a condition in conifers before, nor had he ever heard of such a thing. He was disbelieving his senses, but there were the bees, coming, feeding, and going, apparently loaded with wanted supplies of some kind. Then, too, there was that smell of warm honey. He followed the bees in the direction of their travels and within some few hundred feet came to a rocky eminence where stood a number of great pine-forest giants, gnarled, twisted, and cracked with many years of combat with natural forces.

Bees were entering and coming out of numerous cracks and openings in those trees. The honey smell was strong—and then Walker had an inspiration.

When the Bonneville force had been in some timberland on their way from Fort Osage toward the Green River rendezvous area, they came into a bee tree area and by considerable labor had secured a large amount of wild-bee honey.

It had been at Walker's suggestion that a large portion of the Bonneville trade goods had consisted of high-powered alcohol. High-powered so that it could be diluted to one-sixth or one-eighth power and still have plenty of potency for the Indian and mountain trapper trade. Arriving late at the rendezvous, the trading had been about over with, for all the liquid goods of the earlier traders had already been consumed. On arrival at the rendezvous, one, the smallest, Bonneville container of alcohol had been broached and copiously mixed with water and good amounts of the honey for sweetening. The people at the rendezvous, traders, white-squaw men and their mates, Indian warriors and their women, had all taken to that honey-sweetened drink as a flock of ducks take to water after a long dry journey. Trappers, both red and white, had found pelts and peltries that they had been saving for swapping after recovering sobriety after their drinking pleasures were over. For some time the revelers had been getting more peeved with the traders, for the liquor became ever less potent by reason of more water being added between every round.

Walker apparently was a natural trader. He had handled the situation like an old master. He had thinned the alcohol and honey mixture so that it was potent, but not too potent; just right, so that the trappers, both white and red, thirsted for more and more, and when finally they had nothing more to offer in trade, Bonneville had been surprised at how little of the pure alcohol had been taken from the cask. White men and red alike, together with their women, had declared that his liquor was the best of anything they had ever drunk, and that occurrence came brightly now into Walker's mind.

If, by good fortune, the trading at this year's rendezvous had not progressed too far, this honey and plenty of water mixed with some of that alcohol could go far toward recouping some of the faltering fortunes of the Bonneville enterprise, and, as has been previously stated, when good fortune once begins to smile on one for a change, good fortune is persistent. For various and sundry reasons, Sublette, Fitzpatrick, and other traders had not yet arrived at this year's rendezvous site, and later, when they did arrive, they were simply too late. The mountain men and the red men had disposed of all their better furs for the wonderful concoction mixed by the clever Walker. All that was left was the least worthy of their peltries. The late traders were forced to do the best they could, which they did without any ill will whatsoever. This year it was their turn for ill fortune. Next year could be better. They arranged to carry the Bonneville furs to the St. Louis markets, where Walker, who went along, would dispose of them to the best advantage and forward the funds received to the credit of the Bonneville enterprise.

With nothing of interest to keep them, the trappers soon left the rendezvous. Walker and the furs were gone. More trappers were recruited and assigned to various Bonneville groups who would trap in areas best suited this season for the business of gathering furs. And now, with autumn approaching, Bonneville again began to yearn for a sight of those wonderfully colored horses that Lewis and Clark had spoken of so highly. That meant that he would have to go among the Lower Nez Percé who grazed their horses in the great plains along the Columbia.

The next year's rendezvous had already been determined (there was still plenty of that good alcohol remaining). Bonneville went on an excursion, establishing trapping parties in some favored locations, then made a long turn to the left, meeting the rest of his forces up in the mountain country of the high Bitter Roots, leaving some small trapping parties in some sheltered valleys there, where there was scant likelihood of their being troubled by marauding Indians during the trapping season.

9

Captain Bonneville Finds Horses

There had been much talk of late, especially among the new trappers, of great trapping waters in lands formerly overrun by the Snakes, but recently these Indians had been so decimated by smallpox and measles, by too much fire water and continuous battle, that their waters were now, and had been for some years, completely neglected. So Bonneville headed for the waters along the Boisee and other tributaries of the great Snake River, planning on leaving the balance of his trappers there, and then proceeding to the Lower Nez Percé by way of the Snake River.

It was a large country and a long way to go from up in the high Bitter Roots to the lower areas of the Boisee, and as he came to the upper reaches of the Snake, winter was coming on. Much of the district along that portion of the Snake lands was an arid, and sometimes rocky, volcanic area. Heading for the main river, the party became entangled in the mazes of recent (apparently) lava flows that, following cooling, had been tumbled about by obscure forces into a nightmare terrain. Aside from himself, Bonneville had only three men. They were all mounted, and had three pack horses to carry their supplies. Coming into the immediate area of the great river, they found it beneath great cliffs, with springs gushing out in great numbers from fissures and other places. Bonneville estimated that the area had a thousand springs and that land is known today as the Land of a Thousand Springs.

Turning then northward along with the flow of the Snake, after some days they came upon a group of Digger Indians, a most woeful and degraded looking lot. Mostly they were naked and without food, with their habitation consisting of little more than brush shelters. To give you an idea of their circumstances and conventions, one old woman wore, as her complete apparel, a string around her neck to which had been threaded an elk's tooth. Most of them seemed to be so destitute that the white men took pity on them and made some short hunts to secure them meat, which the Indians relished very much, wasting not a single portion of the animal. When the marrow had been cleaned out, the bones were boiled for soup. Bonneville, later, became so disgusted with the Diggers that he avoided them whenever possible; and then, one evening, he had a pleasant surprise. As supper was being prepared, quite a force of Digger Indians rode up, mounted on good-looking ponies. Later they said that they had been given the horses by the Nez Percé. The captain was somewhat doubtful about the gifting of such fine animals, until he had time for reflection, and then he realized that such gifts were possible from the Nez Percé. He had found them to be a very kind-hearted and generous people.

A few days later winter came. Snow began to fall, and the water along the river banks froze several feet from shore. Ofttimes snow would fall for a day or two, and the weather became really frigid, then, after some great variation of temperature, winter was there to stay for the season. Snow came down for days. It drifted in great drifts and piled up deep in the gullies. The weather turned cold and then colder. After some weeks of tough going, the party came to a deep gorge where the vertical cliffs seemed to dispute the river's right-of-way. The river was impassable. To the right, the cliffs towered to great heights. The men could not see the great mountains above them, but they knew that they were there. Across the river toward the west, the mountains also towered high, but after consideration and looking the terrain over carefully, it was concluded that those western ridges could be climbed. It was decided to go in that direction, but first the men had to retrace their path to a site where the ice on the river would be strong enough to hold up their horses. So back they went and managed a crossing without difficulty, except for the sleekness of the ice. The winds had swept the snow away and the ice was sleeker than a polished dance floor. However, with the exception of some skinned knees and bloody noses among the horses, they made it across without difficulty.

They scrambled their way up the mountain through light, soft snow for almost two full days. The three horses gave them the most trouble. The horses could not make it upwards until a path had been trampled in the deep snow for them. With the timber up above now in plain sight, the men came to the edge of a gorge. To the right the river lay far below them. It seemed like miles down there, looking down over drifted snow. There was just a little ledge. But maybe they could make it. There was no way toward the left. The mountain there loomed so high above them they all knew that they could never make it up there, with or without the horses. They had some poles that they had used to help them up the steep climb just below. The captain tried the narrow ledge with a pole, clearing off the snow some. It looked as though it might be all right. Anyway, that was the only way. It was that or turn back, and Captain Bonneville was not the man to turn back as long as there was a chance. They had left a horse down on the mountainside in the deep snow, hoping to go back later, maybe, and bring him up. There were his tie ropes. They were brought up. The captain tied the short lengths together, then fastened the rope around his waist. The other men (there were three) took a wrap around an old snag and let out rope as the captain edged along that narrow ledge, testing the way before each step. Apparently it was a solid ledge with the snow snugly in place. The captain was not so careful on the way back. It was fine. He took the first horse over, working his way along to some wider space. Next came the man that was strongest, and he was packing a heavy load. He made it fine. The man that had crossed put down his pack and pulled on the rope, starting the second horse. That one was packed light, with the food and the cooking utensils. The last man was weak. He had not been feeling well and had about played out the day before. He held on to the horse's tail to steady his way across the ledge. When they were well out on the ledge, the snow fell right out from under them and man and horse

fell into the abyss, the jerk on the rope almost taking the man holding it along with them. There was nothing to see of horse or man.
They were simply gone. The last man was still over on the other
side of the narrow ledge with the last horse, and that one was loaded
with the bedding. As it was now along towards night and everyone
was completely worn out, each man camped where he was, in the
deep snow, overnight, hoping to devise some safe way to bring the
last man and horse over the next morning. The captain and the
man over with him unpacked the horse and used the tarp covering
as bedding. It was not a cozy situation, but they were so tired that
they slept the night through. In the morning the horse and man
beyond that narrow ledge were not in sight. Holler and yell as the
others would they could not raise an answer. The man with the
horse must have gotten cold feet and turned back. The captain
hoped that he would be all right. As for the two that were across
the ledge, there was now nothing but sloping ice on that ledge and
they had no means with which to remove it. All they could do was
go on.

Six weeks later, actually, it can be said, more dead than alive,
they came to the summit of the mountains (the Blue Mountain
Range). Timber hid the view toward the south, but to the north
the land dropped away in pleasant slopes. A little valley led toward the northwest and a Chinook wind came up from that way,
thawing the crust that had formed some weeks before. As they
rested there, their minds were not clear and they were uncertain
which way to go. They broke some twigs from some mountain
willows for the horse and, finding pitch in a limb hole in a great
pine, made a fire and cooked some tree moss for a snack. The captain managed that; his companion, Bud, was down and wouldn't
even stir at the captain's pleading. Over about forty feet, the tips
of some willow brush stuck up above the snow and the captain collected what willow buds and tips he could and added that to the
moss. After that had boiled for some time he got some of it down
Bud and later raised him up into sitting position, but Bud was
poorly, very poorly. The horse was moved over now in the hope
that Bud could be gotten underway by his holding on to the horse's

tail, but as the captain was trying to get that going, the snow crust broke away, and then the horse, too, was down.

The captain was never too certain about what happened afterwards, but that about finished him off too. He had noticed for the past several days that Bud and he had not been understanding each other at all. In his better moments the captain had worried some that both of their minds were wandering and had figured then that they both were about through. Actually, the captain had been moving ahead the last couple of days without any conscious knowledge of what was going on. Will power alone had been carrying him on. But now, just as the captain's mind was slipping into a blank, Bud roused and spoke. The captain couldn't understand what Bud was trying to say, but whatever it was it called forth just enough remaining life to carry him along. He never did remember getting the horse out of the snow, but somehow, maybe it was the effects of the tree moss and the willow buds, he found himself, later, bellying himself across soft snow in an effort to make the crust-pack hard enough for the horse to move along. Somehow they got to a small stream that was coming out of a snow bank. Bud followed suit. Somehow they got the snow packed so that the horse, too, made it to the small stream. Along the bank, under the snow, at the water's edge, they found green grass. The horse found it right away and managed to stay upright enough to eat. Just some feet away some willows at the stream edge, bowed over by the weight of past winters' snow, were within easy reach, but now Bud was down again.

The Chinook was warm enough to melt the snow, but when it hit the men it went right through the captain's worn and torn clothes, and maybe, too, his weak condition had something to do with it, but the wind that melted the snow had a chill to it that drove right through to the heart, or so it seemed.

Later the captain was all right again. He could stand up and move about. The snow had settled under the Chinook so that it held his weight. Anyway, there wasn't much of him to hold up just then. He realized that his mind was wandering again, and brought all of his concentration to hold what there was left. Dizzy with the strain, he stumbled and slid off the bank into the creek. The cold spring water coming to his knees shocked him into near normalcy, but as he leaned against the bank, steadying himself, his head seemed to spin some. Then, as he looked down at the shallow pool in which he was standing, he found that he was standing in a bed of watercress. If he could get some of that boiled and down into Bud, Bud would be all right again, and some of that wouldn't do him any great harm either, although he didn't feel hungry; only so terribly weak.

Thirty feet away lay a little pack containing all their worldly goods. Among them was a thin camp kettle. The captain crawled there on his hands and knees and if the snow was cold, he did not notice it. Coming back to the creek he scooped up handfuls of the cress, getting most of it into the small kettle, and as he did so, he thought something surely was wrong with his head again. The cress seemed to be alive and wriggling. He scooped out of the water all the cress that his kettle would hold. It still wiggled, and then Bonneville noticed that the wiggling was perpetrated by hundreds of small fresh-water shrimps. They were small, but the captain sat there on the snowbank of the creek and although it was a frustrating job, he got a few of them into his mouth and they went right down, wiggling and all. Of a sudden now (it must have been some minutes) some strength seemed to work up from his belly. He shook his head to clear it, and there lay Bud just some feet way. Bud was very still. Maybe if he could get a few of those shrimps down into him it might help. He never remembered how he got there, but soon the captain was forcing a few shrimps into Bud's slack mouth. The Chinook had swung away some and the sun, out in full sight now and shining brightly, warmed the captain's hands, so that he managed to trap a few shrimps quite readily. He got six down into Bud, maybe eight, but now his arms were too weak. He had to stop and rest.

A snag, maybe twenty feet high, had splintered as the top had broken away in its fall. The sun was shining on the side that the captain was facing and old gobs of pitch had collected in some of the cracks in the wood after the tree had fallen. He inched his way over to the snag and finding a little dry wood just underneath a slab of dead bark, he put that on a piece of dry bark on the snow, gathered some drops of dry, hard pitch, then, using his flint and steel, he knocked sparks into that tinder until it began to blaze. In minutes then he had a good hot fire.

Pulling off slabs of dry bark from the far side of the snag, he fixed a dry place for Bud to lie in. When he got to Bud, the latter was conscious. His eyes were open, but held no expression. He might have been dreaming for all the captain could tell, but as Bonneville tugged at him to bring him over to the fire, Bud was able to help along some. The bark bed wouldn't be at all comfortable but it was fairly dry. The fire was now beginning to take a hold on the snag. For the first time in weeks the captain knew what warmth felt like. He started a small fire, away from the snag, got the kettle with the watercress and shrimps on it, and fixed it so that it wouldn't tip and spill. His hands were better now. He managed to down a few more wiggling shrimps, then, with his kettle snug on the fire, he stumbled on his knees over to the pack on the creek bank and tugged out the last frayed remnants of tarp there.

Then he found he could make it to his feet and he made better time getting over to Bud, who apparently was fast asleep. Although, if he was breathing, there was no sign of it. There was, though, the least sign of a pulse near an eye. There was life there. The color was better than it had been an hour before. Bud would be all right.

Taking care of the fire around the kettle, the captain happened to wonder about the horse. He looked for him, and it seemed as though the horse was leaning against the creek bank. His head was hanging low. Alarm struck the captain. He hurried as fast as he could to the horse and found that the animal was resting, with his side nestled against the creek bank and his chin resting on some mud alongside the water. The captain noticed then that the horse too had been eating the watercress. A few mouthfuls had, apparently, given him some strength and he was resting snugly against the bank.

When the captain got back to the fire, the kettle was boiling right merrily. The shrimps had all stopped wiggling. He stumbled back to the saddle pack and brought over a wooden fork and spoon, and then, quite suddenly, the captain knew that the worst was over. He noted how dirty the forks and spoons were. For some days, apparently, little cleaning had been done to their eating utensils.

The next morning, when he awoke, the captain was somewhat surprised to find himself snuggled up against Bud, underneath a piece of tarp, and comfortably warm. He could not remember ever having felt so wonderfully cozy. Bud was snoring, ever so slightly, so that was all right. He himself was feeling fine, but as he tried to move, he found that even just stirring was beyond his strength just then. He managed to get his head out from under the blanket and as he stared up into the trees, he noted that the tree tops were waving. The Chinook was still blowing. He was hungry, but somehow he didn't feel as though he wanted any more cress and shrimp this morning. Apparently he had overeaten on them yesterday. He felt as weak just then as he imagined their last cup of tea had been, and was surprised that he could remember that tea. He felt terribly weak, but that was merely a sort of languid feeling. The thing that was pestering him then was hunger. For the first time that he could remember in a long time he was actually feeling hungry. He had been hungry, he knew, but that had been a different feeling. It had gnawed at him before, tearing him down little by little. It had grown into a sick feeling. Now he was just plain hungry.

He thought about the horse, and turning his head in an attempt to see him, he found himself looking at a large clump of rosebush, the leaves still on it and somewhat green underneath. Red rose hips gleamed brightly under the morning sun. The captain's mind was bright and sharp this morning, for he was able to figure out that snow had covered that rosebush before hard-killing frosts had come in the autumn. Of a sudden he knew what he would have for breakfast. Rose hips were good. He had eaten them as a boy.

But getting up was another matter. He had once seen a man trying to get to his feet after having been badly beaten in a long fight. The captain, as he tried to struggle to his feet, realized that he must look much the same as that man. His first two attempts were total failures, but he tried again, and after that, at each try, he was doing better. Before he succeeded Bud woke up and was eyeing him, but making not a move. Bud really was tired. He was all in.

But Bonneville was persistent. At every try he appeared to get just a trifle stronger, and then, at long last, he was on his feet, and arranging the smoldering fire that was still feebly burning at the base of the snag. He was surprised to find the camp kettle empty. He didn't remember eating the last of that cress.

With kettle in hand, he went slowly over to that clump of rose-bush and began gathering the hips, finding them surprisingly firm. At home they had always mushed up before spring. The soil must be good here, he thought, the hips were large and very red. He slipped one into his mouth and chewed on it just slightly. There was flavor there, just as he remembered. He hurried with his picking.

He made a mistake. He had put a lot more of water into the kettle than he should have. The hips would be nothing but a watery soup. The captain didn't like that idea at all. He drained off all the water he handily could, but even then he didn't like what would be coming up. Then he remembered the willows. He found that the willow buds had already begun to swell and that the Chinook wasn't yet a full day old. He had his knife out and was cutting away the tenderest-looking top twigs, and when he had quite a large handful he went back to the fire and the cooking kettle. Steam was already coming from the kettle. He stripped off all the willow buds he could manage handily, then whittled away at the soft bark at the tip, putting it into the pot in small pieces. The fire was getting low, but there was no wind there to bother that morning, so a large fire was not needed. He nestled the kettle down a little deeper into red-hot coals and right soon the willow buds began giving off a pleasant odor.

He called to the horse, but the horse did not raise its head. Either it was feeding on cress, he decided, or was saving even such of its strength as lifting its head would have required. That horse really was low. And now the captain had to do something about Bud. But Bud was content to lie beneath that warm blanket. He hadn't felt so comfortable since he could remember. He was going to lie right there and die in comfort. He knew that he couldn't go any farther anyway. The captain knew just how Bud felt. He had felt the same way just after he had awakened. But that wouldn't do. He wasn't going to allow Bud to lie there and die. Besides, he might need him. "Come on, Bud. Roll out." But Bud wasn't having any of that. At the captain's efforts to roll him out, he remained as limp as a wet dish rag. But the captain was resourceful.

Shaking a frayed sleeve down over his left hand, he picked up the kettle of boiling stew and then, sitting down as close to Bud as he could, he began to stir the stew. Now, that stew had neither salt or other condiment for seasoning, but maybe the captain's hunger was all the seasoning required. At any rate, in just one minute, spoons full of that stew were finding their way into the captain's mouth. It was hot. The captain smacked his lips loudly. Between the odor of the stew and the smacking of the captain's lips, the combination was too much for Bud. In just minutes he was taking spoonfuls of that stew when administered by Bonneville, and before the meal was over he was sitting up and doing full justice to his share.

Lower down the trail the going got tough again, and regardless of how well the two men had felt at the conclusion of breakfast, they found that getting the horse out of the creek and saddled with the pack saddle and their few possessions had taken away what little strength they had acquired. Down below, the Chinook had not had much effect—just enough to soften the crust, so that the horse broke through it at almost every step. They finally got him into the water of the creek, but then both of the men were down. Their knees just wouldn't hold them upright. It seemed so silly. Neither of them were in any pain, except for the terrible feeling of total weakness. Bud was willing to call it a day. From where they now were all that they could see ahead was more timber, with a winding opening always there before them as they progressed downward. But Bud was no quitter. He had simply come to the end of his rope. He was all played out and he was through.

Bonneville, wisely, had gathered a few handfuls of the rose hips before starting away from camp that morning. There were some mushed up in his one good pocket, but they weren't too bad. Not if you were hungry enough. The captain was sure that if they could only go on just one more day they would find aid.

One at a time, as best he might, he fed single rose hips into Bud's mouth. The poorest-looking, those mushed up and somewhat dirty, he fed to himself. The horse was finding something to nibble at. He was a sorry-looking animal now, but they needed the pack that he was carrying.

Bud resisted as best he might, but Bonneville got him to his feet, as much by threats as by giving him strength. The captain had no strength to offer. What had worked best were his threats to roll Bud into the icy waters of the creek if he didn't help get himself up. Once on his feet, Bud seemed now to be the stronger of the two.

Toward evening they saw rose bushes ahead, and the captain began to think of supper. But alas, they found that there was competition for those rose hips. A flock of large blue grouse was feeding there. By resting his gun over Bud's shoulder, the captain got off a lucky shot and knocked a bird out of a tree. The rest just craned their necks, looking around stupidly. The captain got another with another shot, but after that he couldn't load the gun. His arms shook so from weakness that he was afraid he would spill powder trying to load the gun, and he couldn't afford to waste any.

The horse had gone down twice during the day, and it looked like he was about done in, but there were cottonwoods near. If they could only get him to the cottonwoods, or get some cottonwood to him, there still might be a chance. It wasn't really thawing, but the weather had lost its worst winter chill. Bud went for the two birds, while the captain rested on his gun. Then, when Bud got back, the captain started slowly for the cottonwoods. The horse was down now, its nose resting on the snow. Bud had brought back a good stick when he brought the birds and that was a great help to Bonneville. He made it to the cottonwood trees, but could not find the strength to reach up and break a wig or peel any bark.

Leaning against the tree then, in the sun, he, as he managed to raise his head, found that a good green-branched limb had broken away from that tree, probably because of heavy snow. He managed to wiggle it free and then found that towing it toward the horse was easier than walking free. He found rest by leaning on that limb between steps. The horse was able to nibble on slivers of bark, and Bud fed him while the captain prepared the birds for supper.

Lower down the going got tougher again. They had come to an area where the snow was deeper, but the horse was still on its feet and Bud was able to get along by hanging onto its tail. Toward evening they came to a perfect maze of rabbits' tracks. There were well-trodden deep trails in the snow. They even jumped some as they struggled slowly along, but neither man was strong enough now to point the gun. That evening though, Bud set some snares, and after an hour or so they had a timber rabbit caught in a snare. A fire was burning and they prepared to cook that rabbit right way.

Some folks do not care for rabbit meat. I detest it. But those two hungry men never had better meat in their lives. Nothing much was wasted. The captain even chewed up the bones. The horse, though down, was staunchly trying to eat the last of that cotton-wood.

About the next midday, out of the snow now but so weak that their imaginations were playing tricks on them, and with Bud still hanging onto the horse's tail, they rounded a bend, and some distance away, coming up the trail, was a man on horseback. At first Bonneville thought his imagination had reached a new high, but of a sudden he was sure. The rider had seen them, too, and had stopped his horse, and that restive stallion, seeing a horse up ahead, was immediately interested and stomped about as it was being held back. There could not be any further doubt. There before them really was a man on horseback.

No one will ever know which of the three was the most surprised. The rider's horse had by now gradually pranced forward, twisting and squirming, prancing and turning, and then the captain had a good look at that horse. It was the most beautiful horse he had ever seen, being neatly and compactly built and covered with round spots much like those displayed by a baby deer. The spots were white against a dark background.

As the captain looked with mouth wide open in surprise (the captain was so weak that he didn't have good control any more) the rider rode up close and stopped.

Bonneville actually had been the life of the party. No matter who was down, hoping never to get up again, he always had somehow, somewhere, managed to find the strength to rally his men and get them going. Now the trials were over. As the captain stood there, wavering slightly because of weakness, he suddenly collapsed on the trail; falling in a heap as does a bullock when a bullet enters the brain.

Bud stepped up to offer help to the captain, and then the Indian, realizing that these two could offer no trouble, rode up close, dismounted, and tried to be of help also. A little later, all three sitting in the sun, the Indian rolled out of some covering quite a large chunk of dried salmon, offering most of it to his two visitors, who began doing their best to tear their chunks of fish into small enough pieces so that they could get them into their mouths. The only one of the entire group that was disappointed was the Indian's mount. That stallion had determined long before then that the other horse there was of no interest to him. The captain's horse was a gelding.

Just before dark they all made it down to a crude bark shelter, where the men fed on boiled smoked salmon and their horse chewed contentedly upon cottonwood bark.

Captain Bonneville and his good man Bud were very ill for some weeks after their rescue by the Nez Percé Indian. As far as the two recuperating men were concerned there were no symptoms or indications of illness, except for the fact that they were unable to eat enough to bring back strength. It could have been that their long journey over the great Blue Mountains, fighting deep snow during a most severe winter, with almost no food at all, had upset their digestive tracts to such an extent that it would take some time for a readjustment of their inner mechanism. Then too, the family of

the Indian that had found them were people in the poorest of Nez
Percé circumstances, living a considerable distance removed from
even the scant amenities of the crudest of the Nez Percé villages.
The winter was then drawing near its end and the food that had
been stored by the Indians for that season was now but a remnant
of what even normally would have been the poorest of the dried
or smoked salmon and jerked venison, which, though capable of
digestion by a strong man, was certainly no proper food to set before two persons in such straits as the good captain and his friend
were in.

Now with the terrors of their experiences behind them and
without the demand upon them both to steel themselves for a
supreme test every living day, they could not summon the forti-
tude to swallow any considerable quantity of such fare, and what
they did get down apparently did them very little good, actually
creating a morbid condition which nearly brought them to their
final straits. But the old man of the camp, becoming alarmed, traveled far down to a village near Fort Walla Walla where a sister of
his was in the employ of the Hudson's Bay Company, and she, good
heart, rode back to the camp astride behind her brother on his
horse, bringing with her certain remedies, together with some supply of foods of the kind she used in feeding, occasionally, ailing
children and babies of the wives of the important men of the
Hudson's Bay establishment.

We gather from what the captain has told that this sister was a
somewhat aged and decrepit crone. She was not by any stretch of
the imagination a belle of the frontier, no matter how remote and
meager its situation or poor its circumstances, nor would she have
been of interest to even the poorest of the trappers of the mountains as a means of tending his camp fires or providing other home
comforts, but the captain claims that when it came to a matter of
faithful efficient care, of attention, of careful and proper feeding,
the woman deserves a place among the immortals of lady-hood. In
fact, the good captain's opinion of these Indian friends, actually of
all the Nez Percé people with whom he came into contact as a whole,
was so laudatory that I will refrain from giving it here, as it may

seem that I—who grew up among them—am partial and supplying the words for his pen.

The two full pages in his notes the captain devotes to the Nez Percé people, eulogizing their virtues, are written in words of such depth of sincere feeling, with such rhythm of composition, that I consider myself unfit to even copy them here.

Captain Bonneville knew well the American Indian, from the east coast almost to the west coast of the continent. His opinions of some of them are expressed in phrases that might well delight Lucifer himself; but his words in praise of the Nez Percé should be read by every American citizen as a matter of belated justice to an Indian people, who, however they tried, could but fail to satisfy the corrupt baseness of the white men they were forced to deal with, at a time when failure to assent to unjust and arbitrary demands meant death and extinction to a way of life that they knew well and held dear.

Under the attentions and administrations of the sister, the two sick white men began to improve almost immediately, and in a couple of weeks the captain was hunting in the woods, bringing fresh meat for the wickiup camp. Shortly thereafter he was being taught the mysteries of how to snatch salmon out of the streams. The captain would have enjoyed staying there forever, for, as he says, "that were heaven enough for any man," but now, with the two white men well, and word having come by messenger that her various mistresses were awaiting impatiently her return, it was time for the nurse to go. The captain, under the escort of their nurse's nephew and all mounted on fresh steeds, started for the Hudson's Bay station at Fort Walla Walla.

The siege of illness the captain had just gone through had taken the urge to see the beautiful Nez Percé horses out of his mind for the time being, but as they swung along the lower Snake for a stretch, a band of Pintos across the river hightailed it down over the high bank for water. That sight brought his hand down so tightly against the mouth rope that it stopped his horse right in its tracks. The captain feasted his eyes upon that swarm of horses rushing down from the high bank, with heads a-tossing, manes a-flying,

and tails a-swinging, until they hit bottom and started to drink.
His mount wanted to go on. It was heading towards its home
grounds. The captain just reined that horse in tight and watched
those drinking horses. Those critters got to frisking as they finished their drinking. They sure were a sight for eyes that but some
weeks before had given up all dreams of ever seeing them. The captain would have liked to move right in among them, but duty called
and he knew in his heart that the likes of that were not for him.
Some Indian boys high up on the bank began having fun with those
Pinto horses, sailing flat shale rock and similar objects at them
and a-hollering. The horses took off upstream on the dead run,
and full of frolic. They didn't fear the boys, or even mind them.
They were just full of fun and frolic from a free life on the prairies
of the Columbia Basin. The captain watched them until they disappeared around the bend, then, with just a little sigh of regret, he
slacked away on his rein string and proceeded on towards Walla
Walla.

He had not, though, seen his last of gorgeous Nez Percé ponies. A
little farther to the west, the Snake makes a bend toward the north
to receive the waters of the Palouse River. Along to the west though,
along the south bottom lands of the river, lie wide areas of grazing
lands as fine as any in the entire Palouse country. The Nez Percé
secured whatever they needed for the happiness of life and their
women from the Hudson's Bay Company by swapping the company
manager some horses from time to time, so large bands were kept
south of the river as a supply convenient to the needs of those company people. The captain had never seen so many horses, nor would
he ever again see such beautiful horses. He used to dream about
them in later years, and was known to have muttered about them
in his sleep, as does many a lonesome soldier, far from home, mut-
ter in his sleep about some cherished memory.

The captain spent a pleasant week in and about Fort Walla Walla,
but the people there in charge of the establishment, though polite,
were not friendly. It was their purpose to discourage any American penetration of that part of the West. The British still had hopes

of possessing all of that territory and wished that the Americans, for gosh sake's, would stay away.

The captain, though, had heard of a wonderful valley, far to the west, in Oregon. He was going to investigate that section of country so that he might include some information of its circumstances in his reports to his superior officers He therefore outfitted himself as best he could, and he and Bud started out that way.

Below the frontier village, just lately become known as The Dalles, they came to such rugged banks along the Columbia as to make that route seem impractical for common pioneer travel along the river, in fact so impractical that the captain decided to see if a more satisfactory route could not be found by going directly west of the Blue Mountains. He and Bud therefore turned back toward the east, going up the John Day River, that came in from the south. Then, after a day's travel coming into highlands that led directly to the summit lands of the Blues, they turned and made their way east to the Snake, a short distance above where their troubles had commenced the winter before. After crossing that river, the captain collected his trapper bands who were heading for the rendezvous, and then, with his western enterprise completed, he started for the east, for he already was long overdue in reporting to his superior army officers. And with that he passes out of our consideration anent western horses.

10

ANOTHER SEARCH FOR WILD HORSES

In the year 1832 Washington Irving, a gentleman who delighted in hunting in the game lands of eastern North America, and who possessed a wonderful command of the English language as it was spoken in America, together with a most facile pen, was well and favorably known to a host of readers because of his pleasing exposition of big-game hunting conditions in America.

He had been requested by many friends and a host of mere readers to make, and describe, a hunting expedition in the great hunting areas west of the Mississippi River, for in those days, as well as at the present time, many who dream of forays into the land of big game are unable to indulge their desire, but can enjoy reading the writing of some competent hunter who combines prowess as a hunter with a well-worded and interesting account of a big-game hunt.

The American public, especially those of the people who, for whatever reason, are unable to enjoy the hunt themselves, has ever enjoyed reading of the experiences of those more fortunate. Because of that, it had become practically a demand that the admittedly good hunter and prominent author, Washington Irving, should make and describe such a hunt in the big-game areas of western America, which in those days meant a hunt in the great western plains country, the Rocky Mountains at that time being so little known that they did not then enter into consideration. That demand for an Irving hunt was based upon the fact that he was known as a man of good judgment in his presentation of any circumstances, not subject to flights of fancy or fiction, yet well able

136

to compose an interesting story out of whatever circumstances were available.

And so, in the late summer of 1832, in the company of the newly appointed Commissioner of Indian Affairs and his party, who were starting upon a journey through the lands of the still wild Indian Territory, for the purpose of adjusting certain difficulties between the Indians there and the whites who were crowding in and dispossessing many Indians, with the result that much bickering and some fighting had been going on for some years, Irving set forth.

They made their start from the frontier town of St. Louis, State of Missouri, situated on the west bank of the Mississippi, near to the junction of the Missouri River with that stream. They wended their way through the settlements, coming after a time into the lands of Arkansas, and in due time attained their first objective, Fort Gibson, situated close to the east of the junction of the Arkansas and Neosha Rivers.

It is something of a coincidence that one of the principal reasons for Irving's visit to the Indian Territory was his desire to see the great number of mustangs that were reputed to have been, and to still be, in the process of being moved northward to the Indians much farther north by Indians from lands much farther to the south. Irving was a great lover of horses and envisioned with delight great herds of horses rushing northward over the plains in circumstances as free as was possible under the conditions of the times. Among his notes, after he left Fort Gibson, are several entries that they were nearing the wild-horse lands. Unfortunately for him, the party seems never to have actually come into those wild-horse lands. True, four wild horses, captured singly, were taken on their way through all of that wild area, and to make matters even worse from his viewpoint, three of those horses taken were obviously not wild horses at all; merely eastern horses that somehow had escaped their masters and were roaming the country. Those three so evidently had no desire to avoid capture that there was neither fun nor excitement in taking them. The fourth horse was a different matter. He was one of a wild band of six, the only wild band that was seen, and the chase was long and thrilling. Thank goodness, for Irving's sake, that they ran into that band, or he would not have had the memory even of those few wild prairie horses to lend a remembrance of wild horses for his consideration.

True, at various times word that wild horses were near was passed along the line of march, but unfortunately for our writer, he never was able to find any indication that wild horses were, or even had been, near in any part of that country. Mr. Irving was no scouting Indian with all-seeing eyes for signs, but he was hunting man enough to know when there was a complete lack of evidence of any horses having passed that way.

One day there did rush into camp a number of rookie horse-men from the fort, with word that a great herd of wild horses was passing through a nearby forest. There was a great to-do among the army escort in a frenzy of preparing the camp for a ride after those wild horses. By that stage of the expedition, Irving had be-come somewhat disillusioned about the numbers of wild horses that had been thought to exist in these wild Indian lands and would have been content to keep on with the making of notes in his memo book, but a favorite attendant of his was so urgent that he come to see the fun that he somewhat reluctantly mounted and followed him. As the group charged wildly east to make a great capture, whom should they meet coming out of that forest but a company of horsemen who had been on another assignment at the time the Commissioner had departed from Fort Gibson, and who now had caught up with their advance party! That was a great letdown for most of the members of the army, but you may have noticed herein before that Mr. Irving was a man of considerable judgment. He had gone along just for the ride, and principally to please his cook.

In justice to the Commissioner though, it should be said that the party did see bands of traveling Indians sometime later, but sad to relate, they were almost all entirely on foot. They also found some Indians in camps, but sad to relate too, there were but few horses about any of those camps, and those seen were but the scrubbiest of horseflesh. Mr. Irving was glad indeed when the hunt-ing petered out, and, with snow in the air, the party made a swing to the south as a prelude to their return to Fort Gibson.

In the spring of 1832, Captain Bonneville and his party had crossed the plains from near St. Louis into the far reaches of the Windy Mountain range of the Rockies, before they came onto great numbers of Indian horses. Then, in the autumn, in a region some 200 miles farther south, a contingent of the army, together with Washington Irving, who was on the watch for wild horses being taken to the north, crossed the plains country into the foothills of the Rockies, and saw, sensibly speaking, no wild horses worth considering. Where, oh where, were the wild horses that were supposed to be going north? The answer is simple. In 1832 there were no such wild horses.

President Polk about then had dreams of the U.S. acquiring more territory along the western borders of the country. It has been said by one illustrious historian that the President must have believed in dreams, for some weeks before few thought that war with Mexico was imminent, he, in some correspondence with his good friend of the young State of Missouri, advised the governor of that state to speedily acquire enough mounts for a regiment of cavalry, and enough pack mules to carry needed supplies for them over western desert areas.

On May 13, 1846 the United States government declared war against the government of Mexico, on whatever pretext that might sound logical and seem laudable. It has been said that no real attempt was made to hide the fact that the President was after California. One of the earliest programs for the prosecution of that war was the formation of a western army that was to proceed as quickly as was feasible from Ft. Leavenworth, which stood along the Missouri not too far from St. Louis, slightly south of west across the great plains country to Fort Bent, a U.S. installation for the control of western Indians, and from there into New Mexico, a Mexican province; to seize Santa Fe, the capital of the province, for the U.S., hold it against whatever attacks might be brought against the place, and form an American government for the entire province. After accomplishing this, the commander of the U.S. forces, if he believed it feasible, was to proceed to California, using whatever ways and means necessary to accomplish the purpose, which was the seizure and holding of that territory.

The preparation for these projects were most certainly advanced by the foresightedness and actions of the President in having his expedition's route follow the old Santa Fe trail of traders going into Mexico. The trail had been in operation for many years. The route had been selected in years past as the passage best suited for travel because of the satisfactory presence of grass and water, a situation highly conducive to the maintenance of horse bands, both those controlled by Indians or white men and those on the loose. The road was no straight line laid out by a surveyor's transit, but followed the route of greatest convenience for those passing either to the north or the south, taking advantage of streams of water, or water holes, and providing pasturage for the animals en route. Those water holes and that lush pasturage should, in the spring, beckon to any wild horses, as a white light at night beckons to a weary traveler. If any of the early traders that used that trail ever saw any great herds of horses as they passed along that route, surely some records to that effect should exist. Diligent search on my part has failed to produce any such evidence.

The First Dragoons was the crack regiment of the entire U.S. Army, either cavalry or infantry. With them on this march were civilian scouts, mostly mountain men, whose names and experiences in crossing the plains country in early times, north and south, east and west, and in the mountain regions beyond, fill some of the most thrilling pages of American history. The First Dragoons was on the watch for horses, for, almost from the first day on the march, the volunteer mounted infantry began losing horses. The First Dragoons found no horses worthy of mention during their entire march to Santa Fe.

By the time General Kearny's forces were in camp at Ft. Bent, having crossed the easiest stages on the way to Santa Fe, more than one-third of his mounts were missing. The general was heard to remark about that situation something to the effect that it looked very much as though his mounted men would all be marching on foot before they arrived at Santa Fe; and he was so very nearly right. Had his First U.S. Dragoons or his plains-wise scouts been able to find many horses, either on the loose or in the possession of either Indians or white men, they would have brought them in as remounts.

Various museums throughout the Middle West are replete with letters and various documents dealing with that long march across the plains. Those papers deal with every imaginable situation of that march, from lack of soldiery discipline to swarms of mosquitoes. They tell of ground squirrels, of amusing experiences with stray skunks, of drinking filthy water from chance water holes, and of sleeping out under the stars at night. But mention of droves of wild horses is sadly lacking.

There is one record of wild horses in the archives. It tells of a single small band of wild horses, less than a dozen in number, who were found standing in a shallow water hole, the only water that had been seen in miles and miles. Those horses were fouling up that water in the ways customary to horses the world over when they have satisfied their thirst and are resting content. Some splashed around, making a muddy mess of the water, others relieved their bodies in their customary ways. Had those men had their ammunition with them, they would have killed every one of those few horses with pleasure. They chased them out of there and the men with the strongest stomachs quenched their thirst as best they might. Yes, there were some horses seen during that march, but the situation was so unusual, the circumstance was worthy of a letter home to brother, and I have been told that that letter may be seen in some museum in Missouri. (I hope sometime to see it.)

Bernard De Voto, in his book *The Year of Decision*, gives us some details of the First Missouri Mounted Infantry, a regiment of mounted troops recruited by the governor of Missouri before the declaration of war, at the request of President Polk. His record is both amusing and pathetic. There can be no doubt that the regiment could have used remounts long before it ever came to Ft. Bent. Readjustment of the various contingents while at Ft. Bent left the First Missouri Mounted Infantry without mounts. Yes, the expedition to Santa Fe and California could well have used any stray horses that were on the plains during the regiment's crossing.

True, there may have been other things on those soldiers' minds. You know how it is when men in the army are on a rugged march. Let's check just a little further.

A certain gentleman trader, Magoffin by name, one of several brothers who had for years been prominent in trading ventures in far Mexican lands, had for some years been becoming increasingly dissatisfied with trading conditions existing under Mexican rule, and was most anxious that much of that country should come under American rule. This particular brother had been in Washington during the winter, holding some confidential conferences with the President, and with others who might help rearrange matters. Business there had delayed his return west for so long that his brothers had taken their wagon train out in advance of the declaration of war. Too, in the south, a delayed journey would have been a serious problem to them because of lack of water and feed for their animals as summer drought came on. This Mr. Magoffin tagged along behind the army, making himself popular with the officers through a plentiful supply of various liquors and a hospitable nature. It may have been just as well that he tagged along in the rear of the army in a leisurely fashion, for he had brought his young wife with him on this journey. He had objected to her coming along most strongly, for the young lady was in a most delicate condition, but she had insisted on going with him. At first she enjoyed the journey a great deal, but being alone in her carriage much of the time—her husband was an important man, of much experience along this trail, and had of necessity to hold many conferences with the expedition's officers—the young lady eventually became most lonely and in order to pass the time wrote many letters home to her people in Kentucky.

The lady was a Kentuckian, born and bred. She knew just about all there was to know about horses, and she loved them. In addition to her husband's conveyances, she had with her, for her sole use and convenience, a carriage and matched pair, and also a riding pony that she had ridden for some years before her marriage. After some days on the road her condition became such that her husband forbade her to ride the pony any more. In her letters home she lamented about missing her rides on that pony, and, being lonely, wrote about nearly everything that was of interest to her.

She told about the uncouth language of some of the army stragglers, their lack of consideration, their profanity, and other matters. In practically every letter she moaned about her inability to spend some hours daily on her pony. She wrote about everything she could think of. Of how one evening, near a water hole, the mosquitoes swarmed in such numbers underneath her petticoats that she screamed in agony, and of how a kind officer rushed up, carried her to the water hole, dunked her, feet first, into the water, and helped keep her there until all those pestering mosquitoes were drowned. Yes, she wrote of everything, but never once did she mention seeing wild horses.

Now, a Kentucky girl, lonesome and pining for a ride upon her pony, would certainly have written about the matter had she ever seen wild horses during that trip. That observation, certainly, calls for no bright deduction. She never did.

With affairs in Santa Fe well in hand, General Kearny was ready to start for California, but first he had to equip his force with horses. His buyers worked every available source. Santa Fe was literally full of Comanche and Pawnee warriors at the time. They were expecting to profit handsomely from the American occupation. They missed a bet. They should have been raiding for horses down in Mexico. In Santa Fe those Indians, stated to be the notorious raiders of the Mexican lands, had not a horse to offer. The best Kearny could do in gathering a force together from all sources, including the dismounting of some cavalry that would not accompany them, was approximately 500 horses, and with those he started west to conquer California for the United States.

A further indication of General Kearny's efforts in the horse situation following his turning the New Mexico province into an American territory was somewhat as follows: With his affairs well in hand, the general was ready to fulfill the final clause of his orders—to go on, if possible, to California and place that area under the protection of the American flag. The general was all ready, except for needed horses. His quartermasters scoured the country with no success. There were some mules in Santa Fe, but somehow the price had gone up so high that the general refused to pay the prices asked. He would not requisition the mules without payment, for it was his aim to make friends of the Santa Fe people. Santa Fe was actually crowded with Pawnee and Comanche Indian braves. Those vaunted raiders of Mexican haciendas and towns had flocked there, after the American army came, for purposes still unknown. There had been plenty of time for them to raid south of the border and bring horses there, to Santa Fe, and they surely knew that the American army needed horses. Not even a dimwit could have escaped achieving that knowledge, for the cavalry situation of the American force was a joke throughout the entire army. Much of the cavalry had come into town on foot, and the American soldiers could not resist making a joke out of that situation. The general dismounted the officers, used every suitable horse in his command, and managed to field approximately 500 horses. He started west with that many mounted men, and a pack string of mules, to conquer California for his country.

The journey of these 500 men through trackless desert wastes is an epic of man's endurance in the face of hopeless odds. The perversities of nature probably never have been exceeded in any journey in any land. More than a month later, their horses all in, their food supplies long gone, their lips cracked and their tongues swollen because of thirst, they came to a trickle of water that in time became quite a river. Two scouts, moving like worn-out ghosts, made a search for some sort of food up ahead a mile or so. They found no trace of food, but they did discover where a great number of horses had, during the early morning, apparently taken off up a canyon.

Such horses as could travel at all were mounted by some scarecrow men and took off up the canyon with all the speed that they could muster. About two miles up the canyon—it proved to be a box canyon, with water at the cliff that formed the box—and there, on fair pasture, they found more than a 1,000 horses being guarded by four Spaniards. The Spaniards were taking the horses to the City of the Angels (Los Angeles), they said.

Those horses had not been brought in by Indian raiders, but by four, practically unarmed, Spaniards from away down Chihuahua way. Kearny and his men made it to California, and it puzzles me: How did those Spaniards get paid for those 1,000 horses, out there in the middle of a great and tortuous desert? But more to the point, in my consideration of horse raiding in Mexican lands—Chihuahua has often been reported as a favorite raiding ground for Apache and other Indians from more northern areas, and how could four practically unarmed Spaniards drive such a great herd of horses over a thousand miles? Yet, the entire situation is a matter of recorded history.

11
CONTINUING SEARCH

George Frederick Ruxton left his native England at the age of seventeen, in 1839, to fight in the Carlist Wars in Spain, possibly on a matter of importance for his queen. The Queen of Spain, following the fighting, pinned upon his boyish chest one of the highest treasures of Spain's considerable list of decorations, the right for his acceptance being granted him by Her Gracious Majesty, Queen Victoria.

Thereafter, he spent some years in obscure parts of Her Majesty's more remote lands, all of them, it is thought, in the service of his country and queen. In 1846 he landed in Mexico upon some service for his queen. What his business was is still an unsolved mystery, but most likely it had to do with some situation in regard to western American lands.

For some reason, Ruxton preferred to travel the Indian and bandit-infested trails of Mexico all alone, except for an occasional hired servant. How he made it unharmed across and up over all of northern Mexico and into Santa Fe in the new United States territory of New Mexico makes a more interesting tale than the story of the Arabian Nights, but make it he did, not without many inconveniences but without the least harm from either Indians or bandits, either and both of whom were spreading injury, death, and terror much of the way along the trails leading into the north.

While traveling in Mexico, he made notes of Indian raids for horses and other plunder, but regarded such raids as being mainly for the purpose of stealing horses and mules. He suggests a rather small figure for the annual toll of such raids, mentioning a figure that is conservative when compared with some given by others, who laid claims to having much longer experience in such matters.

Ruxton suggests an annual toll to Mexico of possibly 10,000 head a year. I detest such smooth round figures in estimates, even though the numerals do not suggest a very great high. In another paragraph he tells of an Indian raid that netted the raiders an even 150 mules. The next winter, up in America, he estimates the gain on another Indian raid as an even 150 horses. Mr. Ruxton is a most interesting writer, but, again, I detest such soothing round numbers. In my business experiences I usually have found inventory numbers of such round, even numbers to be in error when the items so listed were rechecked. Be that as it may, Ruxton arrived in Santa Fe, still fancy free and with an unpunctured skin, although it must be admitted that he by then bore the marks of some contusions and abrasions.

Until perusing Ruxton's tales of his experiences in Santa Fe and for some months following his leaving that place, one can scarcely appreciate the charming facility of his pen in telling of the atrocities perpetrated by dissident and marauding Indians who had taken to the warpath in an endeavor to right old wrongs, fancied or actual, supposedly imposed upon them by white men or their associates. Commonly, tales of such continuing horrors leave the reader with a queer unsettled feeling in the pit of the stomach. The reader has been known to be unable to go to sleep, and if at last sleep is attained, to wake up later under the pressure of nightmare horrors; but this Mr. Ruxton wields a remarkably different sort of pen. He gives gripping and graphic descriptions of the most horrid tortures and sadistic killings in such words that the reader, instead of becoming a wreck of horror, acquires rather a feeling of having just witnessed a salutary effort of worthwhile endeavor and may actually enjoy the fancied shrieks of imaginary torture and the expiring gasps of the dying victims with considerable delight, just as one views a TV killing with a sound appraisal of the techniques employed by the picture killer. It was a most unique skill.

Shortly after proceeding into the Rocky Mountains to the north of Santa Fe the good Ruxton became entangled among bands of Indians that were busy raiding each other for horses rather than going 1,000 miles to the south in Mexico for the enjoyment of the same pleasures. It was these notes of Ruxton's that suggested to me what had been going on, more or less, among the southern Indians—one band stealing horses from another, and then, maybe in a few days or a few weeks, losing them again to their former owners or some other band of Indians, forming, as it were, a regular merry-go-round of exchanging horses, and giving an appearance of many horses coming into the territories whereas actually the numbers must have been much smaller than they appeared to be at the time of the raiding.

That could be part of the answer to the great number of horses that were supposed to come annually into the northern territories. And now just one more painful illustration of events in 1846.

The winter of 1845-46 was an extremely severe one. During some of the coldest weather the Mormon people and the Mormon Church were driven out of the State of Illinois by hoodlums. The hoodlums could be said to have been completely out of control, but the truth is that no control was attempted, for the local authorities actually urged the hoodlums on, and, whenever opportunity offered, joined the hoodlums in their deviltry.

The wounds suffered by the Mormons in Illinois that winter may never be healed, so maybe the less said about the matter the better. Suffice it to say that it was a time of terrible trouble for the Mormons. The Huns of old could have learned some innovations in their trade if they had been able to see the hoodlums in action in Illinois that winter.

One of the chief situations that brought on the troubles at that time was the fact that the Mormons had, through prodigious and prolonged labor and austere living, managed to procure a considerable number of very fine horses; also, many wagons to be used in their migration to lands farther west. They were not at all sure where they were going, but they were heading west in '46.

The people in several communities had become jealous of the fine horses and staunch equipment that the Mormons had accumulated. A neighbor from a nearby village drove into Nauvoo, the Mormon city. He saw the store windows full of fine goods. Better than he could purchase anywhere else closer than Chicago. Figuring on getting the best of the deal, someone got into a horse swap with a Mormon, only to discover later that he had gotten by far the shortest end of the stick. He raved around home about that. His three large sons, itching for excitement and/or trouble, slipped out the back door. Less than an hour later a large gang of young men sauntered along the main street of Nauvoo. One of the lads threw a boulder through a window of the finest store in town. "Damn the Mormons," he shouted. More windows were crashed. The Mormons were not afraid of a fight. The battle was on.

The people in several nearby villages hated the Mormons with a hate that passeth understanding. Of a sudden, the roads leading into Nauvoo were full of bob sleighs, with one-horse rigs, with cutters, with anything that would travel over snow. Moving in towards Nauvoo. Just as animals of prey can sense a conflict, so the men folk of that area seemed to feel that something was doing. As eagles up high smell fresh blood and set their wings, following the scent, so the neighbors came drifting into Nauvoo.

The Mormons put up a good battle. They had been kicked around the country long enough. This was it. Many determined to win or die. Many died. The attackers were re-enforced from near and far. The Mormons crowded back into the few buildings that were not aflame, hurried their women and children down upon the ice covering the great Mississippi. A few made it on a horse or two. A few teams got across. Some women pulled small sleds piled as high as they could be with personal belongings. One woman was pushing a baby carriage. A last few Mormon men got across the river in the dark. It could have been the end of the Mormon Church, but quite a few men had been away from their home town, working on large farms, in the woods, and on river boats. As the news got around, these men drifted into the camp set up in the brush on the west side of the river.

The weather was extremely cold. People died. Some were buried, but mostly there was no way to get holes into the frozen ground. Many were merely buried in the snow. It was hoped to give them fitting burial when the ground thawed later on. Yes, it was a bad winter for the Mormons. They had not, as yet, really hoped to get started for a new land for a year or more, but now there was no choice. It was go west or perish.

Many parents, too completely miserable to be able to shed a tear, buried a dear one as best they could. A few families lost every child. But the Mormons could survive that, no matter how much they suffered or grieved. Through the Book, the Lord had told them that in heaven there are many mansions, and that there was no sorrow there. The survivors had that much to solace them. They did the best they could. Every man, every woman, every child, each in his own way, did the best he could. A widower could find another wife; a widow would find another husband; and somebody surely would take care of the orphan children; but where would they find horses? Some of them never did.

Later in the winter, as word spread around, a few Elders who were in other areas spreading the Word, and accepting donations, did manage to bring in a few horses. Some people in Illinois, feeling disgraced at the havoc wrought by neighbors, brought a few horses across the river, but the number was pitifully small. Some brought a cow, maybe, or some brought a calf. Some brought chickens. One even brought a lone rooster.

A few of the Mormons camped in the brush on the west side of the river starved to death; some froze; an occasional family was completely wiped out; but as soon as the cold eased some began to move out, heading west. Some of those who got away before the snow melted and the ground became soft in the spring were the most fortunate, for later melting snow softened the soil, some places hip deep, and the traveling was almost impossible for some weeks. But whatever the situation the wishes of most, the prayers of all, were mostly for horses; unfortunately, at that time of year, there were none in the sections of the plains country they traversed. Men and women, sometimes children, helped pull the buggies. One outfit had two weak women pulling on one end of the evener, while at the other end a decrepit cow tugged and pulled along. Wheelbarrows were a common conveyance—mostly homemade too—with bodies of heavy bark and the handles whittled out of willows. And the lady with the three daughters apparently survived the winter, for a woman was seen pushing a baby buggy across the prairie, while three little girls, in single file, hung onto her and each other's skirts as they slowly moved into the west across those endless prairies.

Of course those people prayed for horses. If ever a people of this world were entitled to ask their God for aid, it was those Mormons. But, "God works in mysterious ways His wonders to perform." Their Good Book told them so. At any rate, few of those prayers were answered just then. They struggled on as best they could without horses. They split up along two different routes, the better to find roots for sustenance, and for other reasons. Mostly they just wanted to keep away from the Oregon Trail, for it had been rumored that many people from Illinois and Missouri would be taking the Oregon Trail in the spring, and they had had all they wanted of those people.

The records do not tell of their seeing any unattached horses that spring. Well along in the summer a small band of Indians—Pawnees, I believe—did approach them. Those Indians were villainous-looking and the Mormons were prepared to meet their Maker with prayers on their lips and songs welling up high; but those Pawnees were not on the warpath, and the Mormons did manage to talk them out of some roots and a side of antelope, but failed completely in their pleas for a horse.

Sad to relate, in that spring of 1846, along that section of the plains, from just west of the Mississippi until closely approaching the Rocky Mountains, there were extremely few horses, either running wild or under control of Indians.

12

WHERE ARE THOSE WILD HORSES GOING NORTH?

We have been spending quite a number of pages and a good deal of printer's ink recording our search for wild mustangs being taken towards the far north from Mexico by Comanche and Pawnee Indians, but so far, you will notice, our search has produced very few. However, I consider the refutation of the claims of so many mustangs going north as my contribution to western history, so I am going to use up some more pages in a search for those horses.

A few years after Captain Bonneville's travels across the great plains country, followed very closely by Washington Irving's attempt to find a lot of wild horses going north, we find a record of another expedition across approximately the shortest transverse diameter of those plains, and we will check the report of that expedition into the great plains country. From Captain Nathan Boone's USA journal we select some pertinent entries, to wit: May 14, 1843 to July 31, 1843. ". . . saw in the upper Arkansas River country perhaps 10,000 buffalo feeding on the plains below as far as the eyes could see." "Saw a herd of wild horses about a dozen in number. . . ." Another date: ". . . startled a wild horse today, and one of the officers chasing it fell in with a herd of about 30. . ." Again and later: "Saw plenty of buffalo today, and elk came near our camp this evening." June 28: "Saw buffalo and small herd of wild horses." June 29 into early July, while in the Cimmaron and Canadian River country: ". . . buffalo scarce; saw 7 wild horses today. . ."

Captain Nathan Boone, USA, keeping records for the information of his superiors saw scarcely enough unattached wild horses to be worthy of mention. Be sure that had he seen more he would have included the fact in his records.

The captain apparently was a conscientious and methodical man, for his daily journal of that trip across the plains was filled with so much detailed information that some (so it seems at this time) was of a very trivial nature. One thing is certain; had there been any great number of horses, in any condition, during his journey, he would certainly have made notes in his journal, including a statement of the numbers seen.

That is just one more point scored against some claims that Comanche and Pawnee Indians often drove large numbers of mustangs into the northern plains from out of areas far south in Mexico.

The Nathan Boone contingent, though composed of a small party of men, consisted of frontier men, but they did cross the great plains at approximately the plains area of its shortest transverse diameter, and as they were on the hunt for game, their search must have been satisfactorily thorough, and even though they saw almost no horses, signs of any great numbers of horses having been in that country at any previous time would have been detected by them and have been correctly appraised.

In the decade prior to the Nathan Boone party's travels across and about the plains, the Mexican government was probably in the worst and most chaotic condition of its entire existence. Its politics and its politicians, including the governors of the various states that composed the national government, and even the heads of the national government were in a continual series of messes. The heads of the governments, state and national alike, changed so frequently as almost to require an automatic computer for a proper and correct recording. And to add to the complete malfunctioning of Mexican governments at any level of importance, the changes of governors, and even of some of the heads of the national government, were achieved following periods of personal graft of

government funds and other assets; together with nefarious dealings that cast a stench of irresponsible action over that entire
period in the life of Mexico. The Mexican people, and more particularly those in the horse-producing areas of the north central
portions of the country, were completely defenseless against the
operations of raiders of whatever color for the products that the
raiders most desired.

Such situations were particularly true with regard to the northern and northwestern areas of the country, from prior to the time
the Texans gained their freedom in 1836 until after the American
Army, during the Mexican War, gained control of much of that
territory in 1846-47.

Those years were a time, too, in which horses and mules would
have brought Indian raiders from the south payment in American
dollars, and the honest American dollar of those days was of so
much greater value than Mexican currency that any Indian, with
but a meager number of dollars, would have been rich in the land
below the American border. That feature, because of the circumstances of the Indians of that period and time, was, of course, of
little interest to those who raided the Mexican horse bands.

If there ever had been a good time for the Comanches and Pawnees to bring horses north, for gain or any other reason, it would
have been in the years between Daniel Boone's travels about the
plains country and the time of, and immediately following, the war
between the United States and Mexico. The bountiful records about
those decades which cover the circumstances of plains-areas horse
conditions and history do not disclose any such situation as horses
being brought to the north in such predominant numbers as to
entitle such horses to the credit of putting the northern-plains
Indians on horseback.

13
CAPTAINS LEWIS AND CLARK

The first distinct indication, the first impression, that I can recall today of the fact that, probably, the Indian horses of the plains country had not come north out of Mexico, was in the winter of my tenth year—my last full term at school. When the snow became deep, I rode my horse, Spot, to school. Spot was a dark brindle color, with a dark bay spot high on each hip, the position and size being identical. Teacher quickly was interested in those two spots, so I told him what I knew of the spotted horses of the Nez Percé. The next day, teacher brought to school a large book, profusely illustrated with copies of paintings showing Indian horses on the plains.

I remember only two names of the artists whose works were used in those illustrations. One was George Catlin; the other, Alfred Jacob Miller. I remember Catlin well, for he displayed several spotted horses in his paintings. The reason I have been able to remember Miller is because a next-door neighbor was named Jacob Miller.

The teacher lent me the book, so that I might look it over during leisure time at home. Father became as interested in the book as I was, and we looked those pictures over many a time. Because of the Pintos I had known and ridden, I was impressed and pleased with the many Pintos in all the illustrations of horses in the book. I mentioned the great number of Pintos in that book to Father and then he too was surprised. He had spent some years, as a young man, in missionary work among Indians in Mexico, and

155

he knew Mexican horses (mustangs). He said Mexican horses were not Pintos, and we wondered about the paintings together.

Father had some volumes of the *Original Journals of the Lewis and Clark Expedition*. In later years, in the winters, when snow limited my work outside, I often read through those journals. Gradually, as I read those Lewis and Clark journals, I noticed that Lewis and Clark had seen almost no horses on their journey until they came to the Mandan Indians, some 1500 miles up the Missouri River, which indicated that Lewis and Clark had been pretty well across the plains country, really in the foothills of the Rockies, before they saw any horses. I noticed, too, that the Mandans, who had a few horses, said that they had obtained their first horses from the Crows, and that, in response to inquiry, they told Captain Clark that the "Pierced Nose Indians" on the other side of the mountains had plenty of horses.

On May 14, 1804, the Lewis and Clark Expedition started up the Missouri River on their great journey to the Pacific Ocean— the first men of record to make such a journey. They carried with them a large amount of supplies and equipment, including two horses.

As soon as the expedition got past the white settlements, hunters were sent out, both to the right and the left of the river, for the purpose of securing meat, and to look the country over, for Captain Lewis was most anxious to make a thorough report of the area and its assets to President Jefferson, who, through luck, had instigated the proceedings in the land that, unknown to him at the time, had been purchased by two of his representatives in Europe. Quite a furor over the purchase was going on among members of Congress, and, too, among the general public, who in the main believed that the country purchased was a liability rather than an asset, and $15,000,000 in those days was a lot of money indeed. The president hoped that the reports made by Lewis and Clark would lessen the clamor and smooth out the criticisms being tossed about so freely.

Thomas Jefferson, known to his friends as Tom, though of English descent, spent many a pleasant hour at making it tough for the British. He even wrote the American Declaration of Independence and some other important literature; very annoying to the folks across the sea. After Tom became the Honorable Thomas Jefferson, President of the United States of America, the cares of office weighed most heavily upon him, and as there were no golf courses near or available at the time, he had to find his pleasures and relaxation through some other means.

President Jefferson, though somewhat playful in character, was also a man of serious intent and inclination. In order for most of his pleasures to be really enjoyable, they had also to have a utilitarian aspect. At this time he was lucky, and skillful, in arranging such a situation. He took on a job that could be of great benefit to his country, which filled his requirement of serious intent and at the same time could be most annoying to the British, a feature of that work that certainly gave him great pleasure. The affair he had then engineered and set in motion was one of the greatest contributions for the future good of the American people ever inaugurated by any American president.

He sent into the far northwest an expedition for exploration purposes, reasoning that exploration would give the United States prior rights to great areas of still unknown lands. The instructions given to the expedition's commander were for him to keep to the north as far as was practical, exploring as much country to the right and left as was possible, but proceeding to the Pacific Ocean; to establish friendly relations with all the Indians contacted, and impress upon them the fact that the United States was their best friend, and that the Great Father in Washington would continually have their best interests in mind, and to establish whatever facts could be ascertained in all pertinent matters and make reports as feasible.

It was believed by President Jefferson and his confidant, Captain Lewis, that the greatest beaver waters on the continent were in the watersheds of the Missouri and the Columbia Rivers. Fortunately, the styles in Europe still demanded many beaver pelts, and from the constancy of those styles, it seemed that beaver trapping would be a profitable industry for a long time to come. The President too was sure that Canadian waters had been badly over-trapped for years and that the British firms working Canadian waters would be looking elsewhere for new sources for beaver pelts, and for that reason would be crowding more toward the south. In fact, many Canadian trappers were already working along the northern branches of the Missouri and Mr. Jefferson hoped to change that situation. They had not, as far as the president could learn, made any great efforts west of the Rockies and he hoped to beat them to that territory.

Then too, there was the question of the boundary line between the United States and Canada. No boundary line had been established from Lake Superior westward, and each nation wanted all the western land that it could get. That was a potent reason for the President to ask that exploration should cover as much area north as was consistent with good progress toward the west.

The journey was to be kept as much of a secret as possible in order that Great Britain should not become aware of either the expedition or its purpose, so that it would not institute some comparable effort. The expedition was quite a hush-hush affair. Since nothing is more enjoyable to a free people than a matter to be kept a secret, interest in the journey soon was nation-wide. The journey then became a matter of some urgency and President Jefferson wished it to progress with all possible dispatch.

At the time, apparently, the British information service was far short of the efficiency displayed in recent years by that of the Russian Communists, for the affair of the expedition aroused no interest in official circles in London. But now we had better proceed up the Missouri with Captains Lewis and Clark.

After two weeks on the way one stray horse was seen. The men could not catch it, but from the description given, it was but some stray from the settlements. Some 150 miles farther up river they began to see Sioux Indians, sitting high up on the north bank. It developed that these Sioux were an agricultural people, but did not use horses at all in their work. Their farming techniques were very crude, but the soil was excellent and they grew some very fine crops. No horses were seen. For a long way before coming to the Sioux the river had been very crooked and the hunters had been able to range over large areas on both sides of it. Captain Clark, preferring to roam the country rather than ride the slow-moving boats, explored some distant areas that, so they had been informed in St. Louis, would be well worth investigating.

After passing by the Sioux—who were willing to trade whatever they had for whatever trinkets offered—they traversed a long stretch of rough country. Just before they entered that area they saw two horses in possession of Indians.

Having passed through the rough lands they next came to the Arikara Indians. These were a sub-tribe of the Pawnees, whose home areas were considerably to the south, living mostly along the Platte River and its tributaries. The Pawnees were said to have some horses. The Arikaras were now an unimportant people, their numbers having been decimated by smallpox and measles, with those epidemics being followed by depredations by the Minnetaree tribes, so that now the Arikaras and the Mandans had combined their warrior forces the better to withstand mutual enemies. The Arikaras were without horses, and lived in old abandoned Mandan villages, the Mandans having changed their home locations because of attacks by the Sioux, who were a comparatively new people west of the Mississippi.

Captain Lewis made a side journey to the Pawnees. Found that they were growers of corn. Heard about the Kite Indians. There were supposed to be one hundred of them, all with horses. They were supposed to be the fiercest warriors on the plains, but the captain saw neither horses nor horse signs or tracks.

Mr. Durion, who had traded up and down that entire country, said that to the north, where the French and English traded with the Indians for furs, there were very few, if any, horses up in that country; he said horses were not needed, as all traffic was by water and via streams that required very few portages.

After getting above the Arikara lands, the party came to the Mandan Indians. When they first saw those Indians, they too were perched up high on the north bank. Also, they were an agricultural people. One long island was entirely planted to garden sass. Trading was brisk for a few hours. The cooks dished up chow that night that made some of the men feel like boys on the farm once more. Corn and beans and watermelons were among the products traded for. The party had lost one of their two horses and tried here to replace the lost animal, but were unsuccessful.

On up stream, the voyagers approached some large Mandan villages on October 25, and many Indians swarmed down over the bank to see them. Some rode up on horses. These were the first horses in any number at all that the party had seen. Its records show that they were more than 1,500 miles up stream from where they had started. Yet actually, until then, the men had seen only two or three horses other than their own, although they had heard that there were some around. However, since exploring parties had seen neither horses nor horse signs, there seemed to be a slight note of skepticism regarding horses in the area in the way the notes were worded.

After these upper river Mandans had become acquainted with the captain, they revealed the reasons for their old, empty villages lower along the river. They said that smallpox, followed by raids from the Sioux and the Minnetarees, had caused them to abandon those villages some years before, but that now the Sioux were friends and it was hoped that they would be safe and content here where they now were. Visiting here and there the captains found that these Indian villages existed mostly by gardening, and they saw very few horses.

Captain Lewis was most anxious to get messages off to the president, so it was decided to stay here for some time while exhibits were being packed and then to send both the messages and the exhibits down river by their friend and interpreter, the trader, Mr. Durion, who wished to return down river from this place. A few days later the weather turned cold and snow began to fall. The men got a boat down stream with the messages and packed exhibits and then decided it would be best to spend the winter right there. The Mandans seemed to have plenty of corn and other food and were anxious to trade it at a very satisfactory rate of exchange. Staying here for the winter pleased some of the men very much. They had become enamoured with some of the village maidens and were finding them most pleasant and obliging.

A fort and winter quarters were constructed some distance away and across the river. No explanation is given for situating their living quarters so far from their prospective food supply, but the reason could have been the captains' displeasure with some of their men who had taken to spending too much time away from their duties enjoying the attentions of the Indian maidens.

The weather turned very cold and that slowed down the erection of their winter quarters, but they moved into the unfinished quarters just before Christmas, upon which day a good time was had by all. It was a good thing that they moved in, for after Christmas the weather really did get cold. Sometimes the thermometer got down to more than 40 degrees below zero. Captain Lewis apparently was afraid to put down figures much lower than that with much regularity. It seems he was afraid that his figures would be doubted.

The interpreter they had brought up stream with them now being gone, they found in the nearest Mandan village a certain Frenchman, Charboneau by name, who had been in these Indian lands for thirteen years and was said to be fluent in several Indian languages. He was taken before Captain Clark for an audition.

Captain William Clark, as an officer in the United States Army, had been in and around New Orleans for three years on special service for his superiors. His duties had been of a nature that required his wearing civilian attire, he had mingled with the elite of that metropolitan city, and had acquired a certain fluency in the French language. His services there were not needed after the Louisiana territory had been purchased by the U.S.A., but as he had been away from that city less than two years, he believed that his French would still be good enough for him to be able to converse intelligently with this Frenchman, Charboneau.

When Charboneau started spouting French at the captain, that worthy was really startled. That Frenchman talked French so fast that he would be through with a sentence and have begun on another string or two of words before the bewildered captain could get the first few words sorted out. It was a most embarrassing situation for that captain. He really never was sure whether Charboneau had been among the Indians too long, or whether he—the captain—had been long enough in New Orleans. The two were several days getting together on a formula of speech, and the members of the expedition used to enjoy watching them talk, and watching is the right word, for it developed that speech between the two was more a pattern of sign language than an exchange of French phrases.

The two never did agree upon a set of French words, but they did develop a lot of gestures, grimaces, growls, and gutturals, which after some months were more expressive than any French words that they might have conspired, between them, to consider as the French language. Actually, Captain Clark's difficulties with Charboneau's French stemmed from the fact that the interpreter's French was a mixture of frontier colloquial French, heavily interspersed and thoroughly spiced with Indian noises from several different northland tribes, that consisted about as much of sign talk as it did of spoken phrases, but as they managed to get along with each other, it was much better this way. Many was the time later when the men, after a most frustrating day, tired, hungry, and discouraged, without any favorable prospects before them and unable to turn back, would try to get the captain and Charboneau to talking. Pretty nearly every man could forget to worry about tomorrow in an endeavor to disentangle the gushing words and the flitting hands, almost expiring in their efforts to keep their mirth hidden. Life could not be too bad when there were such really amusing diversions.

History tells us that Charboneau was about the most worthless man that ever hired out to do a job of work, but Captain Lewis would not have agreed with that idea. When going on looked so tough—was so tough—that the prospect for the day ahead almost got him down, he would get those two men talking at each other. Then he would be in difficulty, for he had to hide his mirth. Once he released his mirth behind a chokecherry bush. He almost choked himself to death trying to smother the sounds of his laughter; so much so that thereafter, when designating that kind of berry bush or scrub tree, he would use the words chokecherry, and it is believed by some that that is how the chokecherry got its name.

The expedition's records show that the worthless Charboneau was discharged along in the winter, but the word discharged is far too aristocratic for that occasion. He simply was canned. Sgt. Cass's notes betray the fact that some men asked permission to crack a hole in the river ice and then be allowed to dump the interpreter in it, and it was noted that Captain Clark volunteered to help, but Captain Lewis doused the fires of belligerency by opening a fair-sized cask of fire water. Captain Lewis could not think of losing the diversion of seeing those two clowns, Clark and Charboneau, talking at each other, and hoped that later something would come up to put the interpreter back with the expedition; and he was right, for something did.

The circumstances that led to his re-employment were so unusual and led to so much of later interest to the expedition's men that these circumstances should be narrated here.

Some five years before, a band of Shoshoni Indians had been attacked in their home grounds in the Rocky Mountains by a strong Minnetaree war party; many Shoshoni warriors had been killed, and many of the women and children captured and taken into slavery.

Among the children captured had been a maturing girl, Sacajawea by name. She had been the chief's daughter. Sacajawea had been sold and resold several times, each time becoming the slave of another Indian squaw. Some nice things have been said about Indian squaws, in general, about the work they do, the drudgery they must and do endure; how they do not spank their children and such like stuff; but Sacajawea was unfortunate, regardless of what complimentary things may be said of squaws in general. The squaws for whom Sacajawea was forced to labor were tireless in keeping her in endless drudgery, and were sadistic in punishments at the least of imaginary excuses. About a year before the time we are considering Charboneau had purchased her and made her his wife.

Then, shortly after Charboneau had been discharged by Captain Clark, it was learned that Sacajawea's people, the Shoshoni, had some horses and that they lived in an area approaching the Rocky Mountains that would be crossed by the expedition on its way to the Pacific Coast. Sacajawea being a princess of those people, it would be a fine thing were she to accompany the expedition into her homelands. She would, naturally, be the best of interpreters there, and too, her people would be more inclined to be friendly and thus sell the expedition the horses that would be needed to cross the towering Rocky Mountains.

It then became a matter of diplomacy to rehire Charboneau, the French interpreter, husband of Sacajawea, the Shoshoni princess. The situation was somewhat more complicated than it might have been normally by the fact that Sacajawea was then in a rather advanced delicate condition, and the captains were afraid that inept overtures might be very distasteful to the lady, and too, they did not wish Charboneau to get the idea that he was a man of importance, for he had previously shown that he was averse to even the slightest discipline. That situation was resolved by Charboneau going on a hunting expedition with some of the Indians of his village. Meat had become very scarce; buffalos were known to have crossed the Missouri on the ice and were now spending the winter among the cottonwoods and willows up river somewhere near. Charboneau was a member of the Mandan party that went out after some of those buffalos. His lodge was very short of food of any kind and it was necessary to have meat. When the captains discovered that situation, they determined to use their most diplomatic approaches to Sacajawea during Charboneau's absence, with the plan in mind of selling her the idea that the employment of her husband would be a good idea. They wished to have the princess in the most favorable frame of mind toward them in particular, and all white men in general, for it had been intimated to them that it could just be possible that the Indian princess might at this time have a somewhat dim view of white men in general because of some very definite failures of her French husband.

With the help of young Durion, the son of their first interpreter, they held a consultation with the chiefs of Sacajawea's home village and arranged for a succession of affairs during which the princess would be gradually raised in distinction to a position she was entitled to by reason of being the daughter of an important chief. Had not the princess become so gradually enveloped with the attentions of her friends of her home village she might have become alarmed or indisposed at such a rush of attentions, but, as it developed, she accepted all the politeness and civilities extended her as a matter of sincere friendship, which, basically, was indeed the fact, for Sacajawea was beloved by all who had come to know her well. The men did not dare to apply the soothing ointments of popular attention with too great pressure at first, but by now Sacajawea was really enjoying herself for the first time in her life, and she, good lady, was perfectly willing for good fortune to smile as it willed.

By the time Charboneau had returned Sacajawea had indeed formed a very good opinion of the white travelers, especially of Captain Clark, and that situation, in regard to the captain, was most natural. For the captain was such a man that hardly a woman of this world, regardless of race, creed, or position in life, but would most naturally be interested in him. He was tall, something over six feet, and of ideal proportions. His looks, his every move and action, suggested a man of strength and virility. He was by nature among the kindest and most considerate of men. There was no sham about that. He was so by nature, and just now, while we are on a subject not directly pertaining to horses, one might wonder how the captain had escaped the penalties of matrimony for so long a time. Do not misunderstand, please. Although the friendship between him and the Indian Princess Sacajawea grew even stronger as the expedition progressed, it can be truly said that here, for once, in that wild land, a friendship between a woman and a man was truly platonic.

With the return of Charboneau from the buffalo-hunting trip, diplomatic measures went into really high gear, in order to influence him to ask for re-employment as the expedition's interpreter. Before that situation progressed to such a point that the Frenchman's unstable nature would result in an expanded head structure, the princess became ill from morbid conditions associated with her pregnancy. Her Indian friends understood the nature of her ailment, but were unable to suggest any remedy.

The incantations and contortions of sundry Indian medicine men having failed to give the sick woman relief, she had an inspiration and asked her husband to go to the white captains for help. Distasteful as such an errand was to Charboneau, he could understand this one time of emergency and—after all, Sacajawea was his favorite wife—he did hurry to the white men's fort and appeal to the captains for help for his wife.

Now, neither of the captains would have dreamed of laying any claims whatever to being a physician, not by any stretch of their imaginations. They would not even have dreamed of offering, or even accepting, a position even of advisers to a patient in the princess' situation, and were searching their minds for some means to evade the consequences of a refusal, when a runner came from the village with a message for Charboneau that his wife had become worse and was in extremely difficult circumstances.

Of course the erratic and unstable Frenchman now became almost frantic in his pleadings, and Captain Clark, who commonly became brilliant in thought when emergencies pressed him hard, discovered a new approach to the predicament of rehiring Charboneau.

Neither of the captains was a family man, and they were not at all familiar with matters pertaining to such a situation as they now were confronted with, but Clark's mind sparkled to new heights. They had among their literature a volume relating to family ills and suggested home remedies therefor. Clark seized the volume and riffled through its pages until coming to a chapter that was headed "Pregnancy" and "Childbirth." A hurried perusal apprised him that ofttimes in advanced stages of pregnancy an expecting mother's blood might become morbid, even to the extent of causing difficulties, and possibly death. The book suggested hot baths to produce a sweat, and then various medicines, running the full string, from crushed rattlesnake tail buttons down to the use of occasional drops of snakeroot tea every few hours in full glasses of water.

As the two captains looked over those last lines together, Lewis noticed the name of an herb that he knew well, and of which he had a good supply in dry form. He no sooner mentioned that fact than Captain Clark urged him to bring some of that along as quickly as possible, and while tea was being brewed out of that, he broke out of the fort and, at a high gallop, was on the way to getting the princess immersed in the hot baths the prescriptions had advised. The hot baths gave some immediate relief, the dosage of herbs completed the remedy, and the princess was forever grateful. Two days later the interpreter came to the fort and humbly asked Captain Clark for reinstatement in his former position. Then, with the captain being in a preferred position, he had an opportunity to impress upon the applicant that, while he might be convenient to have around upon occasion, his temperament was not at all suited for the job at hand, but that he (the captain) would think it over. At which Charboneau broke down, confessed to his regret at his former behavior, and promised to be a good and faithful servant forever after. So, after letting the man worry for a day, the captain sent word that he was rehired. Another situation that had developed satisfactorily for the progress of the expedition party.

While the above situations had been progressing the weather had steadily grown colder. The weather really got so cold that some of the expedition's members thought that they were freezing to death, although they were in a snug room rolled up in a multiplicity of buffalo robes. During one of those extremely cold days—48 below the thermometer registered—a band of mounted Sioux hunters came into the nearest Mandan villages situated on the river bank, looking for a place to warm up and for a hot meal for a change. Their horses were left standing, unattended and unprotected, out in the cold, without even a handful of cottonwood bark to give them comfort.

While those horses were forming a tight huddle in an effort to secure some warmth from each other's bodies, their tails clamped down tight and their backs humped and shivering, Captains Lewis and Clark came by as they were going to the Mandan chief's home for a visit. The suffering Sioux horses came to the attention of the captains as they passed them, causing the two men some worry, for they themselves did not neglect their animals in any fashion. They were making the visit to the Mandan chief to confer with him on the horse situation as it might be farther west. They had seen so few horses so far on their journey that they were slightly worried as to the horse situation farther west. It was at this visit that the Mandan chief told them of the many horses that the Nez Percé had on the other side of the great mountains, and that they should have little difficulty securing enough horses from the Shoshoni Indians on this side of the mountains to take them over to the other side, where all the rivers ran towards the Stinking Waters (the ocean). He explained that both the Mandans and the Sioux had gotten their first horses from the Crows, but believed that the Crows lived too far north for the party to cross their lands. However, the chief continued, the Crows were such very good friends of his that he would send a token to the great Crow chief so that the chief might know that the white travelers were friends of the Mandans. Then they would have no trouble in getting what horses they needed from the Crows.

14

SACAJAWEA PROVES HER WORTH

The Mandan chief was a garrulous old fellow and most of the afternoon was spent visiting with him. With the visit drawing to an end, the chief filled a ceremonial pipe with tobacco and kinnikinnick, and when it was drawing properly, it was passed around to all, and everyone had a few puffs. Those that used the pipe included York, the Negro servant of Captain Clark, who had accompanied the captains, for they needed him to carry presents to the chief and some supplies and medicines to the Princess Sacajawea.

History has been remiss, or at least negligent, in not giving York, Captain Clark's Negro servant his fair share of recognition in the accomplishments of the Lewis and Clark Expedition. In spite of the fact that he was not carried on the rolls as an enlisted man of the exploration force, he contributed his daily share to the success of the exploration, as well as taking care of the personal needs of Captain Clark.

(My father heard this version of some aspects of the circumstances that led to the master and servant relationship connecting Captain Clark and the Negro York. He heard the story in New Orleans in 1868 while he was working there as a stevedore along the docks pending the arrival of official papers before sailing into lower Mexico to engage in missionary and medical work among the natives there.)

Stationed in New Orleans, upon a special mission, and as a purported private citizen, in 1801, William Clark, at approximately sundown, one day, along a narrow street leading down into the dock area, found that to be a most shabby part of the city. Mr. Clark was to meet an informant who would supply him with papers and information of a secret nature. Unable to contact his party then, he had turned away into Creole Alley (since then renovated and renamed), keeping watch for his party, but without success. Turning a corner, he came sharply upon a vile-looking group that was stringing a darky up by using a rope that they had tossed over some timbers that at one time had supported the ceiling for some original room. The hanging apparently was being carried out under adverse circumstances and in a great hurry, for the Negro was being towed upwards without his hands, or his feet, having been tied, which was evident by the fact that his loose hands were grasping the rope above his head in a desperate attempt to prevent his strangling by the pressure of the rope around his neck, while his legs and feet swung in a macabre sort of dance, just as though they were attempting to climb a rope that was not there.

It was Mr. Clark's nature to think before he acted, but in this situation there was no time to think. If he was going to be of service, he had to act at once. Without a second's hesitation he drew a well-made, fancily decorated, double-barreled derringer from its holster, that was attached to the belt above his left hip, and fired at the tight rope that was doing its best to strangle the darky. The rope parted with a jerk, the break being ragged, and the darky fell with a considerable thud but with less of a bang than would have been the case had he not come down on two or three of his hopeful executioners. Clark rushed up to deliver the other barrel, but as he came up, the last of the would-be executioners was disappearing into an alley of tall weeds just adjacent.

Getting the colored man untangled from the rope, back on his feet, and then completely restoring him with brandy from a small hip flask he carried, Mr. Clark urged the man ahead of him up a street that led to a better section of the city. Having by then arrived at a well-lit corner in a better section of the city, Mr. Clark was turning away, but the colored man, noting this, came closer and made a plea that the man who had saved his life employ him as a servant; to which plea Mr. Clark replied that such a procedure would be against the law, as no man was permitted to hire a fugitive slave without the consent of the owner. The colored man replied that he had been on his own in this city for as long as he could remember, and was not beholden to any man. If his parents had been slaves, he had no true knowledge of the fact. He stated further that his friends and acquaintances knew him to be a free man and that he had worked about the docks off and on for some years now and to the full satisfaction of his employers. His words were not at all correct, nor his grammar very precise, but in his darky lingo he put his ideas across with Mr. Clark so well that the gentleman had not the least difficulty in understanding. Mr. Clark was a Virginian and familiar with darky jabber. Later that evening, in more convenient circumstances, the deal was made. York (Mr. Clark's name for his servant) got along very well, and no record has ever been discovered that either party ever was dissatisfied with the arrangement. Ever since that night, York was a most faithful and efficient servant, and on the way up the Missouri River did his share of work with any man, in addition to taking care of Captain Clark's own personal needs.

As the conference over the question of horses toward the west between Captains Lewis and Clark and the Mandan chief drew to a close, Clark nodded to York, who had carried gifts for the chief. In response to the nod, York began to unwrap the gifts, but quite suddenly all action was halted by uproar and bickering that could be heard, and was apparently issuing, from the dwelling next in line toward the north.

The uproar was so great that the two captains failed to hide their surprise at the furor. The chief, in turn, could not hide his annoyance at the unseemly disturbance within his village. After they all listened in astonishment to the tumult for some moments, the volume of noise subsided, but continued yips and yaps of drunken Indians came with considerable regularity. Altogether the racket carried the suggestion of a drunken brawl, and that was displeasing not only to the captains, but was also most annoying to the chief, who offered an apology through the interpreter, young Durion.

After the Mandan chieftain had his gifts in hand, had admired them, and given his thanks, the captains said good-day and withdrew. As they came outside, followed closely by York, they paused to consider the shivering, humpbacked, nearly frozen horses, as they fastened their own collars against the outside cold. They were growling their disgust at the owners of horses who would treat their mounts in such poor fashion, when a series of yells and war whoops sounded close to them on their right. Turning to check on the commotion they saw a wild-eyed, mostly naked, savage, with his right hand raised high in the act of throwing his tomahawk right at Captain Clark. Before Captain Clark could move a muscle in defense, York drew a throwing knife from some recess in his clothing and cast it, whirling at high speed, with such skill and artistry that its point slipped into that warrior so smoothly that there was not even a hiss of sound to give notice that a knife had found its mark. The warrior's war cry stopped short with not even a quaver following the crescendo of sound, and he fell to the snow as though he had been pole axed.

Fortunately for the captains, and for York too, those inside the dwelling that had erupted the yelling Indian were still interested chiefly in consuming the rest of the firewater therein, so that they did not know at once of the occurrence outside, or it might have gone ill for the three. With complete presence of mind, Captain Clark quickly stepped back inside the Mandan chieftain's domicile and through Durion explained what had happened. In a moment Durion was outside calling to the Mandan warriors to come, and come quickly, prepared for battle.

A block of Mandan warriors was set up across the doorway of the dwelling that housed the still celebrating Sioux, and then, as the victim was examined and the circumstances were explained by Durion, both the Mandan warriors and the many women who had gathered sized up York in awed wonder. They were amazed at the dexterity he had shown in making such an amazing throw, and at the neatness with which the heavy knife had entered that drunken warrior's heart.

The two captains were somewhat mortified, but neither one could really blame the colored servant, for it had been all too evident that the drunken Sioux had been about to throw that tomahawk, and he had been too close to miss.

Arrangements were made with the Mandan chieftain to give the remaining Sioux gifts and whatever other amelioration was needed, and the white men promised to settle the score.

The weeks passed by, and then, as happens in those far-north Dakotas, as happens also in more salubrious climes, winter began to slip away, both under foot and in the air. The expedition members began prying their boats free of the ice, repairs were begun, and, as the days slipped by, the task became ever more urgent.

A boat was prepared for the return trip down stream. It was to carry exhibits to the President as well as the reports of Captain Lewis. Then, overhead, up high against a clear blue sky, a great V of geese went skimming by towards the far north, not noisy and talkative now as they had been the past autumn as they took their way leisurely toward the southlands. Then they were going south to sport away the winter. A fashion and custom they had since a time before the coming of man upon the earth. And man, who is supposed to be all-wise, has finally just become wise enough, of late years, to attempt to follow their feathered wings upon the sturdy wings of jets.

Going north that spring though, with their winter pleasures behind them, there were no lingering gossip sessions. An urgency drove them steadily northward, and the oldest, oft-mated, goose, as well as the youngest of the virgins, chattered with impatience if the lead gander as much as slowed down to look far below at some favored watering place. And then, early of an April morning, robins were flitting about among the cottonwoods and willows, perking their heads for the early morning worms, and it was time to go. The long boat, heading down stream under the command of the French engage, young Durion, was pushed from shore, while

the Indians lining the bank waved good-bye and the whites waved
and shrilled and whistled a happy good wish and good-bye. And
Captain Clark looked over his small number of boats with an ap-
praising eye and gave the order to cast off. It was April 7, 1805,
and it would be many a day before the people back home, or the
world at large, would again hear from the expedition of Captains
Lewis and Clark.

The boats that were carrying the party heading west shoved off,
all ready to hoist the sails and with the oars giving a spurt to their
take-off. The Lewis and Clark Expedition was then on its way again,
heading for the Pacific. An ocean that had been beckoning to
Europeans for almost a thousand years before them. The number
of persons aboard was thirty-two, and that includes the Princess
Sacajawea and her baby, Pompey.

This article is supposed to be about western North American
horses and the only excuse we can give for dragging this expedition into the narrative is that we are in the process of proving that
the horse ridden by the northern plains Indians came from northwest America, not in predominant numbers from Mexico far to the
south. We are claiming that the Lewis and Clark party saw almost
no horses on their journey west until they came to the higher foothills of the Rocky Mountains, and, to demonstrate how great an
interest they had been building up in horse numbers, we are going
to show their great need for horses, which should vouch for the
fact that if horses in any numbers had been seen as they proceeded
toward those mountains, their appearance would most certainly
have been noted in their records. Captain Lewis was the officer
who was to make and keep the reports for the President, and he
was a most meticulous recorder of everything noticed, from the
sex of pestering mosquitoes to the mention of geysers and of
towering, snow-covered mountains.

It is true, and I can understand the reason too, that a narrative, slightly historical in nature, should cling quite closely to as
bare a statement of facts as circumstances will allow, but what can
one do when one's pen comes up against a personage such as

Sacajawea, Princess of the Shoshoni, and guarantee that the expedition shall achieve its purpose. There is nothing that a writer can do in such circumstances, except be careful of his words, but allow the pen whatever leeway it needs to do her womanhood justice.

No tale of the Lewis and Clark Expedition, no matter how condensed or abbreviated it may be, should be written without due consideration being given to Sacajawea, Princess of the Shoshoni Indians and the good angel of Lewis and Clark.

During the preparations for going up stream, Captain Lewis had been busy compiling notes for the President and superintending the packing of the exhibits, while Clark had been very occupied with getting the boats and supplies ready for the journey. He had been too busy to even change his socks much less pay attention to his moccasins. The boats had not been on the way up river an hour before Sacajawea was starting on a new pair of footgear for the captain. He tried to get her to use a needle and thread, but the lady preferred to use her primitive bone awl and deer sinews. Before she had finished the moccasins, another man had torn a great rip in his deerskin pants leg and Sacajawea got busy patching that. After that, sewing up the rips in clothes and repairing and making moccasins kept her busy. So busy that many a time Captain Clark was tending her baby for her. She was forever as busy as a beaver. The party could not have gotten along without her.

Along that part of the Missouri there are more horseshoe bends in the river's course than there are bends in the shoes of a team of horses, but the explorers did all right. The river was high with the spring run-off of snow water, so the riffles were high and smoothed out because of the near flood of water. After about ten days they came into a long, flooded area. The water flooded all of the valley along there and was full of much debris, drowned buffalos and other defunct animals. There was no game along there, so the men had to subsist on the food carried in the boats.

Getting up the river above the flooded area, they came to an easy stretch of traveling; the finest they were to have on the river.

They saw signs of a large Indian encampment along the bank. The Indians had not been gone long. The party was glad to have missed them. The lady judged from discarded moccasins that those Indians had been Minnetarees, and they were a troublesome lot, apparently looking for trouble. No horse sign is mentioned; neither hoof-prints or other signs. Had there been any, someone would have made a record, for the reports are full of things of every description, some of the most trivial kind. Had horse signs been seen, someone would surely have noted the fact in the records. The river was roily and very murky. No luck fishing.

The river continued to be very crooked, but the current was very smooth and easy, and soon they began to see great herds of buffalos. There were so many dead ones along the river banks that some wondered how there could be so many left alive. The land spread out along there and the whole country swarmed with buffalos. It was a land, on both sides of the river, of low dips and swales fairly cluttered with cottonwoods and different kinds of willow. Buffalos and other animals, probably elk and deer, had been browsing on that growth all winter, apparently, for the fine top growths had mostly all been eaten away.

Here they began to see many wolves. The wolves waxed fat on the defunct buffalos. And then they saw their first huge white bear (grizzly). Apparently one look was enough for the guy that first saw that bear, for he hit the river, stepping high and fast with Mr. Bear right after him. Guns were handy, so that evening they tried out their first grizzly steaks. Not too bad either. The records say that they secured eight gallons of oil from that critter. Some bear.

The meat of a young grizzly is among the tenderest and most flavorsome meat in all the woodlands, but the meat of an old bear is something different, and that's for sure. It is not at all like old shoe leather, but it resists mastication much like (I imagine) foam rubber would. (I don't know about foam rubber, but I do know about old bear.) The longer one chews upon a bite of it, the larger the bite of meat becomes—and try and swallow it! Especially is that so if the meat is cooked before and around a campfire; the meat on stakes, not so close to the fire as to char it, yet close enough to give it sufficient heat to cook the meat soft and tender (you hope).

The meat in that case does grow sizzling hot, but the juices that should tenderize it drip away, leaving the meat a tough, spongy mass that resists a knife as completely as it does strong jaws and sharp teeth. The men found that out. They were extra hungry and had a try at the bear meat before it was away from the flames long enough to fail in burning their tongues and mouths inside, as well as their over-eager ups.

Sacajawea had been active in the butchering, saving the liver, the upper entrails, and other parts most favored by Indians. While the cooks were struggling with their own efforts at cooking up the bear meat, Sacajawea had been persuading her reluctant husband to bring up some of the heaviest limb wood and poles and had gotten quite a fire going in a cooking spot of her own. Then, with the edge of her fire dying down into beds of hot cinders, she charred thick slices of the meat in the hottest coals, then, cleaning away small areas right among the red hot cinders, she put down green-leaved willow twigs on the cleared spots and placed the charred slices on these twigs, adding one twig of young sage brush to each slice, covered them with wet young tule growth out of the slough and raked hot coals over the lot, in the meantime urging some who had become interested to look around and find some watercress or sorrel for seasoning. (The party was without either salt or pepper just then.) The salt had become wet and was still moist and caked. After about an hour, with the men becoming more ravenous by the minute, the coals, no longer red, were raked away, the slabs of meat uncovered, and they found that the old grizzly was pretty good eating. Some claimed it was better than buffalo hump; others, that it was superior to beaver tail. But actually the remarks were few. The men were just too busy eating to waste much time in conversation.

Commonly, in backwoods circumstances diners seldom waste much time in conversation. The day's labors have given them such an appetite and so great a capacity that their time is spent, almost exclusively, in the consumption of the food within reach, and no boarding-house reach was ever able to compete on equal terms with that of a backwoodsman.

Sacajawea had reserved the bear liver for a specific purpose. The French assistant interpreter, Toussaint by name, had been somewhat puny, even before leaving the Mandan villages. No one thought too much of that for the man managed to take care of such duties as were required of him, but he had become worse the farther up river the party managed to go. The last few days his skin had become yellowish in color. Even the whites of his eyes had turned yellow. The skin of his face looked nasty through his thin black beard. He had been in considerable discomfort, and in some pain for the last day or so. He was bothered with a tight flatulency and could not keep food down. Now, while other men were wolfing down the bear meat, he had crept away into some nearby shrubbery and was hiding out like some wretched, sick wild animal.

Sacajawea had been trying to give him some comfort, but Toussaint had been choleric all day and not amenable to cajolery. Now, with the men eating (she had asked the captains to wait until she cooked the liver), she asked the captains for just a small glass of the spirits they kept for medicinal purposes, then, crushing the bloom from some nearby skunk cabbage, yellow and tender and juicy because of its recent emergence from the swamp, she mixed some of the juice with a goodly portion of the spirits, and then persuaded the sick one to swallow that slowly, washing the vile taste out of his mouth with straight spirits as he did so. While that shot of fire water and skunk cabbage juice was taking hold, she proceeded with the cooking of the liver.

While she had been ministering to the sick man, she had gotten Charboneau to bring from the boats one of the large cast-iron hot-cake griddles and placed it upon a bed of red- hot coals.

That Charboneau had certainly not set a good example of what a fond husband should do to assist a busy wife. It was only after the most persistent urging on the part of Sacajawea that she had prevailed. She would have pleasured in getting the griddle herself but she was extremely busy in preparing the meal. Charboneau resisted manfully, and it is still somewhat a matter of doubt whether he might not have won out, but Captain Clark, wearying of the grumbling, and very hungry, suggested to Charboneau that if he would take care of the baby—it was ailing—he would himself go get the griddle. That suggestion horrified the father. No Indian buck, in camp or in the home wigwam, ever touched his baby. If it suffered, that was just too bad. If it wailed too loudly and too long, the buck merely moved outside, even though a blizzard were a-blowing. It was taboo—against their principles. Taking care of the baby was a woman's work, and no one has ever heard of an uncivilized Missouri Indian buck ever assuming a task reserved for his women. Charboneau, by this time of life, was more of an Indian—especially regarding work—than he was a white man. That Captain Clark was a determined and positive man. The husband stumbled without more argument over to the boat for the griddle, though he grumbled all the way over and back. Sacajawea didn't mind. She was busy and didn't even hear his grumbling.

Then, with the griddle sizzling-hot, Sacajawea doused it liberally with bear grease and placed sliced liver, closely spaced, all along the griddle. She had chopped up some of the skunk cabbage bloom and sprinkled it heavily over some pieces at one end that she was preparing especially for the sick man. With both the captains, and Charboneau, eating, she poured the balance of the spirits down the sick man and then, while that was getting in its soothing, healing action, she loaded a bark plate with generous portions of the specially prepared liver and carried it to the sick man, who, following that last drink, had emerged from the shrubbery and was now looking with some expectancy toward the lady cook.

A slight shudder shook him before the first bite, but as the meal progressed, either that last drink, or maybe a certain intake of bear grease, inherent in such cookery, lubricated his elbow joints, for his hands began feeding his face with considerable dispatch and regularity of movement. By the time he had finished his bark plate was empty.

The next morning the sick man was much better and Captain Lewis marveled, and in consequence made additional memos in his notebook. Sacajawea prepared one meal a day of that bear liver for two days, and by that time the now well man, being slightly fed up on bear liver, was allowed to subsist on other diet. In less than a week he felt so much better that he was able to spend a considerable part of each day at the oars. He thought of his cure as something of a miracle, and thereafter became another man to chant praises for the angel of the expedition.

Up the river a few days later there was discovered an Indian woman draped in her funeral finery robes, raised high on a platform, away from despoiling by wolves or other feral creatures. Beneath her couch was placed her winter sled, her personal possessions, and other treasured belongings. None of these included anything that could have indicated the possession of a saddle or a horse. A feature that later was so common in Indian burials.

Along the river now, in every glade or open area of land, the buffalo and elk and deer were so plentiful that only the choicest of the meat was used, the balance being left to feed the ever numerous wolves and other varmints. The captains, being thoughtful of the future, did pause in one pleasant place to jerk and dry a lot of meat in case of need at some future time, but that was thought by most to be a useless thoughtfulness.

And then, with the warming temperatures of advancing spring, gnats and mosquitoes came in swarms and clouds. After that, about the time that these seemed unbearable, the deerflies and the other stinging insects swarmed in to give assistance to other stinging pests. The men had but one resource against those pests. Sacajawea mixed hot bear grease with soft clay and smeared that liberally over any parts of her body not protected by her clothing. The mosquitoes, the gnats, even the deerflies, could not penetrate such a protective coating. Soon all the rest of the party were smearing their bodies with that misery-allaying compound, and that certainly was a life-saver, for with the weather warm, and because of the efforts at the oars and the tow ropes, the men had to shed much of their clothing.

During the warmth of the day, most of the men wore little more than wraparounds around their thighs, only as a concession to modesty because of the woman with them. That bear grease and mud coating were another benefit they had derived because the princess of the Shoshoni was with them.

From that time on that expedition's personnel consisted of about the dirtiest men that had ever forced their way up any river. And soon now a shortage of provisions began to plague them. Because of an unfortunate circumstance involving the boat that carried their supply of cured meat, they had lost all of that supply, and the deerflies and other pests had driven the deer and elk to higher areas, and, naturally, the bears had mostly disappeared with them. They were now out of the buffalo ranges, and the ducks and geese were hidden in areas suitable for nesting. Food rapidly became a problem. A few of the men, those that could be spared from the oars or tow ropes, hunted along both sides of the river. There were no beaver ponds, so no beaver, a favorite source of meat, and from that time on food became an ever-increasing and serious problem.

The hunters came in with little to satisfy the hungry men, and they forced their way up stream as best they could.

No Indians had been seen since a few days after they had left the Mandan villages, and though they found now, along the river banks, the trails left by traveling Indians, there is no record at all of horse tracks or any other horse sign. They were approaching a wilderness country. One day they did get a few ducks, one goose, and a few muskrats, but what they needed was something filling.

Hungry and gaunt they tied up one evening, just below a slide area of the river bank. The river some years before had cut a new channel and the old channel was a mere slough that was just a mass of decaying tules. Some new tule growth was already protruding above the water. While everyone rested for some moments after the anchors had been dropped, a lone old buffalo bull, decrepit, and with eyes so dim he had not seen them, began to swim across the river toward their side of the water. He paid no attention to them whatsoever. The current carried him down stream past them as the men scrambled for their guns, the while he landed on the bank below them. As he came close to the shore, Sgt. Cass looked to the priming of his rifle, and then, as the old bull began to stagger up the bank, knocked the old fellow over with one well-placed bullet. The bull didn't stay down though. Struggling erect, he scrambled around, finally made it to the top of the bank, and started away for the protection of some nearby brush, but some-one took a shot at him through the willows. This time he dropped straight down, just as though someone had pulled his feet right out from under him.

His hind quarters were useless, but by the time someone got to him he was up on his front legs and his eyes glared red as blood because of the rays of the westering sun. Someone finished the job, and then everyone thought of eating. Someone laid open the area above the hump meat and cut out a hunk. Somebody was working on the other side before that was done. Someone else rustled about and found some dead, dry willows, and a fire soon was burning. Dry willow sticks were brought and eager hands fastened chunks of meat upon them and these were set up so that the heat of the fire could work on them. Troubles were speedily being forgotten, as everyone wanted to get his meat roasting at the same time in the heat of the fire.

Here was meat, and jollity reigned supreme, but only for about one-half minute; then it tapered away quickly. Some mouths that had been drooling in anticipation now began to pucker in distaste. A terrible stench was coming out of the roasting area. They didn't know just yet what was wrong, but they knew something awful was surely happening. A slight breeze was blowing away from the man who first got his meat cooking. He was famished. He couldn't wait any longer. He waved his charred hunk of meat in the air a couple of times to cool it some, and then took a hungry man's bite. Dismay and disbelief spread across his face. All of a sudden that bite of meat spurted out of his mouth and he was running for water to wash out his mouth.

Captain Clark had one failing uncommon with mountain men; he had a queasy stomach and had walked away as the butchering started, but York, the captain's large darky servant, was one of the first to get his meat cooking. At last, he too could wait no longer.

Dancing about in glee as he waved his meat to cool, he hurriedly took a good big bite. York had jaws as powerful as a gorilla and he bit through that meat as neatly as though he had been using a cleaver, then, eyes closed tight in anticipation, he began to chew his meat. That was a mistake. Had he swallowed that bit whole, he might have gotten by with it, but as he tried to chew that meat, every chew made that mouthful swell up and grow larger; then too, he got a taste of what he had been chewing.

Now, York was not noted for any fastidiousness. At a table he could clean up what other diners had discarded, but now he tried to get rid of that piece of meat in such a hurry he got all mixed up in his reflexes. Instead of the meat trying to come out, it started to go down, and poor York almost strangled before he got that meat out of his mouth. If the taste hadn't been forcing him to gag so badly, that piece of meat might actually have strangled him. York sure was one sick man.

He wasn't alone though. Nearly everyone around was feeling pretty sick too. They had been expecting a fine meal and now this! It was just too much. Some of the men, for the first time on this journey, wished that they had never left home.

Anyone with more experience in the buffalo country could have told them just what they should have expected. Buffalo bulls, from the month of May and on into the month of October, are unfit to eat. Even wolves will pass bulls up at that time of the year, and although this bull was so old he was most likely impotent, age apparently had not changed that condition. That, added to his age, simply put that bull's meat beyond consumption, but Sacajawea was already working out a solution for that sorry problem.

By then some of the men, holding their nostrils closed because of the stench, rushed, with bursts of speed, to grab their meat sticks away from the fire, and cast them into the river, glad to be, once and for all, rid of such foulness.

15

SACAJAWEA: COOK EXTRAORDINARY

Sacajawea had been doing the drudgery for squaws for five years before she became the preferred wife of Charboneau's lodge. In the days before horses were common, and there was no meat in the lodge, Sioux squaws liked to keep close to their hunter husbands. That's the surest way for them to get something to eat, and anyway, there was that slave girl to carry their packs around, so a-hunting they would go.

Once, on the prairie, her squaw's lord and master had killed an old bull, just about like this one here, over in some cottonwoods near a water hole close to the Cheyenne River. A preliminary feast of liver and muntins had been attempted, for everyone was hungry, but of a sudden they gave that up in a hurry. The beast had smelled bad enough, the girl had thought, to discourage a polecat. That old bull was simply impossible even for their ravenous Indian appetites. But the boss squaw wasn't stumped for more than a few minutes. There would have been no hesitation at all, but she had been forced to recover her breath.

Ordering her slave girl to gather the wood for a large fire, she had contrived to cook that old bull so well that it wasn't bad eating at all. Sacajawea had done practically all of the work, so she knew very well how to go about such an effort now.

She now spoke rapidly and at some length to Charboneau, and he in turn spoke rapidly in French to Captain Clark. (Some hand signs were very revealing.) Everything moved fast after that. Someone helped Charboneau line up some rocks (Sacajawea supervising) in three rows, the rows eight inches apart and six feet long. While that operation proceeded, two men were sent over to the largest boat and they brought back with them the two iron grates used by the expedition in cooking over camp fires. Two men went over to the south slope of the nearby hill and started plucking dwarf sage, called pisco by the Sioux. Another went over to a supply boat and brought back one of the two corn-husk mattresses used by the captains; another brought over a jar of salt (or so they hoped, for they had collected it just the day before from a white incrustation along the river's edge, and although it tasted much like Epsom salts, Sacajawea hoped that it would do). There was some hot pepper that Captain Clark had brought north with him from New Orleans, but was so terrifically hot that it had never been used.

When the rocks had been put down to suit Sacajawea, she had the iron grates placed properly, then, on each of the three rows of rocks, she placed a row of meat chunks that the most hardy of the men had got ready. She sprinkled all of them heavily with both salt and the hot pepper, then covered them thickly with the fragrant sage, seeing to it that it was properly put on, so that all the meat would be covered, then covered all three rows of rocks with a thick covering of corn husks. She repeated layer after layer until all the meat was in position for cooking.

While she was placing the meat, others had brought up long, dead, dry willow withes. Sacajawea was happy now. She could easily see that everyone was watching her with interest and anxiety, and for once she was ordering Charboneau about, instead of him shouting instructions at her. She was chattering happily, telling him what she wanted done.

Those dry willows burned with a hot, small flame, not charring the meat too much, but sending up a lot of heat. Some men had been pulling tule growth out of the water. It was a pretty, light green, but slippery as the dickens, and every rush was heavy with its content of water. The pool was near, and although the tules slipped around some, they all managed to get some up to Sacajawea. Those tules were pliable and porous, and wherever the stems were crushed they oozed a little water. She used those rushes to cover the three rows of meat, the soft tip-ends reaching over and down the outside rows. With everything now in readiness, the long thin willow withes were slipped into the spaces between the rows of rocks, and plenty were placed along the sides, then the fires were started, and pretty soon steam was coming up through the tules and moisture was then dripping back down upon the cooking meat.

For some little time there was nothing appealing in the smell from that cooking meat, an opposite term could well be used without a person being at all critical, but after a time the cooking odor gave off a more pleasing aroma.

York, having recovered from his previous experience, now was ready to make another try at that meat—he sure was hungry—but Sacajawea shooed him away. She wasn't going to allow anyone to spoil her cooking. She shooed him away just as does a bantam hen a rooster she doesn't want around, and York, a full three times the size of the lady cook, accepted her action with a pretty fair-sized grin.

By bedtime everyone, including the two captains, was hanging around that cooking fire. Gee, but that cooking smelled good. But Sacajawea got rid of them all. She sent them for more willow wood, for she had to cook that meat most of the night. At her request, the sergeant of the guard, late that night, stood guard over the cooking fires so that no one could rifle the grills before Sacajawea was satisfied with the cooking.

The next morning everyone ate, and ate, and ate. They even gnawed upon the gristle about the bones. York even gnawed on the bones; he said the flavor went right through them. And nobody became ill either, although it did seem later as though a good part of that salty flavoring had possibly contained some Epsom salts all right. Sacajawea had cooked that old bull into a perfect meal.

It is necessary that we leave Sacajawea now, for a time at least. Even at this early time of the expedition's progress we can understand why that Shoshoni princess had been called the angel of the Lewis and Clark Expedition.

16

SACAJAWEA COMES HOME

We will now have to skip many a mile and several weeks in the journey of Lewis and Clark, and take up again when they at last find the Shoshoni Indians. These Shoshoni were frightened people at first, because of several bad raids against them by hands from other Indian tribes. After having overcome their fear, they became quite friendly, but the chief of the band found by Captain Lewis did not wish to sell any horses. They did not have many, he said, and also that they were about to start for their buffalo-hunting grounds. But when Sacajawea came up, the chief and the princess recognized each other, as did also some of the women. Sacajawea was the long-lost sister of the chief. The chief then was willing to let the white men have all the horses that his band could spare, but that number was woefully small. The expedition needed horses if they were going to get over the Rockies, so the chief promised to find other Shoshoni bands and get horses from them. Captain Clark went along, and between them they did get a few horses. Not even the minimum number needed, but they did get a few.

Upon being questioned, the Shoshoni chief said that they got their horses from the Spanish settlements, about five days' journey away. This statement has been accepted as a statement of fact, but let us check this claim in an effort to find what credence, if any, can be given the Shoshoni claim that they got their horses from the Spanish settlements, "five or six sleeps away." It is this Shoshoni claim of getting their horses from the Spanish settlements that could have added to the belief that the horses of the northern Indians came, predominantly, from Mexico.

Lewis and Clark were horsemen. They had known horses from their earliest boyhood. They were natives of Virginia and had spent most of their lives in that province. They not only were horsemen, but they had a very sharp eye when it came to sizing up a horse, as witness a certain statement in one of Captain Lewis's reports to the President, to wit: ". . . the Shoshoni have no need to trim or otherwise shorten their horses tails. . . ." That short part of a sentence is a dead giveaway as to where the Shoshoni got their horses. Had their horses been Mexican, or Spanish horses from Mexico, they would have been mustangs, or, as mustangs are commonly called, "broom tails," with their tails so long that they would have been coated with dirt and mud. The only horses in the west in those days that were not broom tails were the spotted horses and the Nez Percé horses produced by the Nez Percé Indians.

Later, when Lewis and Clark presented their old Shoshoni guide to some Nez Percé chiefs, the chiefs were not at all friendly to that Shoshoni. They displayed their distaste for that guide so plainly that Lewis and Clark asked the chiefs for the reason for such an unpleasant demeanor, and they were told that they did not like the Shoshoni Indians because they stole Nez Percé horses. In 1832 or '33, Nez Percé traveling with Captain Bonneville (recalling what has already appeared herein) told the captain that they did not like the Shoshoni, for they stole Nez Percé horses.

As I recall the situation, neither Captains Lewis or Clark comment to any extent as to the quality of the horses they procured from the Shoshoni Indians. Possibly they were too anxious to secure more to make any comment on quality; however, the tone of their later notes regarding the horses is far from enthusiastic. That would be only natural, for the lands occupied by the Shoshoni bands at the time the captains passed through the Shoshoni home areas were poor beyond belief in natural resources, so, naturally, the best of horses would after too long a time show the effects of considerably inferior circumstances.

The Shoshoni bands had retired to high, rugged, and rock-strewn lands among remote mountains because of fear of marauding Indians. At the time of the Lewis and Clark visit through their lands, the people, from the chiefs down through the warrior classes and including the women, were in a constantly jittery state because of their fears of more raids from more eastern Indians. That was the daily Shoshoni fear, the theme of much of their talks with Lewis and Clark, and as warrant for the justification of their fears we have the situation of Sacajawea, their long-lost princess, who was stolen from the tribe during an Indian raid some five or six years before.

Merely as an indication backing up the claims of the Nez Percé that the Shoshoni stole their horses from them, we would like to ask how people, who at that time were actually afraid of shadows, and without either many horses and with nothing with which to trade, could travel all the way to the Spanish settlements for horses. Such a feat is quite beyond understanding. The only reference that Captain Lewis entered in his note regarding the living circumstances of those Shoshoni is that they were very poor; too poor to have anything to trade for tobacco.

Another situation that would be most puzzling, did it not fit in with other adverse observations against the Shoshoni claims that they got their horses from the Spanish settlements far to the south, was their statement that the journey to those settlements was of five days' duration. That statement reveals a total lack of any knowledge whatsoever as to the distance to, or location of, such Spanish settlements. That distance was more than 1,200 miles of tortuous travel from where the Shoshonis then lived to the settlement of Santa Fe, the closest Spanish or Mexican trading center. A journey of five weeks, in their circumstances, might have been possible; a journey of five days, impossible. Our conclusion, following long and detailed investigation and consideration of the matter, leads us to the conviction that the Nez Percé were correct when they claimed that the Shoshoni Indians got their horses from the Nez Percé.

It is my contention that claims issuing from other sources have no more merit than the statements of the Shoshoni as regards the movements of large numbers of horses northward out of Mexico, and that therefore such claims are of little or no value in determining where the northern plains Indians actually got their horses.

It is now high time that we again proceed with Lewis and Clark's journey into a multitudinous horse land, but first we would like to say a few kind words for the Shoshoni.

Although Captains Lewis and Clark are very conservative in their statements regarding the merits of the Shoshoni, the lower echelons of the expedition speak highly of them. Speak of them as being kind, considerate, and very generous, considering their poor circumstances; and then there is Sacajawea.

Sacajawea was a family member of the very band of Shoshoni Indians that our Lewis and Clark party first met. All the records of that lady's experiences and behavior during the long trek to the Pacific Ocean and the return, statements as to her character and worth, portray her as being entitled to a high position among the immortals of this earth. Never once is there even a whisper that would suggest an impropriety. Never once is there anything but praise; much of it fulsome in the original journals. Without her, the expedition might well have foundered early in 1805, and could easily have disappeared without a trace—a situation that was commonly believed to have happened by the time 1806 brought a change in the calendars; her practical approach to confusing circumstance, her encouragement at times of such discouragement that even the two captains had thoughts of turning back, carried the expedition through to complete and glorious success.

The names of Lewis and Clark will stand bright forever in the annals of the west, and deservedly so. A grateful people could do worse than grant the Shoshoni princess, Sacajawea, honors scarcely less than those bestowed upon the two great captains. May she ever grace the Happy Hunting Grounds among the spirits of her people.

17

Captains Lewis and Clark Find the Nez Percé

Proceeding onwards, Captain Clark buried the goods he couldn't take with him because of a shortage of horses, loaded up what had to be taken, mounted his weakest men on horseback, and then the expedition started over the Rockies. The highest summits lay before them. Not even their guides could find them a reasonable route. Without food much of the time, often without water, and scarcely an hour's comfort, they pressed on as best they could. Weeks later, starved and weak as they were, another day might have finished them; their horses were fewer than ever—some had been stolen, several had been eaten, some had strayed, with no one strong enough to hunt for them. Then Captain Clark came upon a camp of Nez Percé Indians who had arrived at the Weippe prairies just the evening before to dig camas roots for their winter's supply.

Even the most sedate of peoples achieve their share of misfortune. When the Nez Percé had arrived at the camas grounds late in the afternoon before, they found that flooding waters in the spring had destroyed their food cache and they had been, and still were, out of food, although hunters had hurried out at daybreak in a search for game. They did, however, have many fat dogs. The Nez Percé made no practical use of their dogs, merely allowing them to play around and reproduce. Charboneau, in his association with various Indian peoples, had become very fond of dog meat. He was not at all a bashful man. Without waiting for instructions, his hands began talking to the village chief, suggesting that the visitors would be happy to have some of those dogs for food.

The chief was in a quandary for a few moments. Some of those dogs were children's pets. A fight between several curs broke out at his feet just then, and the chief, losing his dignity in the furor about his feet, motioned with his hands for Charboneau to help himself. With the exception of Captain Clark, all of the expedition's members dined to repletion upon dog meat. Even Sacajawea's baby, Pompey, had the pleasure of sucking on a knuckle bone. It was a most delightful repast—that is, except for Captain Clark. That worthy visited with the chief in an endeavor to avoid hearing the sound of smacking lips and other gustatory indications.

During that time of hunger and complete frustration for Captain Clark, an Indian lad, as bare as September Morn except for his G-string, came sauntering proudly into camp with one blue grouse and five pine squirrels hanging from the crotch of a willow twig. Of course the lad was practically overawed at seeing white men, and more especially so because of the wonderful appearance of the blonde giant, Clark. It was an easy matter for the captain to trade the lad out of the blue grouse and two of the squirrels, so the captain also dined that evening and had food as well for the morrow.

A couple of days rest and recuperation, together with plenty of food—there was a swarm of dogs about and the hunters came in with an elk and a fine young brown bear—and then Clark had to be up and doing.

The captain had been more than intrigued at the Indian horses in and about the Indian camp. There were Pintos and all sorts of horses, and although there were no herders, the animals did not seem to stray too far. Usually, once each day, some youngster would ride out and turn back any such horses as seemed to be inclined to get too far away from camp.

The chief's horse, a gorgeous spotted stallion, was taken care of by the chief's oldest son, who seemed to love that stallion. In return, that creature seemed to be very fond of the lad. Whenever the boy mounted him to ride out to graze, the horse showed his great pleasure by cavorting all over the place, displaying his delight in no uncertain way.

Horses, and more horses, had been the acme of the captain's need and ambitions for most of the past summer. He had worn out both his moccasins and his powers of persuasion in endeavors to secure more of them from the Shoshoni. Now, here, the quite extensive prairie was fairly overrun with horses. Beautiful, wonderful horses.

Toussaint, one of the interpreters, did not seem to hit it off with this Nez Percé chief. It seemed as though there was some sort of personal, natural antagonism between them, so the captain had to turn to Charboneau for assistance. Now, the captain and Charboneau had been out of harmony, out of rapport let us say, since some time before the expedition left the Mandan villages early the past April, not only in the interpreter phases, but in every other angle or phase of human existence. The captain was a Virginian born and bred, and although he never considered his people to be of the aristocracy, they were people of good family and circumstances. They were fond of their women folk and considered strenuous manual labor as beneath their position in the community, the women having either slaves or other servants to take care of the more menial duties of the household.

Charboneau, on the other hand, except for moments of passion, never considered his wife—as was the Indian custom—except as a slave, believing, actually, that the greater her drudgery the more faithful and better a wife she would be. Shortly after the expedition left the Mandan villages early the past April, Charboneau started to chastise Sacajawea for some fancied negligence, but Clark happened to be near and he put a stop to Charboneau's belaboring of Sacajawea with such a burst of anger and such ferocity that Charboneau had never had the courage to attempt chastisement again. But even so, the captain had little use for the puny, weasely Frenchmen, believing his French to be both shocking and ineffective and the man's instincts to be of the lowest.

But since coming into this Nez Percé camp, Charboneau and the Indian chief had hit it off in great fashion. It was just as if two souls had been separated for too long a time, and now that they were together again they were going to make up for lost time.

Charboneau had been spending nearly all of his time since coming into this camp in the presence of this chief, talking at great speed and some length, never ceasing his growls and gutturals, until the arms and hands he used to give coherence to his vocalizing had become worn out with exertion.

Then, wishing to learn more about those wonderful Nez Percé horses, Clark set Charboneau to talking horses with the chief. The captain wanted to know a lot about those horses. Where the Indians got them—how come so many Pintos (Calicos, he called them)? How many horses did they have and where did they pasture them? Each answer seemed to lead to further questioning. Could he see them? The captain, ever since he had slogged over the Rockies, never seemed to tire of thinking of, and yearning to see, horses.

And for once it was a pleasure to watch Charboneau talking. His changes of facial expression, the movements of his hands, even the twisting of his body, all expressed ideas so graphically that even the captain could follow his talking with ease. When the chieftain made a deep, waving motion with both hands and indicated a large area in conjunction therewith, and Charboneau repeated the waving motions in confirmation that he understood, it was as plain as plain could be that the two were speaking of great rolling prairie lands with not the least suggestion that they might have been describing a rolling, tempestuous sea.

In reply to Charboneau's question about the numbers of the horses, the chief, in answering, opened up the fingers of his clenched fists very rapidly, closing them alternately, then brought both arms up into an inclusive gesture that described as plainly as any words ever could that the horses were beyond numbering. In response to the query as to whether the captain could see those horses, the chief turned to Clark with a pleasant and inviting smile and signified that it would be a pleasure to show him the horses at any time of the captain's convenience.

That was one time when Charboneau's interpretative talking was really worth the money, and its satisfactory conclusion should have caused the captain to have a kindlier opinion of the little Frenchman, but the captain was not a man of facile emotions, and it would take more than one success to bring any changes in his opinion regarding his interpreter.

The next day then, the captain, under the escort of some warriors, and including the boy hunter, at the captain's request, were on their way to see the horse bands. They crossed some small streams, one fair-sized river, and then, to their front and to their right and left, stretched a prairie land farther than eyes could see, and in nearly all directions bands of horses were grazing over much of that area.

Records as to the number of horses the Nez Percé had at that time seem to vary with the individual reports of the expedition's members. One man says that there were so many that he couldn't count them in a week. Another says that they were like the white caps breaking in a stormy sea, just everywhere as far as the eyes could see. (The men saw the horse bands some weeks later than did Captain Clark.) If Clark was not wrong in his figures, he was told that individuals among the Nez Percé tribes owned as many as 1,500 horses. Regardless of numbers, it was very evident that these Nez Percé had many, many horses. The captain himself was almost speechless. In describing his sight of so many horses, later to Captain Lewis, about all he could say was: "Thousands and thousands of beautiful horses with more colors than has a rainbow."

Ironically, now that the captain could have had any number of horses that he wanted, he really needed not even one more. From the Weippe prairie it was but a small distance to flowing water, the Clearwater River, which in turn flowed into the Lewis River (now the Snake) and from there on into the Columbia and the sea.

Some weeks later the expedition, proceeding via boats on the Snake River, camped for the afternoon on a sandbar along the north bank of the river, below the site where it took its great sweep toward the west. Captain Clark wished that Captain Lewis might see those great bands of Nez Percé horses on their home plains. Some mounted Nez Percé were riding down the high encampment that towered above the river on the north and after they had been greeted the captain arranged to borrow two of their horses.

They hadn't far to ride before, topping a rise in the prairie, they saw spread out before them leagues and leagues of land that fairly swarmed with horses—and what horses they were! Captain Clark had called them beautiful when describing them to Lewis after his previous sight of them, and now Captain Lewis could understand what he had meant. There was color there. Color and beauty; beauty of color and form and beauty that comes only from the grace of splendid movement and action. The captains stared at all that sight for some minutes, before Lewis suddenly recalled his duty and reached for his notebook. Out of what he wrote we will give just a few lines—and we quote: ". . . The horse is confined principally to the nations inhabiting the great plains of the Columbia . . . and [these nations] possess immense numbers."

"They [the horses] appear to be an excellent race, lofty and elegantly formed, active and endurable; many of them appear like fine English coursers; many of them are pied with large spots of white, irregularly scattered and intermixed with a dark brown bay, the greater part, however, are of uniform color, *marked with stars and white feet*, and resemble in fleetness and bottom, as well as in form and color, the best blooded horses in Virginia." End of quote.

That description, coming impromptu and from one not specially trained in horse nomenclature, is a very fair description, coming as it did from a man who was very much surprised at the entire situation. It would indeed require a man with a very fluent pen to give a better unstudied description of swarms of moving Nez Percé horses, and it cannot, without stretching the imagination, be considered a description of mustang horses.

The captains on that day must really have been looking at quite a number of Appaloosa horses, for in further notes Captain Lewis continues, saying—and again we quote verbatim: "The natives . . . appear to take no pains in selecting their male horses for breed; and indeed those of that class appear much the most indifferent."

The Appaloosa is the only horse in which the male is inferior (indifferent, in Captain Lewis's words) to the female. There can be not the least doubt that the two captains were, on that day, looking at a considerable number of Appaloosas. The stars that Lewis describes, the inferiority of the males, and the white feet are exclusive features of those Appaloosas, except for an occasional white hoof among the Pintos. And with this observation we believe it will be proper to leave Captains Lewis and Clark, and their good angel Sacajawea, to continue their journey without further attention to their efforts. History tells of their trials and troubles and of their final successes. But before turning to other considerations we would like to mention Captain Clark just once again.

After the celebrations and receptions following his return were over, ofttimes, when the captain thought over his journey into the west and reminisced among his friends, a sparkle would come into his eyes, he would lose his customary casual manner, and his features would become animated, assuming in their combination a look of wonder, as he told of those swarms of beautiful horses in the lands of the Nez Percé; as though those sights were then again before him and were almost too wonderful to be true.

And now, as further confirmation of the Nez Percé having so many horses in the first years of the 1800s, we would like to give a short sketch of incidents upholding that fact.

18
Captain Ross Gets Horses

The Nez Percé Indians were the parent people of a large family of northwestern Indians that lived almost entirely within the Columbia River basin. Sociologists have named those people the Shahaptian family of Indians, and have said that they were a different people from other Indians anywhere in the entire northwest. Among the family of Shahaptian people was a large nearby tribe known as the Yakima Indians. Being direct descendants of the original Nez Percé of the territory, and always closely allied to them, they had their full share of Nez Percé horses, but, for some reason, at the time the white men came into their lands there does not appear to have been a great many Appaloosas among them.

Following the visit of Lewis and Clark, the next white man of importance to visit the Nez Percé lands and make a report of his visit, his experiences, and associated events, was a certain Captain Ross, who was in command of a trapper force in the employ of a British-Canadian fur company that was acting in concert with British government desires for the exploration of the lands to the north and west of the Columbia River, as an act in opposition of claims to such lands by the United States as a result of the explorations by Captains Lewis and Clark.

In 1810 Captain Ross worked his way west by streams that kept his route pretty well to the north of the present U.S.-Canadian border, but as he came into the foothills of the Rockies, he found that he was too far north for his purpose. He then turned south-west via the Kootenai River, coming into present U.S. territory while on that river; then, before that river turns directly to the north, he took a tributary to the south that led through the Cabinet Mountains and a short portage across some easy packing to the banks of the Clark Fork River. Coming to that river, he found that it also flowed almost directly northward, so he crossed the Clark Fork and took a tributary that flowed down into it from the southwest, and later, by another short portage, came into the headwaters of the Little Spokane River, which stream flowed almost directly south into the Spokane, which, in turn flowed directly west, entering the Columbia just about where that mighty river makes its great turn to the west, leading into the Grand Coulee territory, and on farther west to where that river again turns directly south until it again turns westward at the Oregon State line.

Coming to the junction of the Little Spokane with the Spokane River, Captain Ross established there a trading post he named Spokane House. That was the first successful inland trading post west of the Rocky Mountains.

Having established that post, the captain went on west to where the Okanogan comes into the Columbia from directly north and began establishing a trading post there. With progress there being satisfactory, the captain's thoughts turned towards the second purpose of the expedition—the exploration of the lands westward to the Pacific Ocean. The Indians at Ft. Okanogan, his trading post, told him that the contemplated journey directly west was almost impossible to accomplish, and advised him to take the Columbia on his journey to the ocean.

Inasmuch as his purpose was secret, the captain could not tell those Indians that such a course would not meet his purpose, and was directly opposite to his instructions, and in order to secure a successful conclusion to the enterprise, he decided to obtain some horses with which to make the journey overland and westward.

On his way west from the Kootenai to the Spokane River, the captain's party had passed close to the land of the Pend Oreille Indians (friends and relatives of the Nez Percé), who had plenty of horses. The captain must have noticed plenty of horse signs, or it may be that the Spokanes had told him of such; anyway, he made a journey back to Spokane House in an endeavor to find horses. Unsuccessful in that, he turned back to Ft. Okanogan and attempted a journey on foot westward to the coast, but was forced to turn back before achieving his goal.

When he was again back at Ft. Okanogan, the Indians there finally revealed to him that the E-Yakimas, far to the south and west of the Columbia, had many horses. The captain was very annoyed that the Okanogans had not told him of this before; to which the Indians politely replied that they had not been asked about the matter. And they were correct. Apparently the captain had not as yet heard of the Nez Percé horses. The Okanogans told him further that the E-Yakima horses would do him no good, for the reason that those Indians were a warlike and terrible tribe, always killing anyone coming to their land for horses, and would kill him too, if he went there.

Captain Ross was a staunch soul, with plenty of determination, and as no other prospect was at hand, he persuaded a few Okanogans to go with him and took off overland for the land of the E-Yakimas. After tough going over some rough and rugged mountains, he came down to the edge of the mountain timber and looked across a large valley extending miles to the south and many miles to the west. That valley is now known as the Kittitas Valley. At that time its expanse of fine grazing land must have surprised the captain, and the herds of horses he saw filling those plains (as he says) away into the distance actually astounded him. The figures he gives are interesting but probably should not be checked too closely, for after all, the captain had been looking for horses for a long time.

The captain and his little party of Okanogans had a rough time of it for some hours (the Yakima squaws wanted to use their knives on them, the captain relates), but a small bottle of firewater warmed the chief's heart, and after a couple of days the captain's courage impressed the Yakima bucks and the captain finally got the horses he needed.

Going back to the Okanogan took much more time than the captain had planned on using because of a very heavy snowstorm. The snow came down so heavily that even his Indian guides could not be sure of their way, so that by the time he got to where his supplies were the entire country was snowed in.

It now appears as though that unfortunate trip back to Spokane House in search of Pend Oreille horses may have saved much northern territory for Uncle Sam.

The Captain Ross story has been entered here to show additional evidence that the Nez Percé did have a whale of a lot of horses at a time when Indians far to the east, and some fairly well south too, were entirely without horses.

And now, with this presentation of the horse situation with Captain Ross, we wish to rest our case of the Nez Percé horse versus the mustang as the predominant factor in placing the plains Indians on horseback, changing those Indians from foot-bound scavengers of the dregs of existence into the paladins of the west.

There is more, much more, that could be said. For instance: As late as the 1850s, in the plains country, it was not too unusual to find aged or otherwise incapacitated Indians abandoned by their families to die of hunger and thirst, unless by some fortunate circumstance some carnivorous predator released them from their misery. A circumstance of plains existence that disappeared as the Indians acquired the horse. But now, enough of such things.

19

NEITHER TIME NOR NATURE PAUSES

The tides of the ocean ebb and flow forever with the passage of time, but often some tide builds up into a crest that suddenly comes up high and overcomes all that formerly had contained it, and the coast line ever after has a new look and a different situation.

Tidal waves are not confined to the oceans alone. There also are tides in the lives of all God's creatures. Just recently, in the span of but a few generations, circumstances in life have reached such a crest that their tide crested high and then receded quickly, leaving scarce a trace.

Such a circumstance of quite recent occurrence is illustrated in the history of the American wild pigeon. The wild pigeons of the western plains country, during the times of the first crossings of the Mississippi by white men, were building up into a tidal wave so great that their numbers, in flights of individual flocks, or the spread of their wings, obscured the sun for hours. Each year they migrated to and from the Indian lands. Their coming was a life saver for many a destitute Indian. And then, as the white men surged across the Mississippi and the Nez Percé horses came in from the west, in one season the wild pigeon reached such a crest that nature recoiled and the wild pigeon disappeared forever. But a benign Creator, or a refulgent nature, if you so prefer, that has watched over human beings since the beginning, came to the aid of another segment of the people, for at the time the wild pigeon disappeared, the American buffalo too reached the crest of its numbers and again the Indian of the plains was well-fed and content.

During those times of the late eighteenth and early nineteenth centuries, a tidal wave of human circumstances was building up in many and various areas of the world. In the British Isles, in Europe, in areas as far distant as China, conflicting ideas in political beliefs and religious convictions, a surplus of humans, and a lack of opportunity sent many people to the New World, and a great share of these came to the United States. America was the lodestar that drew people from many parts of the Old World by the millions. The Revolutionary War set up a block against western expansion for a time, but the War of 1812 erased much of the Indian threat, the journey of Lewis and Clark ignited the spark, and a tide of white people quickly burst across the wide Mississippi. (That tide has not reached its crest even to this day.)

As the tide of white men surged westward, a tide of Nez Percé and Cayuse horses was surging eastward to join the surge of humanity moving westward, and the two joined together into the power that settled the west.

We have accounted for the surge of humanity moving into the west, but the sudden surge of the Pinto—and other Cayuses—within the expanse of but some few years—is a little more difficult to ascertain. True, at the time of Lewis and Clark, the Columbia Basin lands were pasturing so many Nez Percé horses that their numbers must, sooner or later, have become a burden, and after all, the have-nots of this world are forever grasping at the assets of those who have. As has been noted, even before the time of the Lewis and Clark venture, the Indians farther to the east already were making inroads into the bands of the Nez Percé horses. Then, when the white men came, there was no stopping the situation. The Nez Percé horse quickly spread throughout the plains country, helping the white men develop the land and build his cities, and soon then, as does the high crest of an ocean tidal wave, the tide of the Cayuse horse began slowly to recede under the pressure of mechanical equipment. Then came the internal combustion engine, the tractors, and other innovations, and the wave of the Nez Percé horses collapsed as completely throughout the west as does an ocean tidal wave in the bosom of the seas.

The high tide of the Nez Percé people too is gone, and they are of the past, which is mostly forgotten, but a few Nez Percé horses still remain to bring back memories of boyhood days to a few old-timers.

Even this winter, looking north out of my living room window, across the valley and high up against the south exposure of Selah Mountain, I can see on occasion, a small band of original Nez Percé horses. I can note their areas of varied coloration through my glasses, but so far have been unable to pick up any brands or other markings that would denote human ownership. Their homelands must have become untenable under the pressure of horse hunters who supply the dog-food canneries. Maybe an age-old horse instinct has suggested a refuge close to many human beings.

Some few bands—very few—still roam the Yakima Indian Reservation. Their color blazes in the sun with all its old-time variations and attraction.

To the north, up near the Canadian border, on the Colville Reservation, some few small bands of the Nez Percé horse still may be found. Much of that reservation's land is still as primitive as in the days when white men first passed that Way.

Should you wish for a last look at an animal that soon may be extinct, allow me to suggest that you go up to the Reynolds Resort on Buffalo Lake, slip a boat into the water, and enjoy a day of good fishing. On that day, while you are filling the icebox with your limit of nice trout, if you are lucky, you will see coming down to water a band of original-blood Nez Percé horses. Some of their coloring is as beautiful as such horses ever displayed since their beginning. One band has a beautifully marked black-and-white Pinto stallion. Black-and-white is a rare pinto-color pattern, and he is a very beautiful animal. Try to pick him out of that band of Nez Percé horses from some distance away. He is neither superior to his mares, nor is he inferior to them, a characteristic among horses only of the Nez Percé breed; a progeny resulting from an Appaloosa and Spanish mare cross in a small band of such horses that escaped both the Aztec Indians and the Conquistadors during the time of the Cortés fighting in Mexico City in 1520.

20

We Backtrack a Trifle

Our placing of the origin of the Pinto horse later in this writing than may be justified by proper continuity is for the reason that we wish to show that Captains Lewis and Clark saw them, along with great numbers of Appaloosas, in Nez Percé horse bands in the Palouse country of what is now the southeast part of Washington in the year of 1805, at a time when native horses were still extremely scarce west of the Mississippi River.

We also wish to have you apprised of the fact that Captain Lewis in his report to President Jefferson on the wonderful horse situation of the Nez Percé Indians, expressly calls the President's attention to the fact that the horses that he then had under observation disclosed a very unusual characteristic, in that the males were inferior to the females. (This in support of my construction of Appaloosa original conformation, conceived and so constructed by me long before I ever saw that report of Captain Lewis to President Jefferson.) And further, to call your attention to Captain Clark's enthusiasm regarding the many wonderful Pintos he saw in close proximity to the Appaloosas Captain Lewis was describing to the President.

The reason that Lewis and Clark found such great numbers of Pintos and Appaloosas among the Nez Percé after having found almost no horses farther to the east was due to circumstances previously outlined herein, to the Nez Percé breeding of their first horses, and continued later breeding system.

205

The original cross was the mating of an Appaloosa stallion with some Spanish mares and following that first cross some selective breeding practices with the progeny of that continued cross together with the progeny of some Appaloosa mares. That selective breeding continued the Appaloosa breed in its original Asian conformation and color patterns, and the cross breeding of the Spanish mares and their mixed progeny produced the Nez Percé horse, and that strain of horses leaned heavily to Pinto coloration. Quite likely, selective breeding by the party in charge of the original breeding program handled affairs so that the Pinto coloration and ratio became pretty well stabilized in the Nez Percé horses.

That program must have been put in operation by someone not only familiar with horses but who also had had considerable experience in European systems of horse breeding. Such a person would coincide exactly with the veterinarian of the Cortés expedition into Mexico, one Juan Alvarado by name, who beyond a doubt must have spent the rest of his life in teaching his Indian friends how to carry on his program. Juan Alvarado disappeared during the second day's fighting in Mexico City as the Aztec attacked the Spaniards in their Old Palace grounds. I have never read of his body having been found, and I have read every book that I could find on the fighting in Mexico City.

The cross between the Appaloosa stallion and a few Spanish mares, together with the controlled later breeding, including the progeny of the first cross, resulted quite soon thereafter in an entirely new breed of horses, which became known shortly after the white men found them as the Nez Percé. An important percentage of the Nez Percé were of Pinto coloration, and without doubt had the Pinto conformation and characteristics. The exact percentage can never be known, but the Pinto was impressive in numbers among Nez Percé horses at the time Captain Clark found them in Nez Percé lands in 1805, numerous and impressive enough to hold Captain Clark's quite exclusive attention the while Captain Lewis, some weeks later, was concentrating upon bands of Appaloosas somewhere close to bands of the Nez Percé horses.

I am certain that the original Appaloosa stallion cross with Spanish mares produced the Nez Percé horse, and of course the Nez Percé horse characteristics could have been firmly fixed by some immediately following selected breeding. I am particularly certain of the original cross used in producing the Pinto for two specific reasons, namely: that the Appaloosa stallion of undiluted Asian parentage was inferior to the mares of that breed not because of any deterioration in Appaloosa circumstances but under a decree of nature and for nature's specific reason. The same inferiority of the male is found in pre-horse ancestors of the horse genus.

Man in Europe, for some hundreds of years and thousands of generations of horse existence, had used selective breeding methods in the production and improvement, for his special need, of European horses. In their system of producing horses, the male was the important figure, so naturally, the stallion, after a time, became the superior of the two sexes. Those European horses included native Spanish horses. The fact that by the time of Cortés the Spanish horse was not as important in conformation as some other European horses was due solely to poor conditions for the existence of horses in Spain, and not to any deterioration of the blood lines of the Spanish horse. In other words, the stallions of the Spanish horse were, in general, much superior in conformation to the mares, which was also true of the more favored horses of Central Europe and the British Isles.

The Appaloosa stallion, his heritage unsullied by alien blood, was of a type that should have produced Appaloosa characteristics in his genes. On the other hand, the Spanish mares of that cross would have the tendency to produce foals with European horse characteristics, or stallions which would be greatly superior to the mares.

The genes of both parents combined in a compromise of that situation, a circumstance that is common in breeding. In that situation the males of the resulting progeny were neither inferior nor superior to the females produced by that cross. That fact is evident in such bands of undiluted Nez Percé blood lines that exist today.

Fifty years ago the Yakima Indian Reservation was dotted with bands of Nez Percé horses of the old pure strain. Even twenty-five years ago there were still some bands to be seen. Now they are almost all gone. But there is still one band that may, on occasion, be seen from the Satus Highway. The stallion of that band must be seen quite close in order to pick him out of the band. Another interesting feature of that band is that almost every horse is a Pinto.

The Colville Indian Reservation, extending from Grand Coulee on the south to approximately half-way to the Canadian border on the north, is a great area of much land still in its natural state, and several bands of the old-time pure Nez Percé horses may be seen there at opportune times. On a summer day—should you be interested—drive up to the Fred Reynolds Fishing Resort on Buffalo Lake, 13 miles northeast of Grand Coulee Dam. Fish a while and if the day is warm you will most likely see one or two bands of pure-blooded Nez Percé horses coming down to the lake for water. Approach them as closely as you can, it will still be difficult for you to pick out the stallions of those bands. They compare exactly with the mares in size and general conformation. If you watch them for a time, the stallion will be noticeable for, sooner or later, he will assert his position as leader of the band by herding his harem in the direction he wishes them to go.

The fact that there are any Nez Percé horses of the original bloodline left at all in these times speaks well for the tenacity of the breed and of nature's determination to avoid the extinction of a form of life that is not inimical to other forms of life.

The fact of the continued existence of pure-blooded horses at this time is the more remarkable when we become familiar with certain circumstances that have been building up ever, since white men began coming into Nez Percé horse territory. Even before the coming of the first pioneers, trappers, mounted on stallions and/or mares of European bloodlines from the eastern United States, began to dilute the Nez Percé horse blood. But that process was slow until the main emigration toward the west came along and surmounted the Blue Mountains of Oregon Trail fame. The circumstances effecting the matter are substantially as follows:

As the Nez Percé Indians grew in numbers, certain families, for one reason or another, split from the chief Nez Percé home sites and chose other areas as home locations for certain seasons of the year. Sometime in the earliest years of the nineteenth century a group of Nez Percé began using a certain summit area of the Blue Mountains as their summer home and autumn hunting grounds. It was an ideal situation from almost any standpoint of view. The summits of the Blues there contain wide areas of wonderful meadow-like areas of splendid grazing lands, an area interspersed with occasional groups of fine, tall conifers. It was then, and still is today, a wonderful area for summer living.

It so happened that when Joe Meek, old-time trapper and Mountain man of an excellence never surpassed, took the first wagon over the route that later became the Oregon Trail over the Blue Mountains, his horses were practically worn out by the time his outfit attained the summit of those Blues. At the summit, Old Joe came to the very area that those summering Nez Percé families used as their summer home, and Joe had hardly unhitched his horses before those Nez Percé found him.

Joe Meek knew western Indians from top to bottom; inside and out; male or female, but he never was a man who could learn new languages easily. He was handy at sign talk with any Indian, but their vocal lingo was beyond his understanding. Very shortly after getting together with those Nez Percé at the summit there, he was busy working up a trade of his worn-out plugs for a couple of fresh Nez Percé horses. A trade was worked out all right, with each side figuring that they had the best of the bargain, so both were satisfied, but Joe couldn't make out exactly what name that band of Indians called themselves, and ended by calling them Cayuses. Then, before leaving, he named the pleasant creek along which he had camped "Cayuse Creek," and later, when he came again among white men down near the Columbia, he called the Indians with whom he had traded Cayuses, and that name has stuck with those Nez Percé that used that area as a seasonal home. The Nez Percé of that summit area thus became known as Cayuses. Not long thereafter some people began to use Joe Meek's route on their way to the settlements in the Willamette Valley in western Oregon, and, just as in Joe's circumstances, these later travelers' horses would be worn out by the time they reached the summit of the Blues. For that reason the summit area there became a great trading place with the Indians, and because of the name given the Indians by Joe Meek, that Cayuse name stuck and became well known to anyone becoming interested in the Oregon country. Because of the Cayuse name of the Indians, the pioneers gave the name "Cayuse" to the horses that the Indians traded there.

Because of the Cayuse name for those Indian horses, the name "Nez Percé" horse soon was out of fashion, and truly, it may have been just as well, for it wasn't many years before the mixed-breed horses that followed that trading with the Cayuse Indians were considerably different from the true Nez Percé horse. The mixed breed, the Cayuse, was a somewhat larger horse than the old Nez Percé, with longer legs and a less tractable disposition. The Cayuse wasn't the old Nez Percé anymore, but the new mixed-breed Cayuse became very popular among western pioneers because of its greater size and its greater power in breaking up the soil of the new west. As the Midwest plains began to be broken up for farming, great numbers of Cayuses were driven to that area. There, added infusions of eastern bloodlines increased the size and strength of the Cayuse and by the time of the Spanish-American War the old-time Cayuse was a rarity nearly everywhere. Along with the changed bloodlines, the Pinto coloration so common among the Nez Percé horses also appeared less often, so that the Cayuse had a very low incidence of Pinto coloration. Also, I noticed years ago that the white and sometimes laminated hoofs seen at times in the Appaloosas did not appear in the Cayuse bands in the northwest in the 1890s, and of late years we do not see the white hoof as often as we formerly did in the Pinto. Probably, through the years, small infusions of other bloodlines have diluted the genes of the original Nez Percé strain to such an extent that such features may disappear entirely.

When the Spanish-American War began in 1898, there was a great movement of horses into army services from the West and far west. By that time horse raising in the Yakima valley was almost an obsolete industry. The *Carex filifolia* areas of the great Columbia basin (principally in Lincoln County) were being plowed and heavy horses were needed for that heavy work. Some few years later the combine harvester came into northwestern grain lands. It took heavy and very strong horses to lug against a combine for ten hours many a day. The Cayuse could not qualify. They were good though on the roads as eight-horse teams pulled the grain wagons from the ranches to shipping points, but then came the automobile, and the trucks. Soon nobody even drove a Cayuse hitched to a buggy, rubber-tired or not. The day of the Cayuse was over, and so was the day of the Nez Percé horse; cattlemen needed his remaining grazing lands upon which to grow beef. Horse hunters herded them into shipping pens, and the day of the Nez Percé horse soon was over.

Religious beliefs vary among the peoples of many lands and different races. It may be said that few neighbors have exactly the same ideas of the hereafter, and it is right that each and every person should be entitled to a truly individual idea of a future existence. The Indians of the west in the glory of their days upon a horse believed in a happy hunting grounds in their hereafter, in which their buffalo horses crowded close to fleeing herds of buffalos rushing on, maybe just out of reach of his arrow, forever notched upon the whang string of an ever-arching bow; or perhaps his brother featured himself upon a spotted war horse, with feathers braided in both mane and tail and with nostrils expanded to the limit to give it speed forever, chasing an ever-retreating foe that fled just beyond the point of his ever questing lance.

Such a heaven is not for me. Could I spend eternity, forever, amid bands of brightly colored horses such I knew when but a boy, that would be heaven enough for me, and I would not dare ask for a better.

I had planned the words just above as the completion of this manuscript, but upon further consideration I find that there is too much left unwritten about the mysterious horses of western North America.

A friend asks me how it happened that the Nez Percé Indians had such great numbers of beautiful horses for so long a time before other western Indians overran the Nez Percé, took those horses for their own, and began to scatter them across the west in many new sections. That is a good question and I shall answer it.

Then too, I had used in the earlier pages quotations from other authors as proof that my claims regarding mysterious horse circumstances were correct. I had disregarded those items that would have a contradictory effect, honestly believing that they were the result of incorrect or misleading observations. Now it occurs to me that other readers may not have the same opinion. The result could be a lack of faith in my presentation of certain horse circumstances that involve the movement of horses to the north out of Mexico. Also, I know from experience that statistics are mighty poor and uninteresting reading to people who are active with horses. In consequence, I am going to give a summary of the horse situation in Spain from the times of the earliest known records to the time when those mustangs were supposed to be coming into far northern areas out of Mexico, and that will definitely conclude this writing. The facts regarding horse circumstances in Spain and in the Colonies under the control of Spain during that long period of time will be the best possible insurance for the acceptance of my presentation of mysterious horses of western North America. And now for Nez Percé horse circumstances.

21

Nez Percé Isolation

The principal reason that the Nez Percé circumstances in connection with horses were unknown for so long was merely a matter of the location of those Indians. The permanent homelands of the true Nez Percé were in the most isolated district of the entire northwest.

The original party of Indians that came from the far south in Mexico and finally settled permanently in the northwest chose as their final homelands an area closely adjacent to the Salmon River where that stream flows into the Snake River below Hell's Canyon. Hell's Canyon is one of the greatest, if not actually the greatest, canyon known at the present time. No more isolated area can be found on the North American continent, and it is a part of the Columbia River watershed.

The Columbia River Basin is an immense expanse of land that comprises the greater part of central Washington State and also extensive areas in both Idaho and Oregon States. With the exception of the foothills areas of the mountain ranges that encircle the basin, the area in general is almost entirely without timber even along the banks of its most important rivers.

Very little moisture either as snow or rain comes into the basin areas, for the entire perimeter of the basin consists of great ranges of high mountains. To the west towers the high Cascade Mountain Range, with its many high peaks covered with snow the entire year. That range of mountains, aided first by the great Olympic Range farther to the west, permits little moisture to come from the west.

Then, having crossed the border into Canada, one finds a series of mountain ranges that tie in with the Cascades on the west and branch off from the Rocky Mountains in the east. Very little moisture comes into the basin from the north. To the east of the basin the towering escarpments of the high Rockies stand almost directly north and south, with the most rugged range, the Bitter Roots, standing close and very high directly to the east of the Nez Percé homelands. Even at this late date no feasible route for a road has been found that might lead to those Indian lands, and that in spite of one of the greatest gold strikes in the west in Nez Percé lands in the early 1860s. Even the high foothills leading west from those Nez Percé lands to the summits of the Bitter Roots are so dry for much of each year that the timber growth consists of specialized conifers that can exist in almost and situations. Certainly little moisture comes into the basin from the east.

In the Hell's Canyon area to the south of the Nez Percé homelands, towering mountain spurs jut out westward to where the Snake River finds a way northward through the precipitous walls of Hell's Canyon. Immediately to the west, though some distance to the north, the Powder River Range of the Blue Mountains in Oregon thrusts high pinnacles almost to the Snake River, forming with the great Blue Mountain Range a great barrier to the south for any moisture that might be seeking a way into Columbia River Basin lands.

In all of the semi-arid areas of the Columbia Basin there is one very pleasant situation. Almost directly north of the gap in the mountains to the south that forms the Hell's Canyon gorge through which the Snake River flows to the north, and almost directly east of the gap in the high Cascade Mountains where the Columbia River flows on to the west and the Pacific Ocean, moisture-loaded winds apparently bump into each other and dump moisture in considerable amounts. That situation has existed for eons of time, for the soil for a large area is a loam that was deposited there in bygone ages. The combination of that loam and the plentiful moisture of the area has formed a pasture land for horses that probably has been unsurpassed anywhere in the world.

That district lies extensively in Whitman County in southeastern Washington, but extends also into great areas of eastern Idaho. The tract is known as the Palouse country, and was the grazing grounds for the Nez Percé horses.

In the central areas of the basin an annual moisture supply of four inches is common; moisture content of eleven inches per annum is very rare. With the exception of certain areas of lava flows and protruding basalt formations, much of the central area has a soil structure so light that the moisture from a good rain on uncultivated areas seems to disappear entirely in almost one night. The combination of such circumstances protected the Nez Percé homelands from encroachment by roving Indians in pre-pioneer times, and also prevented too much pressure from the white pioneers in more recent time.

Added to that situation one finds in considerable areas of the central basin quite extensive lava flows and protruding basalt formations. The remaining area of the central part of the basin is covered with a soil formation that is so light in structure that the moisture from a good rain will disappear overnight, leaving the top soil in a seemingly hopeless aridity completely unfit for farming.

Such a combination of natural circumstances was an effective barrier against the encroachment of outsiders from a great area to the north of the Snake River, a stream which in that part of its flow toward the Columbia had no fording places whatever. The Nez Percé were quite safe from intruders from any direction because of the deterrents to settlers we have already mentioned, but there was another and most aggravating deterrent to add to those with which we are now familiar.

True, not all of the central basin area is now an empty waste. Great areas of Lincoln County, Washington, comprise most of the central basin lands. Much of that area is featured by gently rounded hills, but these are interspersed with hills that tower high, and ofttimes an elevation would be so steep that its summit would seem, for all the world, to overhang. Occasionally, between those hills there would be a valley of considerable width and length. The moisture would seep down out of the higher ground and much of those valley areas would have sufficient moisture to produce fine crops. A favorite crop was wheat. Those valleys were settled, but the population of Lincoln County was quite limited, because such valleys were rare. One could ride all day, in some areas, and never see a shack or a person. But the crops did so well in those few valleys that of course pioneers began homesteading the hills. But those hills, unless one knew the true circumstances, had the worst deterrent to farming that a pioneer ever knew. That deterrent in Lincoln County was *Carex filifolia.*

You do not recognize the name? You don't know what *Carex filifolia* is? Well, I'm just the one to tell you. *Carex filifolia* is a plant, and when a homesteader, avid for land to plow, first stepped upon some *Carex* sod he believed that he had found a paradise, for the plant grew so thick as to form a sod as pleasant in the early springtime as any Kentucky Blue Grass.

The plant grew to four inches, sometimes a little more in height, was as thick as it was possible for it to stand, and made a perfect footing for anyone. Beneath the ground though it was of a different character. Its roots were a mass of coarse, tough fibers about the thickness of common No. 10 wire and it looked exactly like the kinkiest, woolliest head of hair that any darky ever wore. To the local people the plant became known as "nigger wool," and that was a perfect name. Any good pair of pliers can cut No. 10 wire, but no pliers ever could cut the roots of nigger wool. If a man's hands were strong enough, the roots might be broken one by one with pliers, but they could not be cut.

It is true that a brand-new plowshare with a very sharp cutting edge could cut some of those roots if plenty of power was attached to the plow beam, but the sharpest share in those early times would not cut a furrow longer than 8 or 10 feet. By that time the edge of the plowshare would be so dull that the roots would only break— not cut. After that not all the men that could line up on the plow beam could hold that plow in the ground. The plow, the moldboard, share and all, would come right up and slide along on the ground. If the horses attached to the plow were weak for any reason, or if they were averse to any heavy pull, they would stop before that happened. Either way the results were the same. You couldn't plow those great fields of *Carex filifolia*, and that drove those pioneer men to distraction.

Such situations drove many a pioneer nuts. Worse yet, some of the more nervous went stark, raving crazy. Such as could not be handled without serious difficulty were taken to the insane asylum at Medical Lake, and word got around that the asylum didn't want any more of those characters if they could avoid taking them in. They simply were too hard to handle. Later, after the *Carex* troubles were over, many of those unfortunate men recovered and were returned to their families.

In the meantime many methods were tried in attempts to farm those *Carex*-infested lands, but all attempts failed. The plant was worthless as pasture land, for neither horses nor cows would eat the grass.

Failing in that too, a movement was started to give the *Carex* lands back to the Indians. Sy Slocum, a former mining man up in the Idaho gold fields, had married a widow who had large holdings of land, including some good valleys that raised wheat and several other crops to perfection. It was a common rumor that the new wife, shortly after a few days of honeymooning, had assumed complete command over Sy's every thought and action, but be that as it may, the lady was a life savior for anyone destitute within driving distance of her home.

In spite of the fact that every man there knew that the Indians were too smart to accept that *Carex* area back as a gift, or under any conditions, quite a movement was worked up with some such object in mind. Sy was the leader in the movement, and, privately, some folks wondered at Sy. He was quite a practical man about most other things.

To make matters worse, the summer that the giveaway program was suggested was the driest season that any old-timer in all the country round about could remember. Up in Sprague, the county seat, it was claimed to be the driest season on record. It became so dry and so hot not even the jack rabbits could stand it. They were

seen in droves migrating towards the Columbia, and someone said
that they were headed for the Willamette Valley in western Oregon.
A land, it was said, where it rained so often that the hens got as
web-footed as the ducks. It got so dry in our country that summer
that sand was known to have blown up off the Columbia River, and
no country in the world ever got any drier than that.

Sy Slocum kept pushing, on the sly maybe, the idea of getting
the Indians to take that land back, and some of the folks got to
kidding about it. About then Sy saw an article in the weekly paper
that came to his house—the only paper in the entire township. The
article told of a great potlatch that was to be held in the Long House
near Lewiston, Idaho, ten days from then, by the surviving
members of the Nez Percé and other Indian tribes. That article in
the paper gave Sy a bright idea, and the next day, after he held
some rather furtive consultations with some of his neighbor men,
a meeting was held in his house and it was agreed that a delegation be dispatched to that Long House Indian meeting to lay the
land proposition before those Indians.

Smallpox, measles, and great and interesting varieties of sick-
ness had almost wiped out the Nez Percé people and the tribe had
been disbanded just a year or two before. Sy claimed that they had
lots of money from royalties from the Idaho gold fields (the very
homelands of the Nez Percé) and insisted that a determined effort
might induce the Indians to consider his proposition. Of course he
had his tongue in his cheek at the time and nearly bit it off, but the
men formed a delegation of all who could manage to get away from
their families, and at the proper time the delegation left for
Lewiston, with the express purpose of playing a dirty trick on those
friendly Nez Percé Indians.

The delegation found the site of the potlatch very easily, having
first taken care of their horses, but they were very unfortunate as
to the time element. Had the white men arrived early, on the first
day of the Indian gathering, they might have received a polite re-
ception from the more important of the Indians, but arriving towards noon of the second day of the Indian gathering, they found

some of the Indian bucks either engaged in consuming firewater or absent in the search for such liquid refreshment. Since the tribe had been disbanded, they were on their own, so it was merely a matter of finding a sociable purveyor of the stuff who might have a supply available, for the city government was against the Indians having any liquor for distraction; trouble invaded the town whenever any Indians became liquored up, and the town marshal was a man who believed it proper to enforce the law.

Now, an Indian buck who is filled with firewater can, and most often does, become a nuisance, and that is very bad, but an Indian who gets just a few drinks inside himself and cannot secure more is really something of a menace to society. Therefore, the edict had gone out before these Indians had come into town. The marshal served notice on every joint in town; "not a drop to any of those Indians."

The Indians that had gone into town with refreshments on their minds simply had not had the proper connections, so came back without any liquor and dry of gullet. In order to hide their disgrace from their squaws they had slunk into the shaded area of the Long House and were trying to overcome their craving for something refreshing by getting a few hours' sleep.

While those Nez Percé had been uptown in a fruitless endeavor to find some poison, two bucks from over on Slick Water Creek, some miles west of Clarkston in Washington State, the sister town of Lewiston, just across the Snake River, had made connections with their favorite bootlegger (he made the stuff himself and man, did it have a wallop!); unfortunately they had only been able to snag a couple of quarts, but that was the real stuff. It hadn't been cut down a bit and two snorts of that liquor would lay anybody out whose stomach wasn't fashioned out of solid, pure monel metal. The two had been firm in their resolve not to pull a cork until that evening, at which time the festivities in the Long House would begin. Then they would tackle the hootch and have a wonderful time. Sad to relate, that day was about the hottest of the long, hot summer. The two had neither saddle nor saddle blanket and the sweat from their horses' backs began to burn their bottoms. Sweat ran down into their eyes, and salty sweat into the corners of their mouths; pressing need overcame their so firm resolutions, made in the cool of the morning, and they each began to take swigs out of their bottles. Now, that hootch was really Christmas liquor, meant to warm a chilly Santa on a Christmas Eve, and how it did warm those two up. By the time they got to the Long House and flopped off their horses into the shade of some poplar trees they were a couple of very sick men and made no attempts whatever to hide that fact. Their retching and puking noises riled the despondent, disappointed Indians trying to sleep in that Long House and they began to gather and store up so much irascibility that the amounts stored for the future surely were to mean grief to someone.

The women of the camp were lucky to be away at the time. Part of them, the older ones, who from time to time had earned an honest dime by doing washing and sundry other chores for some of the important women of the town, were wending their way up into the city precincts in which those ladies lived, with the intent of securing many and sundry items of eatables that would lend a piquant variety to the menus of the tables in the Long House for the next few days. Those Indian squaws were not particular, nor were they choosy; if the ladies had little to spare from their iceboxes maybe the garbage cans would fill their needs, and they were quite content with the prospects.

The young women and the girls were over against a side hill, just a hundred yards or so east of the Long House grounds. The slope was steep there and irregular and chokecherries and service berries grew there in great abundance. Up there, picking cherries, some of the girls could hear the noises made by the two drunks down in the shade near the Long House, but it didn't bother them at all. They had heard such things before. Down near the creek across the road, quite a distance away, the mature women were picking thorn apples. It was just a trifle early for those thorn apples just then. There were more red ones than ripe blue ones, but they all would go good with the camas roots that the children were rooting up out of some scab-rock areas on the bank above the river.

There was so much of good things to gather near there and round about that all the young folks were happy. Some of the sagebrush was green, and there were wild onions and green willows, young and tender, near the water. They would add seasoning.

The girls picking chokecherries were young, happy, and feeling sportive. One among them stuffed her mouth full of ripe chokecherries, mushed them up there, and then squirted chokecherry juice in the face of an unsuspecting sister. Quicker than it takes to tell this, every one of those chokecherry-picking girls was squirting chokecherry juice at someone. They were having lots of fun, albeit some of them were getting rather messy, what with chokecherry juice and pulp. They were by now having a hilarious time. So naturally the girls picking thorn apples just a piece away across the road must get into the fun, and you can believe there really was a riot there for a time.

It has been recorded that the women of the Shahaptian people were more chaste and industrious than were the women of some other Indian peoples (that is mentioned in the Lewis and Clark journals). It was said that the maidens were most reluctant to receive the attentions of the white youths without the sanction of their mothers.

The Nez Percé maidens who minutes before had been squirting chokecherry juice at each other were now down in the creek that meandered along on its way into the river, which flowed just a little distance below. Two of the maidens had fallen into the water during the playing that went on down there and their water-soaked, and scanty, clothing did very little in the way of concealing their lovely and voluptuous forms, and just then two young men on foot, hiking their way from Clarkston to Lewiston and distressed by the heat, dropped into the creek from alongside the road and found themselves in close proximity to that bevy of lovely maidens.

The young men of that vicinity and pioneer time must have been much like the young men the world over when the opportunity comes for some flirtatious behavior, but their wolf whistles, inducements, and other blandishments bringing no pleasing results, they proceeded on into town, hiding their chagrin as best they could.

There was a large crate of dried, smoked salmon over near a door of the Long House. That would be the favored course for the big dinner that would climax the potlatch. Although there were a lot of large flies buzzing near and settling on the comatose Indians that had been overcome with firewater, there were no flies near that smoked salmon. Apparently insects did not like the salmon smoked by the Indian method. Along with the goulash of roots and service berries, the chokecherries and thorn apples, these salmon would be the main portion of the food served at the great dinner coming up; but the dinner, the squaws knew, had better be postponed until most of the wayward bucks had dried up all possible sources of the potent and disabling fire water.

Two of the delegation members had separated, by stealth, from the rest of the delegation at an opportune time as they passed a group of shrubbery following the stabling of the delegation's horses, and now, as other members became aware of that, there was some hesitation in their progress as they looked about in superficial search for the absent members. And then, as they approached the area of the Long House, from the city side, from the south, an old Indian warrior in a frock coat that had once been a deep black but now was so faded one would never have believed it, and with no pants on, but with a ragged scarf tied around his waist in such a manner that the long coat concealed his breechclout, and as barefooted as any coon that ever trailed along a stream, mounted the old crate filled with the salmon and began to preach against the evils of strong drink and of wild white women. He was really spouting off. The retching drunks, who had collapsed in the shade of the poplar trees that shaded the Long House, made some very disgusting noises, but after the preacher began to preach in his native language, with its gurgling and queer nuances of sound, the retching, at certain periods, mingled quite nicely with that gurgling when the preacher ran out of breath.

Now, this delegation had known all the time that their mission was hopeless as far as gaining any results with the Indians was concerned. They knew that the Indians were too smart to accept that *Carex*-infested land even as a gift. The delegation had been conceived and organized by one Sy Slocum, a miner, who had married, by mistake, a widow who was burdened with a large acreage of this no-account area. Even so, he had been more fortunate than the average man, for that acreage had a considerable average of scab-rock land that sloped down into a depression into which moisture from higher areas seeped to such an extent that nigger wool would not grow there. That scab-rock area contained fine pasture for both cattle and horses, and a few patches of ground that produced all manner of garden stuff.

The lady was most generous with the products of her gardens, and furnished free about all of the cows' milk that babies needed for miles around, but she was most domineering in her relations with her husband, Sy. Sy had promoted this idea of giving the land away and back to the Indians, although he and everyone else had known all along that the Indians were far too smart to even consider accepting any such proposition. However, Sy kept promoting the deal among the men folks in the hope that something might materialize. And now all the men of the home area who could manage to get away from their frustrations were at the Indian celebration grounds, and needs must go through with the formula of attempting to get rid of their lands, or, surer than the tax collector or interest to the banks, the women folks—who were suspicious anyhow—would learn of it and there would be the dickens to pay.

For that reason the delegation had persisted in its effort to put their offer of the lands as a gift to influential members of the Indians congregated at the Long House. Therefore they were firm in their intentions, and looked about the grounds, hoping to discover both their missing members and some important-looking Indian bucks.

The way there had been long and wearisome. Although every member had roughed it extensively in his younger days, they had for a long time now enjoyed all the comforts and perquisites of married life, and though their journey, in freedom, had seemed like a lark for some hours, they by this time had had just too much of the free life of the plains. The cooking out in the open over a sagebrush fire, with a hard wind whipping the fire right out from under the skillet, had ceased being a novelty (that's just one example) and they were quite disgusted with the entire trip, wishing that they were home again.

They were somewhat more than a mere trifle out of humor as they looked about them. One of them had a family of twelve, another of thirteen, children. It was surprising how those two missed all those children now. Now that they were free of them. Then, as they looked about in search of some Indians they might proposition, who should come into sight around a corner of the Long House but the two missing members of their party.

They noticed at once that one of the two, Hank Wood by name, wore a silly grin on his face and had difficulty in taking steps evenly and with uniform action and purpose. Although there was no water closer than the Snake River, which flowed about one-half mile to the north, Hank walked as though he were under the impression that he was treading the deck of some small schooner that was weathering some heavy seas. The waiting party looked at Hank with feelings composed about evenly of disgust and envy. Envy, because they realized that Hank had been busily engaged with schooners such as never sailed a sea, and disgust that they had been so unfortunate as not to have been in his place. They were about to take out their spleen on Hank, with each man trying to cough up the dust of the dirt road that had been clogging up his throat and nostrils most of the morning, the better to tell Hank just what they thought of his behavior, but before their throats and nostrils had been relieved of their coatings of dry and somewhat alkaline dust, Sy Slocum, the other missing member was among them.

Sy at just that time was a rather odd-looking creature, though good fortune had just been smiling upon him. It so happened that Sy formerly, when, naturally, he had been considerably younger, had been quite a sport up and down and around the gold-digging grounds not too far away from Lewiston. The very first saloon he had ventured into this day—he was extremely low on funds—he had run smack-dab into an old-time partner of his. When last he had seen that former partner up in some old workings past Grangeville, the partner had just passed through the shocking experience of calling a royal flush with his hand consisting of a measly full house. The partner, Murphy by name, known to one and all simply as Murph, had borrowed all of the gold dust and nuggets in Sy's poke and bet the works on his full house. They both were so broke after that that they had to go back to their claim to wash out some more gold dust, but during the week they had been enjoying the pleasures of Grangeville a half dozen claim jumpers had jumped their claim and were working it with gusto. Both Murph and Sy had staked their shooting hardware and other assets at the Lucky Strike saloon for the wherewithal with which to make a try at recovering their lost gold dust, but they had run into a streak of bad luck and now were in their very own personal diggings without a single chance of recovering them, for the claim jumpers had been men of foresight and had a plentiful arsenal with which to protect their operations. Sy and Murph, loath to lose such a good claim, withdrew without hostilities, or even many words or loud bickering. They had to hatch some kind of plan to recover their own private property, but with nothing liquid on hand and being much too thirsty to properly scheme out a workable plan, they returned to the city with the good intention of securing aid against those so-and-so claim jumpers. What with one thing and another coming up, Sy had ended up in becoming a member of the delegation that was supposed to make a try at giving their worthless land back to the Indians, drunk or sober.

Murph had been more fortunate. He had married Gold Hill Sally, the proud owner and operator of the finest eating-place in all the Idaho gold diggings. They had prospered there so greatly that eventually they had moved their restaurant out of the gold-digging areas (they were petering out at the time), had set up shop in a more civilized location and were prospering greatly, with the missus running the restaurant and Murph operating the saloon they had established.

Murph sure was tickled to see Sy. That old loan and sundry other obligations that were long past due to Sy had bothered him a good deal. Between them the two quickly worked out a sum as payment for the amount fairly due Sy, and Sy, paid in full, had several pockets loaded with heavy coins (paper currency was never used in the west in pioneer times), and every other empty space in his clothes filled with liquor bottles. Even his shirt front was a-bulging.

Murph had not selected the finest of his liquors in stocking up Sy. From old acquaintance, Murph knew that Sy liked his drinks to have a lot of authority, and knew too that Sy thought that the drink was the more perfect the harsher it was. Whiskey that burned its way clear down to his gullet and on down into more lower regions was Sy's idea of a good drink. Consequently, Murph had dug out some potent home-made stuff he had just recently obtained from the same man that had supplied the two Indians now puking up in the shade of the poplars shading the Long House over at the potlatch grounds outside Lewiston.

Up in the diggings, once, after Sy had imbibed plenty of that kind of stuff, he had started to tackle a big grizzly bare-handed, but had been restrained from the certain resulting inconveniences by his buddies.

Now then, Sy was approaching the waiting members of the delegation, looking about for a convenient opportunity to dispose of that potent firewater. The inside of the Long House was the coolest place between Walla Walla, far to the west, and the snow-covered peaks of the high Bitter Roots much farther to the east. Walla Walla's better eating-places and its saloons all had commercial refrigerators, but Lewiston's places of business, except for the most modern, were as yet unable to boast of such modern innovations. The only thing that the less modern places of business on the outskirts of Lewiston could boast of at that time were cooling boxes consisting of a framework of two by twos, covered with gunny sacking with the top formed into a water container. In that container, commonly kept well filled with water, were gunny sacks that stuck up over the edge of the box and were hanging some inches down the sides. The moisture would seep up in the sacking over the edges of the water container, and in seeping down into the sacking siding of the improvised cooler would lower the temperature from 15 to 20 degrees on really hot days.

It so happened that most of the Indian braves also had previously sought the shade of the Long House. That shade not only kept them reasonably cool, and the day was hot, but it also kept them away from the urging of the squaws to get in and help some with the preparations for the coming celebration.

Now, the Indian bucks of that encampment were not especially interested in the potlatch, except for the chances that somehow the celebration might develop into some source of firewater. With the exception of the few miserly fellows who had managed to obtain a very small quantity of the stuff and were now in various stages of intoxication, as has been hereinbefore noted, those in the Long House had found no firewater whatsoever, and they were a morose and frustrated group, who, as the delegation entered the Long House and drew near, merely became more morose, and temporarily hid some very pugnacious feelings.

As Sy came up, helping Hank along, he found there the very opportunity he had been looking for. Shoving the inebriated Hank into the arms of another member of the delegation, he stepped up close to the supinely resting group of braves and began to deliver his opinions and desires, as to the advantages to both sides in the matter, of some trade for the homelands of the delegation's members.

Now good Sy, when he was most earnest and sincere, had his worst moments in the use of the English language. In fact, about the only hilarious times that the colonists of the *Carex*-infested lands had had for a long time was at such times that they could inveigle Sy into some seriously meant dissertation. His command of the English language took such queer and unpredictable mixtures at vocalizing that their use caused some to go into hysterics in efforts to conceal their mirth from Sy and thus keep him at it.

So Sy then, never having been more serious and sincere about a matter in his life, was having a most terrible time in presenting his proposition to those Indians. His hilarious efforts tended quickly to put the delegation members into a humorous and laughing frame of mind, and as a consequence of such doings on the part of the white men, the Indians, already previously out of sorts and itching for trouble, began springing up and taking on a very truculent appearance—and that was where Sy got in his work.

Sy had a great belief in the potency of firewater's power in the quenching of feelings of irritation and promoting a feeling of well-being and comradeship between members of whatever groups represented, regardless of race, creed, or opposing positions between the parties. He was quick to go into action in this situation. Very smoothly and with considerable speed bottles of liquor were withdrawn from the recesses of his clothing, and, with the aid of helping hands, both the Indians and the delegates were gulping down the spirits with great gusto and abandon.

Now, that situation wasn't at all bad for the white men; here, beyond their fondest expectations, was a dream come true. Spirits of any kind or potency had been lacking for a long time in the lands of the *Carex filifolia*. This was a time to be enjoyed. But sad to relate, the situation was completely different with the Indians. Indian bucks, 99 times out of 100, will, as they imbibe firewater, acquire a belligerence that, owing to circumstances, may have been held within, and so gradually build up into such tempers that will blow the lid off any civilized feelings that Indians were supposed to have acquired by that time. Their former and present true natures, atavic through many years of abuse and depredation by white men, were really ready to explode.

Under such conditions, after the Indians had a few drinks, some began to grow belligerent. Soon some became real quarrelsome. Sy was desperately trying to put his proposition across, but by now the mixed-up situation, together with some few drinks he had taken to lubricate his tonsils and organize his thoughts, had affected him so that his English had become strictly a minus quantity, becoming forgotten completely, and his attempted persuasion was being spouted out now in good old-fashioned Swedish.

Now, an Indian brave, either of important lineage or from the lowest ratings of Indian society, detests being made fun of by white men. Nothing else will cause him to so quickly braid feathers into his hair and go upon the warpath. What with the firewater and all, some of those Indians quickly came into such a mood. One thing led to another. Some of the delegation weren't actually fond of Indians under any conditions or circumstances, and very shortly blows were being struck, and a furious battle was in progress. The battle ebbed and flowed, spilling out from the Long House and nearing the county road that passed just outside the fence of the Long House enclosure.

It so happened that just at that time a certain salesman, Mike Clancy by name, had come into town the afternoon before by train, and, having completed his calls upon local firms, was departing by horse and buggy, working his way toward Walla Walla. A short time before a man who was an accomplished metal worker had perfected a certain new type of plowshare out of chilled steel, and had organized a manufacturing company to produce such plowshares for the market. The company was named the "Oliver Chilled Steel Plow Company," and Mike Clancy had been given the western territory as a salesman. Clancy hadn't wasted more than a very few hours in Spokane. The immediate vicinity of Spokane provided no special need for plowblades and really was in no farming area of importance anyway; so Mike had grabbed the first train out that would take him toward Walla Walla, which was the center of a great farming area. He had stopped off in Lewiston, as his train had arrived there early in the morning, and now, having completed his work in Lewiston, he was on his way toward the quite distant Walla Walla, planning to stop at various small towns along the way and quite possibly do some business.

It seems that ofttimes the Power up above is so busy taking care of the universe that the wants of some people, on occasion, may be overlooked. Many people about the world have had that impression, and certainly the farmer folk of the *Carex filifolia* lands would have agreed with that line of thought. But some seer, of so ancient a time as to be beyond my recollection, once said: "Good fortune comes to him who waits"; and in this situation he was so very right, for just as the rowdying Indians and the delegation members were spilling out of the Long House and out onto the sod along the country road, Mike Clancy, the chilled-plowshare salesman, came a-driving by.

Now, Clancy was a typical Irish salesman of the time; slightly red of feature because of a considerable indulgence in spirituous liquors, always ready for a joke or frolic—and a good fight was always a pleasing frolic for Mike. As the ruckus spilled over into the road just in front of his horse, Mike could not fail to become interested, and soon, for whatever reason, he was in just about the middle of it.

A spinster lady, a prim seamstress, was just coming to the area of battle and complete disarray, with a delivery of some lingerie for a customer in town. She was horrified at what she truly believed was a maturing massacre, and whipped her horse on by the struggling men, quickly notifying the local police authorities. Her words were lurid, yet withal seemed to be describing a very menacing situation, so the town marshal quickly deputized all nearby men and hurried to the scene of the terrible conflict.

Well, that fracas ended with every participant being incarcerated within the hoosegow. After a time, when Mike Clancy and a couple of the delegates who had not imbibed any great amount of firewater had gotten various and sundry abrasions and contusions, sort of cleaned up and became less onerous, they got to talking, and of course Mike, a born salesman, was not long in telling of his plows and plowshares that would cut through any sod, and he guaranteed it.

Well, talk about a marvelous circumstance! The marshal was called, explanations were given, and in just a little time Mike Clancy and the delegation members were discussing chilled-steel plowshares over cups of good strong coffee. That chilled-steel plowshare solved the problem of the *Carex filifolia*, and in just a very few years that territory was, and still is, about the best wheat-growing area in the entire United States.

That happened in 1895, as I remember it, and that thought recalls a journey through that *Carex filifolia* area before the chilled-steel plowshare was invented.

22
Early Experiences

My first experiences with nigger wool (*Carex filifolia*) began when I was so young that I am surprised that I remember them now, but they are among my oldest and first memories.

My parents did missionary and medical work in western central Idaho in the early 1890s. I do not remember much of their approximately two years there, for I was too young, and my one winter with the folks spent in that Indian camp was spent by me in the home of other people.

It seems I was a very puny child, subject each winter, following the first chill breeze, to what father called "Lung Fever"—some type of pneumonia I suppose—and as my father was of the homeopathic school of medical practice then, his medical names and terms were somewhat at variance with the names used in these later times. Anyway, it was considered best for me to spend that winter in a much better home and in a much drier location than the wet creek bottom where my parents' temporary shack was situated. I spent that winter on a horse farm that was situated somewhere southeast of Sprague, Washington, and I am sincerely ashamed that I cannot remember the people that took care of me. The only experiences of that horse ranch that I can remember are the bucking horses in the spring and, dimly, how my favorite rider looked. I remember the pitching and the bucking. How, once in a while, some horse would squeal while a cowboy was raking it with the spurs, how they would hump their backs and twist; how they would, occasionally, throw themselves completely backward in attempts to crush their riders. I remember a fall, maybe, though dimly, more than one, and how the worst buckers would try to rub their riders off against the high rail fences. I was very young, but I got so that I could tell which horse was going to really buck by the way it behaved when they put the saddle on the first time. Some that acted up the worst before that weren't the worst buckers at all, but when their eyes glared red and they shivered some as the saddle hit their backs—look out for them. They were wicked.

The boss man—I don't really remember him, but I remember some of the talk about him—always had his horses blindfolded before he hit the saddle, but as he hit the seat the blindfold was yanked off, and, I remember, sometimes his horses bucked something awful. Really, all I remember of my stay at that place are the bucking horses and the riders. I know now that some of those horses were good. I saw a lot of bucking horses as I was growing up. I myself couldn't stick on one too long. If a Cayuse stuck with it long enough, my skinny legs would play out and he'd get rid of me. Sometimes I went high, too, even if not handsome.

Right when the boys were getting well warmed up a-riding, my father came to take me home. He was beginning a circuit, setting up some meeting places, and the wheel tracks we followed were through areas that had never felt a plowshare.

My memories of that journey begin with a meal in a saloon in Sprague, and was I scared. All of my teachings at home, before and since, were that saloons were places that harbored devils, and never, never to go into a saloon. I don't know, even now, why father took me there. I guess it was the only place that he knew at the time where he could get a square meal and some vittles to take for use on the road.

Beginning with that saloon my memory must have improved, for I remember watching to see if our buggy wheels followed exactly in the wheel tracks we were using as a guide. And there were a bunch of Sand Hill cranes some considerable distance away, standing still in the grass on very tall legs. I was all excited and wanted father to shoot one, but father wouldn't. He said their meat wasn't good at that time of year, and anyway, Sand Hill cranes were becoming very rare.

I sure was puzzled about that rare situation. My only experience up to then with anything rare was hearing the talk in the kitchen about my old uncle liking his meat very rare. It's really strange to me that I can still remember such a silly thing.

Father was making a circuit through some areas that had very few settlers. It was a lovely day I remember. It must have been in June. Along in the morning we drove through miles and miles of lupine; lupine as far as our eyes could see. Pink and white and blue and red. It made a gorgeous carpet.

We ate our lunch near an almost dry water hole. Father had trouble getting enough water for the horse. As we came near, the ground, the wheel tracks, and every other place, were filled with frogs leaving that dry hole. As we drove away father tried to pick a road free of moving frogs, so as not to crush them, but he couldn't find any such place. At first, I felt terrible at the buggy wheels crushing so many frogs, but even a little lad can get used to killing, I guess, for pretty soon I went to sleep.

Along in the afternoon we came to an area of lava that father said was quite new. It was blacker than the sides of our buggy and if you rubbed a finger along a chunk freshly turned over, there would be a smudge of soot on that finger. We found a fumarole. As memory recalls it, it must have been a hundred yards, at least, across, seemed perfectly round, and the water was black and completely still. Father said he had been told that some such water holes were practically bottomless. Such things must have been very interesting to a kid, for I remember that well.

I guess I slept some, but I know we drove a very long time, anyway it seemed so to me, and then, quite close up on a slight knoll, we saw a number of men and lots of horses. Some of the horses were ground-tied and some, I still think, were in a rope corral. Father said it was a round-up and stopped our horse to take a look. He hadn't been stopped a minute, it seems to me, when a horse and rider exploded right up from among those men, so it looked like to me.

I had been watching men on bucking horses, sometimes on and sometimes off—off and on all spring—and thought that I was an expert on such. I had seen some fancy bucking, I thought, but this roan was mighty good and exciting. He was the mean, bawling kind; every time his feet hit ground it seemed to bring a bawl right up out of his insides, from way down deep somewheres. That bawling sounded to me just like a buck Indian full of firewater and on the prod. For just a few humps that bawl got meaner and meaner. I began to hold my breath. Something sure was going to happen.

That bronc didn't take off. He bucked right close and tight. I couldn't have put it into words but it seemed to me that roan was just a-warming up. He didn't lunge any, just bucked mostly up and down and sideways and a-twisting. I could see the action from where we were in the buggy. Every time he lit, he bawled. Had a sound to me just like a bear cub up a tree calling its maw. He looked classy to me and the rider was doing all right too. I could see him rake the bronc with his spurs. There was a little scattering of the men watching, and of a sudden that critter, sudden-like, let out a bawl that made our buggy horse get fidgety, went up, nigh straight up, way high, sun fished and came down a-twisting and a-squirming, his nose and his heels so close together it seemed to me the heels would loosen them jaw teeth.

That rider kept on a-going up and up. As he came down, the bronc was a-going up again, and I thought he had struck his head on the saddle seat as he, coming down, and the roan going up came together. I still can hear the smack as the two came together, and for a moment I guess that I was so paralyzed I didn't see the rider slide away and hit the ground, but father quickly handed me the reins to our buggy horse, grabbed his medical bag, and was out of the buggy mighty quick.

I kind of lost my bearings for a moment, and when I was all organized again the bronc was a-bucking over the knoll and someone was dragging the damaged rider out of the way of danger. That roan was still trying to get rid of that saddle the last I saw. I didn't see anything more of father until next morning. After a while, the roustabout, a young fellow twelve, maybe thirteen, years old, came, climbed into the buggy, took me in tow, and showed me around. Took me over to the branding pen, where the help was doing some branding and one thing and another. It was there I first heard the facts of life, saw a man use a knife. Saw a young horse try to thrash around some, heard a fellow say "Pass the salt, and hurry up." Heard the downed horse give a grunt. Saw the knife passed to the helper, all red and messy. Made me kind of sick.

I still don't like the idea of rubbing raw salt into a nasty cut. That's too darned rough for me. I got pretty handy with a knife myself, some years later, but instead of salt I used bluing. Yeah. Plain old household bluing. Best healing agent on a horse I ever used. I learned to use that from an Indian; an old Nez Percé he was. Told me he had been a professional in the old days before Chief Joseph's War. Lots of horses then, he said, all over Idaho.

He was quite a guy and taught me a lot, especially how to take care of a horse after you cut him, and was I ever grateful for that. Told it to me once in words of Frontier English, mixed with Nez Percé and some Chinook jargon. I remember it well, but can't put it down the way he told it to me, but what he hoped he was saying got to me something like this:

"Had a spotted horse once. Used to run him. Heap good horse." Then, getting warmed up, he sped up. "Hyak Kiuitan Klatawa"— meaning, "My horse ran fast." About that time I'd lose him. The best I can do is tell what I think he said in my own words— "Saloon man up to Lewiston had some fast horses. Bet him small bet my horse; short race. His horse won, then I bet him on long race. Maybe a mile, maybe little more. Not mile and half. Bet everything. My horse. My saddle, my outfit, everything.

"Thought maybe lose that bet, but after while my horse ketch up. Me winum. That night saloon man get me drunk, I lose my horse, everything. Can't even catch ride to go home to my wife. Never found another horse like Skookum. Got me job. Been doing this most all a time since."

That Indian didn't look like much, and I don't know whatever became of him, but he taught me a lot about horses. One of his best pointers was the use of household bluing on horse cuts, collar boils, sore necks, or saddle galls and such like ailments. I hope he is treated with as much consideration in his Happy Hunting Grounds as he tried to give to the horses he had to work on. But now I have gotten way off the course. Let's see, where was I? Oh yeah! The young roustabout had me in tow.

Yeah. A guy was rubbing salt into a bad cut. I never used salt. It's just too rough, and I never lost a horse yet. At the time I didn't care for that at all. I had gotten salt into a cut some months before and could still remember how that salt burned and stung.

About dark I got pretty tired, I guess, and somebody must have put me to bed in a pile of blankets, for next morning, Red, the young roustabout, woke me up for breakfast. Breakfast for the men was over, but father was there. Red said he thought that Rod, the spilled rider, was going to get well all right. Later I heard that Rod never did get his voice back. Red told me later that father was asleep. That he had been up all night taking care of Rod. Said that Rod's throat swelled shut so bad that he couldn't breathe, that father had rubbed the throat with his hands and used cold water to keep the swelling down, but that it had been a tight squeeze for Rod.

They didn't have any milk to drink. I didn't like canned cow and I hadn't ever tried coffee yet, so I drank just plain water. All the water at that camp was warm, and I mean real warm. I wondered where they got the cold water to use on Rod's neck, so I asked Red. He said that father had some of the fellows whirl partly filled jugs of water through the air and that somehow the whirling of those jugs had cooled the water real cool. I still think that father's hands were the biggest help. He had hands that eased a body's troubles better than liniment or the use of superheated plates. For rheumatism, or the swellings around broken bones and around and slightly over immature boils, father's hands just simply took away the pain and the nasty colors that accompany bad spots. Funny though. In later years, when father became laid up with rheumatism, his hands couldn't help him a bit.

Before we drove away, Mr. Milke, the boss man, insisted upon paying father for his services to Rod, the injured rider, but father refused to accept any payment. Quite an argument, as I recall, ensued. Father claimed that he was a missionary and not a licensed doctor, but Mr. Milke insisted that father had done a better job than any doctor he ever knew could have done. They both were stubborn and father was just about to drive away when Red approached us leading a horse. The boss man stopped being noisy mighty quick and seemed to get a sort of twinkle in his eyes. He stopped Red, took the lead rope from him, and stepping around to my side of the buggy put the rope into my hands.

Of course father objected, and sincerely too, I still think, but Mr. Milke had, what seemed to me even then, an answer that father could not combat. He said, "You did one of my men a great favor, now I am doing one of yours a favor that I am sure he appreciates. That makes us even." With that, he kind of waved a hand at me and turned and walked away, and all the time I was able to see him he never looked back at us once.

I was now the proud owner of a horse, and what a horse he was! As I recall those minutes now, he was a gelding, but as yet I was not able to fully understand that circumstance. He was a bluish brindle, not an iron gray, but darker, with small black flecks in his hair that reminded me of the fine, small feathers on a chicken's neck. From what I could see of him those first minutes, he had a good-sized, perfectly round, dark bay spot at the hip bone, and I immediately named him Spot. The spot as I remember it now was about the size of a regular tennis ball. Later we discovered that there was an identical spot in exactly the same position on the other hip. I couldn't then figure out a name that would include both spots, so his name continued to be plain Spot.

That horse, I would say now, was a good 15 hands high (a horse always looks tall to a little kid). Neat and trim as to body, with nice, rounding hips, a good saddle, and a small head and ears. His nostrils were so small that I couldn't help noticing that fact when I got a chance to look him over real well. The horses that I had gotten to look at real close at the Indian camp had big, spongy-looking nostrils. A thistle or something had gotten into a nostril once when I was real close trying to feed a mare a handful of clover and she snorted her nose to clean that nostril and blew my hat right off my head. That was the last hat that I ever wore that looked just like a girl's hat. I hated that hat and lost it right then, and maybe that helps me to remember the pair of great nostrils that mare had.

There were no clusters of hair along Spot's legs (no feathers). His feet were so small that even a boy of my age would notice them, and he had one white foot that looked imperfect. One thing—two really; he had almost no mane at all and his tail was so skimpy that I thought something was wrong. Where I had lived during the past winter the driving team stalls had been just adjoining the chicken roosts and that driving team had rubbed much of their upper tails away because of chicken lice, and that made me question, in my mind, whether there wasn't something wrong with Spot, but when I asked my father, he assured me that Spot's tail was natural for an Appaloosa. As we drove along he told me a great deal of what he knew of the spotted horse, which just at that time was becoming known as Appaloosa. Father said that Spot was an Appaloosa and not a Nez Percé horse or a Cayuse, and explained to me the difference between breeds of horses. Those facts remained somewhat hazy for some years but were understood with later experiences.

Spot was a gelding, but some years later, when I learned more about horses and horse circumstances, I discovered that whoever had used the knife on Spot had not done a competent job. As was said among horsemen, Spot had been cut proud. He was impotent, but when mares were in season could, and would, satisfy their desires.

Another queer thing about Spot I discovered later. He was forever bringing colts home from the nearby open range. As I remember it now, I think he brought home about a dozen. He was a regular silly about colts, and when I mentioned that to mother she said Spot was also silly about me. But to return to the journey across those great open spaces. Father told me then about that nigger wool. He didn't give any scientific name to that grass. He probably didn't know it had one, though he was well informed about nearly everything.

Late that afternoon we came to a railroad track. Father said that the railroad had come through just a few years before. There was a sign up the track a slight distance away. Just a board set upright in the ground. There was a word on that board. Father said it read "Davenport." That sign was all there was at that time of the now prosperous little city of Davenport, and nowadays I have to grin, thinking about that, every time I go through the place.

A half mile or a little more up the track, near a spring bordered by some willows and a couple of scrubby cottonwoods nearby, a large camp meeting tent had been set up. Father had arranged for that, so that there would be a gathering of people from great distances around, a large enough gathering for him to organize a church there. There were quite a lot of people, maybe seventy-five, or one hundred. There were a lot of women. I hadn't seen any of them before. Some of them made quite a fuss over me. I guess, now, that maybe being the preacher's son had a lot to do with that. Father said later not to mind that. Some of the women had no boys of their own.

There was a lot of singing that evening as the meeting got under way. Among the singers was a young woman that I never have forgotten. She was young, tall, and very blonde, and she was the best singer of them all. Her sweet, high-toned voice could be heard above all the rest. And somehow, I began to think that she was singing just to me and only for me. Of course that is foolish, but the impression lingers with me still, at times.

Through the years, when riding herd, maybe alone, or hunting bear in far mountain areas, I would hear her singing as she had that evening. Singing just for me.

I was bedded down in some blankets in the back of our buggy before the meeting was over, and as I was slipping into sleep I still could hear the lady singing.

When I awoke in the morning we were well on our way and I never saw the sweet singing lady again; but I never have forgotten her singing. I must have been a very impressed little lad.

It was on that trip that I learned much of what I know about the early Nez Percé and their spotted horses, known now as the

Appaloosa; of the Nez Percé horse and the many Pintos and of the later Cayuse horse and how they came to be, and I hope I have made that situation clear.

23

SPANISH HORSE CIRCUMSTANCES

The horse situation in the early days of Spanish occupation is somewhat obscure, and even confusing, because of some quite fantastic claims about the number of horses brought into Mexican areas during the earliest times of Spanish occupation. Some of the numbers mentioned are so great as to be astonishing. The circumstances that we have herein pictured to the contrary may not carry conviction to everyone, but I feel that a knowledge of Spanish horse circumstances through the years of early history up to the time when Indians were supposed to be running mustangs to the north in numbers attaining hundreds of thousands will be more enlightening and convincing than mere statistics. After all, statistics are more often incorrect than correct, even in times of an inventory, with the facts plainly before the statistician.

The first authentic information we have regarding the Spanish people and their horses comes to us from the time that the Romans occupied the Spanish lands. The Romans completed their conquest of the people of the area and occupied all of the peninsula except the most northern mountains in the third century A.D.

About the time Rome completed her subjugation of the Spanish people the Romans began to have serious difficulties elsewhere. Great numbers of people from somewhere in unknown Asia burst out of their homelands and spread to the boundaries of Roman-occupied territories in south-central Europe. Among those people out of Asia were the Huns, and after they had arrived they began

242

to annoy the Roman legions more than just a little. Matters became so serious that commanders along the border were forced to ask for help, and as the horses of the Huns were the most important element being used against them, the commanders asked for more horses. And they asked for many of them.

The Huns had attacked the Roman legions with their every man mounted upon a sturdy horse, and with many a warrior leading a spare mount. The Hun circumstances were investigated by stealth and it was learned that those people had many horses. Apparently the Huns had moved out of Asia and into Europe as a people in search of a better land and situation. The women and children, even their old folks, were along, and everyone rode a horse. Areas to their rear held great herds of horses under control of herdsmen. When that situation became clear, the commanders of the Roman troops along those borders put in emergency calls for more horses.

Rome had been conquering territories and peoples for some hundreds of years, and as most of those conquered territories contained but limited numbers of horses, the demands of the Roman armies had created a rather severe shortage of horses in strictly Roman territory. In consequence, Imperial headquarters hurried out requests to all the commanders or governors of occupied territories to gather and send to Rome horses suitable for army use.

A demand from Imperial Rome was not to be ignored, even by the governors of such large territories as the Spanish peninsula. The word went out to collect and forward horses in the direction of Rome or, if more convenient, to the northern frontier areas.

New troubles for Rome were coming up pretty much from everywhere about then, but the Hun problem became really serious. These Huns had crowded the Roman legions out of some important territory, and the Roman commanders on that front became really vocal in their requests for horses. These requests were couched in surprisingly strong terms. So strong that there was not the least doubt as to their urgency. Naturally, headquarters in Rome made a check of the areas most likely to produce horses in desirable numbers and in their checking found that the occupied areas of Spain (the peninsula was known as Iberia to the ancient Romans) had delivered but few horses compared to other occupied areas of lesser territory, and very quickly thereafter demands were made upon the governor of the Spanish territory, and in no uncertain words, to deliver more horses, and speedily.

The high Roman command in Spanish lands was an important post in those days of the Roman Empire; not because of their political importance but because of the opportunity for the governor to benefit financially from his position. The governor of that time had not achieved his position by any laxness of forcefulness. After receiving a second demand for horses his demands upon those in subordinate positions were so forceful that Spain, quite soon, became absolutely bare of horses of the quality anywhere near approaching the quality needed by the Roman legions. The demand for horses for the Roman armies never slackened until Imperial Rome fell to pieces as an empire.

It had been no real fault of the Roman command in Spain that satisfactory numbers of horses had not been delivered from there. It was simply a matter of natural circumstances. The Spanish peninsula has never been a country, as a whole, that was highly conducive to horses or horse raising. The circumstances are not complicated.

Along the Mediterranean Sea the Spanish shore rises in pleasant slopes for some few miles in certain areas, none very wide except for some river valleys. A short distance inland from that sea, mountain ranges, mostly precipitate and rugged, compose much of the entire country. The mountain ranges cut off moisture-laden winds from the interior to such an extent that very few areas of any great size are farming districts of any consequence. The more northern provinces of Castile and Estremadura, because of their fortunate situation, are the most important agricultural areas, and they comprise but a small part of Spain.

The greatest part of the interior is a fine land for goats, even mountain goats, and burros and mules. Farming was done either by human labor or with the help of oxen. Transportation then was much the same as it had been ever since, until the last few years of the nineteenth century. The very poor—95 percent of the people, traveled on foot. Those gainfully employed and in better circumstances may have traveled on burros. A well-to-do farmer, to show and display his superior status, would ride a donkey, or, on occasion, a mule. The lesser gentry would travel mostly on horseback, and those people were good and graceful riders. The more wealthy and the nobility would have their carriages, and, of course, their riding horses also.

Farming, on a scale that permitted such extravagance, was done with the aid of oxen; very seldom with a mule or donkey; but in the smaller farms a burro was the only aid in cultivating the soil. Poor folks, not too distant, would deliver produce—milk, cheese, and similar products—either carried by humans or in carts whose motive power might be a goat or a dog. The serious lack of horses in Spain throughout the centuries was not however due to the country's lack of areas pleasing to horses.

Shortly after the Romans moved out of the country, in 703 A.D. to be exact, Moslem armies out of Asia Minor landed on Spanish territory and swarmed into the interior, with the Spanish population powerless to halt them. The difference between the fighting ability of the Moslems and the Spaniards was not the reason for the Moslem success. That success is to be accounted for by difference in the number of good horses that the Moslems possessed.

It is true that in the beginning the Moslems were fierce with fanatical desire to spread their religion far and wide, and that lent power to their armies and to the fury of their attack, but actually that was not a controlling factor for at about that time Christianity had come to the population of Spain and they too were a people firm in their belief and fanatic in their resistance to the Moslems. It really was the superiority in horses that made the difference.

The Moslems forced their way northward through all of Spain until they came to the horse lands of Castile and Estremadura, and there the Spaniards stopped them. Of course Spanish horses were not the chief cause, and the Spanish horses are not entitled to more than their just share of credit in the halt of the Moslem progress northward, for in the several hundred years that the invaders had been pressing toward the north, other wars had drawn the chief Moslem forces elsewhere, and too, with the passing of time the urgency of the Moslem in the spreading of his religion had cooled off. It could have been no mere coincidence however that the Moslem advance toward the north was halted just about at the southern borders of the Castile and Estremadura horse lands.

Of course the hundreds of years of opposition to the advancing Moslems had done nothing to make the position of the Spanish horse any better or more numerous, and one may be assured that there was much fighting to keep the Moslems slowed down in their advance. Nevertheless, as the pleasant living conditions encountered by the Moslems in southern Spain began to influence the important commanders of the Moslem forces, their pressure on the fighting fronts became less severe. Moslem and Christian learned to live in fairly close proximity without the wanton shedding of each other's blood. The northern Spanish potentates, whatever their titles, knew well that the horse was the determining factor in the battles of those times, and, as soon as opportunity offered, efforts to increase Spanish horses in the free lands were augmented as much as possible. The horsemen of Castile and of its northern neighbors who had suitable pasturage began to bring in horses from other areas of Europe: from Catholic Austria and France and even areas farther to the north, for those people knew that it was important that the Moslem tide be checked.

As their resources increased in those northern areas of Spain, intrepid and gallant warriors began to turn back the Moslem masters. A little here, and a little there. Each gain important to the northern Spaniards, but of scant urgency to the Moslem chiefs who had become used to the pleasures of the Spanish shores of the Mediterranean.

In the early years of the fifteenth century a family of Spaniards with extensive holdings of real estate in both Estremadura and Castile began producing quite large numbers of horses. Those many horses gave the family members considerable prestige, and the name of that family, Cortés, sometimes spelled Cortez, has been prominent in Spanish affairs ever since.

In the latter part of the fifteenth century an energetic king of Castile came into prominence because of his forceful handling of the Spanish forces in efforts to expel the Moslems, but by then the efforts of the Spaniards had strengthened the resistance of the Moslems and they refused to retreat farther south. Try as best he might, King John of Castile could not drive the infidels farther south. A lack of good horses was his greatest trouble. Try as he would he could not get enough horses. He had been so very busy fighting that he had neglected to improve his source of horse supply. That was his trouble.

Then, in the late years of that century, as happens to all men, monarch and pauper alike, King John's time on earth began nearing its end. All that any man can do is give his all for his God and his country; King John had done that, and now it was evident that he had. While he lay abed, the fight against the Moslems slackened and then died away just as though important events were awaiting final summons for the king.

King John had a daughter, the beautiful Princess Isabella. The princess spent much of her time on the king's farms, for she loved to be near the horses growing there. Now she was brought in so that her father might see her before he passed on. The king loved his daughter above any mortal thing on earth. She adored her father as only a young maiden can who believes her father to be the paladin of this earth's heroes. Both the king and the princess were most devout Christians, so it was only natural that the princess was very interested in the progress against the Moslems and had done everything in her power to encourage the battle for their complete expulsion from the land of Christian Spain. Her words of comfort to her father were of scant avail, for his failure to completely remove the Moors was a heavy burden upon him. Whenever his mind wandered he would torture himself with his sense of failure and bemoan the fact that only a scarcity of horses had prevented his completing his task. He bewailed that shortage of horses. Then, when he had a lucid moment, as a priest read the prayers for the dying, Princess Isabella, with the jeweled crucifix from the castle's hail of worship in her hands, swore to her dying father that she would continue the work of driving the infidel into a land across the sea, and that her every thought, forsaking all others, her every effort until that was accomplished, would be to that end. And she kissed the crucifix to assure her father that her resolve would never weaken nor her spirit ever falter.

Queen Isabella had several onerous and distasteful duties to perform before her armies prevailed over the Moslems and they were expelled from Europe, but her first duty was accomplished with great pleasure, for her first official act after having become queen of Castile was to proceed to the Cortés estates and there hold a lengthy conference with her friend Manuel Cortés as to the horse situation and such remedies as would cure the lack of horses for her army. That meeting resulted in her giving Cortés *carte-blanche* to collect and secure all horses from anyone in Spanish lands for exclusive army use. No one was to be exempt from that. Immediately thereafter letters of credit to Cortés were issued, enabling him to establish agents in neighboring countries that had horses, and his instructions were to secure all the horses possible, and as quickly as he could arrange for their training and deliver them to the queen's commanders in the battle against her enemy.

It took only a few years and by then Cortés had that horse-procuring project in high gear, and horses were delivered in great numbers to the queen's forces. When letters of credit had expired or were insufficient, the cause of Christian Spain against the infidel Moslems produced thousands of horses on credit. Those horses, all together, gave Queen Isabella the strength that had before been lacking and she thrust the Moslems completely out of Spain.

Queen Isabella's victory over the Moslems came in 1492. Shortly after the surrender of the Moslems, she pawned the last of her jewels to secure the funds needed to send Christopher Columbus on his way to the discovery of a great new world.

Christopher Columbus, the navigator, had never been popular in any court in Europe. His claims of great lands to the west across the sea were looked upon as the dreams of a visionary with but little sense but of a vivid imagination. Queen Isabella's husband, King Ferdinand of Aragon was contemptuous of him and refused to help the queen finance the project. The king really never changed his position in regards to Columbus, not even at the time of Columbus' greatest success, and this brings us now to the first attempts at Spanish colonization of the lands of America.

Good Queen Isabella had given so much of her energy, of her life forces, to the expulsion of the Moslems that shortly after the completion of that task her powers of intelligence and forcefulness went into a severe decline and culminated in her early death. During her period of decline and following her death, Christopher Columbus and his heir, a son, Diego Columbus, experienced some very parlous times.

King Ferdinand of Aragon, husband of Queen Isabella of Castile, had never been too interested in the queen's project of expelling the Moslems. His forebears for several generations had contented themselves with supplying the armies of such Spanish provinces as were engaged in that long conflict with their available supplies for the success of the venture, but only in consideration for money in hand. That policy had enriched the coffers of the Aragon nobility and the rulers of Aragon were among the wealthiest of Spanish monarchs. Young King Ferdinand was not of a disposition inclined to become involved in matters of a serious nature, giving most of his time and talents to the enjoyment of the pleasures of his court. His way of life attracted to his capital and palaces the most profligate young people in all Spain, and more years added little to his wisdom nor changed his way of life. By the time the wars were over and Columbus was preparing to sail west into the unknown seas, the courtiers of King Ferdinand's court were wastrels indeed, with a very low opinion of anybody not actively connected with the goings-on in their court circles. They, along with the king, were opposed to anything connected with Columbus. His successes only added to their detestation of him, and this

situation extended to young Diego Columbus after the admiral's
death.

Their animosity had ruined Columbus, preventing him from
taking any important steps toward the developing of the newly discovered lands.

At the time Queen Isabella had made her contract with Columbus she had granted the navigator, as part of his gains should he
discover land across the seas, the position of viceroy of any such
domains, that position to pass on to his heirs in perpetuity. After
young Columbus had somewhat recovered from his distress at his
father's death he endeavored to begin the colonization of some of
the islands that his father had discovered, but the influence of his
enemies in King Ferdinand's court prevented people with the
necessary funds from contributing to such an enterprise. However,
in 1503 young Diego did manage to dispatch a meager group to the
island of Hispaniola, founding a small colony there. Some years
later he also founded a very weak colony on the island of Cuba.

The circumstances of those young colonies did not warrant the
bringing of many horses to their undeveloped areas. Extremely
short in funds, they had to use their resources for things that would
be of certain benefit to their enterprises, and horses at that time
would not have been of the least benefit in their attempts to develop their surroundings, for horses as they had known them in
Spain were not draft animals and had not been used as motive
power in farming and other pursuits connected with the labor of
production. Horses were not brought into the New World in any
considerable numbers until the fame of the Cortés projects in
Mexico had become known in Spain, and even then the larger part
of the horses brought to the New World did not come to the West
Indies. Rather they passed by the islands and went directly to
Mexico, and shortly thereafter to other areas of the mainland,
especially South America, where sundry Spanish adventurers were
then making a start at the conquest of the Inca civilization in Peru.

Because of the horse situation in Spain it must have been well
into the middle of the sixteenth century before horses in any impressive numbers came into Mexican territory.

Some writers have used the great numbers of wild horses found in the pampas areas of South America some 100 or 150 years later as a measure with which to gauge the arrival of horses into the island colonies of the viceroy, Don Diego Columbus. Actually there was no connection between the arrival of horses in the island colonies at any time and the great numbers of horses found in the pampas in the early 1800s. Nor has it ever had any influence upon, or with, the number of Spanish horses that came into Mexico. The horse situation in Mexico has been, and is today, much the same as the horse situation has been in Spain (the situation in Spain may have improved very recently)—the poor walk to where they hope to go; those in appreciably better circumstances may ride a burro. Some with a little more of this world's goods may have a donkey or a mule, and that's about the horse situation in Mexico today and has been ever since the Spaniards began to settle the country. Of course the hidalgos of some few great haciendas still ride most splendid steeds, but their numbers are few. For long journeys, these days, there are the buses. Bus fares are very low, even in Mexican money, and those that have no other means of transport ride the buses on long journeys. An auto tour through the high central plateau and the western areas of the country will quickly put to rest any lingering doubts that one may entertain as to Mexico being, or ever having been, a horse country that could furnish horses by the hundred thousands annually, as has been suggested by some early writers.

With that explanation of the horse circumstances in Spanish lands, dating from the earliest known times until the quite recent past, we rest our presentation of the circumstances that placed the northern plains Indians of the American west on horseback.

Should there still be doubts in the minds of any reader as to the merits of any claim herein, it might be a good suggestion to read Frank Gilbert Roe's very thorough book on American horses, entitled *The Indian and the Horse*.

I have never had the pleasure of meeting Mr. Roe, but our correspondence, though very limited, has disclosed Mr. Roe to be a gracious, helpful gentleman, and his books bear witness that he is a writer of considerable attainment.

In compiling his book on the American horse, Mr. Roe has included the most thorough bibliography I have ever seen in any book. His chapter on coloration problems, beginning on page 135, should interest anyone who is interested in the breeding of horses. It gives the story of how some people of ancient times tried to increase their number of horses of Pinto coloration, and also of more recent endeavors of some western American Indians along the same lines. The chapter discloses some very confused thinking by those people, especially as regards the Pinto horse. It is our hope that this writing, *Mysterious Horses of Western North America*, will clear up some of the obscure features of horses of both the past and the present.

Appendix

During my reconstruction of early horse circumstances in connection with the central plains Indians, I have, at times, complained about the inability of some writers to see certain facts regarding horses and their situations that should have been obvious to anyone possessing even rudimentary powers of observation. Imagine my chagrin when, after this book was already in the hands of the publishers, I discovered that I myself had been subject to the same fault.

My lack of observation, strangely, has been in connection with the same feature that I had believed some other writers had been most in error about: the situation of the plains Comanche Indians and their supposed running of mustangs north out of Mexico in such predominant numbers as to entitle the mustang to be considered the horse that placed the northern plains Indians on horseback. Because several writers on western horses accepted the earlier writings to that effect as being substantially correct, that situation was the only feature that could be seriously considered as contradicting my statement of facts.

Because of sure knowledge, confined at that time primarily within myself, and contrary to the conclusions expressed by several of the earliest writers on western Indian horses, I was certain that the horses, in predominant numbers, that had placed the northern plains Indians on horseback did not come north out of Mexico, but rather from the Nez Percé Indians whose homelands were in the Columbia Basin areas of the far northwest.

253

According to some early writers the Comanche Indians had
been the prime movers of mustangs into the north, and the picture of the Comanche Indians in that position always had been a
puzzle to me. Those earlier writers had been sincere. There was no
reason for them not to have been, but many of the Comanche horses
had been of pinto coloration, and pinto coloration can be said to
have been, and at present still is, virtually non-existent, to an
extent unusual with any other prominent breed of horses. Too,
George Catlin, the first of several great painters of early Indian
scenes west of the Mississippi, even painted an occasional Appaloosa among the many horses of Pinto coloration. Those Comanche
horses had not come to the north out of Mexico. They were Nez
Percé horses. But how could the early Comanches have raided south
into far Mexico in the late 1700s at a time when none of the more
northern plains Indians had little more than a very few horses, and
how could it have come to pass that those raiding Comanches were
riding Nez Percé horses?

George Catlin, perhaps the greatest early painter of western
Indians and their horses, began painting Indian scenes while he
was among Comanches in 1832 in territory adjacent to the Platte
River, which flows through plains country and empties into the
Missouri River. Among his most frequent horses were Comanche
horses. He depicts many horses with pinto coloring, and at least
one natural Appaloosa, as well as several that had been painted by
Indians to resemble Appaloosa coloring.

According to Webb, in his exhaustive book, *The Great Plains*,
Catlin stated that the Comanches told him that they had but recently come from the far northwest. The Nez Percé Indians were
centrally located in the Pacific northwest.

In Bulletin 30 of the Smithsonian Institution—*Handbook of
American Indians North of Mexico*, volume 1, September, 1912—
beginning with page 327, we find in part the following information: "Comanche—of Shoshonean stock, the only one of that group
living entirely on the plains. Their language and their traditions
show that they are a comparatively recent offshoot of the Shoshoni

of Wyoming. . . . The Wyoming Shoshoni had been driven back farther into the mountains by the Sioux, and the Comanche (Shoshoni) had steadily been driven farther to the south by the same Sioux tribes."

The location of the Shoshoni, including the Comanche tribe of that people, being designated as coming from Wyoming could be very misleading to anyone not familiar with western geographical situations, for Wyoming is composed in part of lands formerly situated within the territory of Idaho. Central Idaho was the homeland of the Nez Percé Indians, who in Lewis and Clark's time there, had more horses than their homelands could handle.

The fact that the Comanches came from the mountainous regions of the northwest should eliminate any doubts as to where they secured their horses.

The Nez Percé told Captains Lewis and Clark in 1805 that they were not really a warring tribe, for the reason that the Shoshoni and the Blackfoot were their only enemies. Both tribes, they said, stole their horses. Although the Blackfoot have always been noted as the worst of the horse- stealing Indians, the Nez Percé claimed that the Shoshoni were the worst of the two tribes.

The further fact that those early writers who saw Comanche raiding parties in southern Texas in the late 1700s saw pintos among their horses attests to the fact that the Comanches horses were Nez Percé and not mustangs, for mustangs as a breed contain fewer animals of pinto coloring than any other modern horses—practically none.

I hope that this Appendix will clinch my case against the myth that Indians raiding into Mexico brought north in predominant numbers the horses that put the northern plains Indians on horseback, and that credit for that achievement will at last be given to the Nez Percé, the people to whom it really belongs.

COACHWHIP PUBLICATIONS

COACHWHIPBOOKS.COM

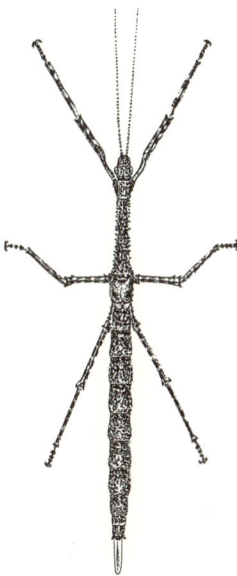

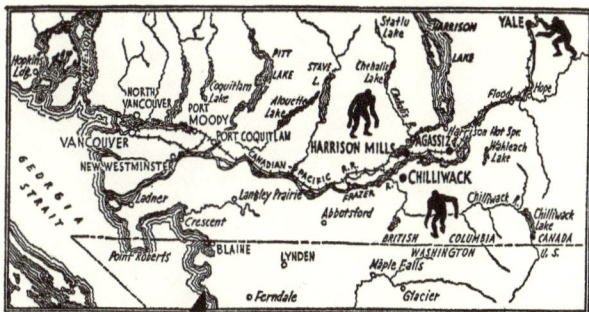

www.ingramcontent.com/pod-product-compliance
Lightning Source LLC
Chambersburg PA
CBHW021049090426
42738CB00006B/248